THE DEVELOPMENTAL COURSE OF ROMANTIC RELATIONSHIPS

This multidisciplinary text highlights the development of romantic relationships, from initiation to commitment or demise, by highlighting the historical context, current research and theory, and diversity of patterns. Engagingly written with colorful examples, the authors examine the joy, stress, power struggles, intimacy, and aggression that characterize these relationships. Readers gain a better understanding as to why, even after the pain and suffering associated with a breakup, most of us go right back out and start again. Relationships are examined through an interdisciplinary lens— psychological, sociological, environmental, and communicative perspectives are all considered. End of chapter summaries, lists of key concepts, and additional readings serve as a review. As a whole, the book explores what precipitates success or failure of these relationships and how this has changed over time.

The book's coverage:

- incorporates both different-sex and same-sex romantic relationships
- examines the roles of gender, race, class, culture, age, and sexuality in relationship development
- looks at multiple types of romantic relationships in emerging adulthood, including dating and cohabitation
- explores both positive and negative relational processes
- analyzes the latest and most important scholarship.

The book opens with an introduction, followed by an historical overview of the development of relationships. Next, relationship development models are examined, including the influence of social factors and the interaction of the partners involved. This volume examines how partners initiate romantic relationships, including infatuation, sexual attraction, and the impact of technology; how cohabitation affects the quality of the future of the relationship; and the individual, social, and circumstantial factors that predict stability or breakups in romantic relationships. The book ends with an examination of the "dark side" of relationships, and suggestions for future research on romantic pairings.

Intended as a supplement for advanced undergraduate or graduate courses in marriage and family, personal/close/intimate relationships, or interpersonal/family communication taught in human development and family studies, psychology, social work, sociology, communication, counseling, and therapy, this book also appeals to researchers and practitioners interested in romantic relationship processes.

Brian G. Ogolsky is Assistant Professor of Human and Community Development at the University of Illinois at Urbana-Champaign.

Sally A. Lloyd is Professor of Women's, Gender, and Sexuality Studies at Miami University.

Rodney M. Cate is Professor Emeritus of Family Studies and Human Development at the University of Arizona.

THE DEVELOPMENTAL COURSE OF ROMANTIC RELATIONSHIPS

Brian G. Ogolsky, Sally A. Lloyd, and Rodney M. Cate

Routledge
Taylor & Francis Group

NEW YORK AND LONDON

First published 2013
by Routledge
711 Third Avenue, New York, NY 10017

Simultaneously published in the UK
by Routledge
27 Church Road, Hove, East Sussex BN3 2FA

Routledge is an imprint of the Taylor & Francis Group, an informa business

© 2013 Psychology Press

The right of Brian G. Ogolsky, Sally A. Lloyd, and Rodney M. Cate
to be identified as authors of this work has been asserted by them in
accordance with sections 77 and 78 of the Copyright, Designs and
Patents Act 1988.

Library of Congress Cataloging in Publication Data
Ogolsky, Brian G.
   The developmental course of romantic relationships / Brian G.
   Ogolsky, University of Illinois at Urbana-Champaign, Sally A. Lloyd,
   Miami University, and Rodney M. Cate, The University of Arizona.
      pages cm
   Includes bibliographical references and index.
   1. Couples.   2. Man-woman relationships.   3. Gay couples.
   4. Courtship.   5. Dating (Social customs)   I. Lloyd, Sally A.
   II. Cate, Rodney M.   III. Title.
   HQ801.O324   2013
   306.7–dc23   2012044869

ISBN: 978–1–84872–929–2 (hbk)
ISBN: 978–1–84872–930–8 (pbk)
ISBN: 978–0–203–38309–4 (ebk)

Typeset in Goudy
by Keystroke, Station Road, Codsall, Wolverhampton

Printed and bound in the United States of America by
Walsworth Publishing Company, Marceline, MO.

This book is dedicated to our families—those that we grew up in, and those that we created. Thank you for showing us how to love and laugh together with those we hold so dear.

CONTENTS

PREFACE

Overview and Contents

The vast majority of the human life course is spent in the context of relationships. Nearly all people form romantic relationships—some of which succeed and some of which fail. What precipitates success or failure of romantic relationships? How has this changed throughout history and how might it change in the future? The answers to these questions are at the crux of the field of relationship science. In this book, we analyze the knowledge base in relationship science by integrating current research and theory explaining the development of romantic relationships. We begin the book with an overview of the historical roots of romantic relationships. We continue with a discussion of relationship initiation, cohabitation, relationship maintenance, and commitment. We then head down the path of the dark side of relationships, attending to research on relationship violence and dissolution. We conclude with a look into the crystal ball of relationship science to predict future directions.

Features

This book has several features that distinguish it from other texts that focus on relationships and families:

- The majority of texts that discuss romantic relationships dedicate, at best, one chapter to research on same-sex couples. This text focuses on all romantic relationships, both different-sex and same-sex.
- This text examines the roles of gender, race, and sexuality in romantic relationship development.
- This text features integrative chapter summaries and key words at the end of each chapter to help assess relevant learning objectives.

Intended Audience

The field of relationship science is inherently interdisciplinary, which creates both opportunities and difficulties. One such difficulty is that relevant research on romantic relationships is published in many different disciplines, which makes it difficult for researchers and students to find. Our book incorporates research from all of the major disciplines. This book is an excellent resource for undergraduate or graduate classes focusing on Intimate Relationships in the fields of family studies, psychology, sociology, communication, social work, marriage and family therapy, gender studies, or other behavioral science fields. This book can be paired with other major texts in the field, including Miller's *Intimate Relationships*, Regan's *Close Relationships*, or Bradbury and Karney's *Intimate Relationships*, to provide a supplemental text highlighting the developmental course of romantic relationships. This book is also an excellent reference for researchers in relationship science.

ACKNOWLEDGMENTS

We would like to thank the anonymous reviewers who provided us with excellent suggestions about the content of the book. We would also like to thank Jill Bowers for reading the entire book and offering countless hours of her time assisting with the organization and flow of the content. We thank Tara Gogolinski for helping with the background research for several of the chapters.

ABOUT THE AUTHORS

Brian G. Ogolsky is Assistant Professor of Human and Community Development at the University of Illinois at Urbana-Champaign. He received his M.S. and Ph.D. in Family Studies and Human Development from the University of Arizona and a B.A. in Psychology from Western Washington University. His research focuses on understanding the maintenance and development of romantic relationships with a specific focus on relational commitment, and research methods for studying couples. In addition to this current work, he has published several book chapters and journal articles. Brian has also received two awards for his teaching and mentoring.

Sally A. Lloyd is Professor of Women's, Gender and Sexuality Studies at Miami University. She received her Ph.D. in Family Studies from Oregon State University. Her scholarship examines violence against women by their intimate partners. Her previous books include *The Handbook of Feminist Family Studies* (co-edited with April Few and Katharine Allen), *The Dark Side of Courtship: Physical and Sexual Aggression* (co-authored with Beth Emery), *Family Violence from a Communication Perspective* (co-edited with Dudley Cahn), and *Courtship* (co-authored with Rodney Cate). While at Miami University, she served as a department chair, director of Women's Studies, associate dean, interim dean, and interim associate vice president for institutional diversity.

Rodney M. Cate has a B.S. in Pharmacy from the University of Texas-Austin, his M.S. in Family Studies from Texas Tech University, and his Ph.D. in Human Development and Family Studies from the Pennsylvania State University-University Park. He is presently Professor Emeritus of Family Studies and Human Development at the University of Arizona. In his 13 years at the University of Arizona, he held teaching, research, and administrative positions. His research interests focused on two areas: the development of premarital relationships, and the association of relationship factors with sexual behavior in romantic relationships. He previously authored one book, *Courtship* (with Sally Lloyd), contributed several chapters to books, and published many juried articles in professional journals. Cate received the Felix Berardo Mentoring Award, given by the National Council on Family Relations, and the James D. Moran Memorial Research Award for Research in Family Studies, from the American Association of Family and Consumer Sciences.

1

INTRODUCTION

Romantic relationships are of fundamental importance to most people in the United States. The vast majority of Americans form long-term romantic relationships, and we derive great satisfaction and many life benefits from being members of such partnerships. Indeed, we find our romantic relationships to be so important that, even after experiencing the pain and suffering associated with the breakup of a dating, cohabiting, or marital relationship, whether same- or different-sex, most of us go right back out and start again. Is it any wonder, then, that we live in a culture that is saturated with images of romance, love, and sexual pleasure, from the magazines we read to the movies and television programs we watch? Romance surrounds us, and we seem to love it.

Romantic relationships are a joy to study, given their central importance in our lives, and the potential of our scholarship to contribute to stronger, healthier, and better relationships. Relationship scholars work across a multitude of disciplines, from communication to family studies to psychology to sociology, which creates a vast and rich multidisciplinary conversation about our work. And the practical, applied significance of our research is critical because the quality of our romantic relationships is closely related to many personal, social, physical, and emotional benefits. For example, people who have higher relationship satisfaction tend to live longer (Orth-Gomer, Wamala, Horsten, Schenck-Gustafsson, Schneiderman, & Mittleman, 2000), have higher life satisfaction (Whisman, Uebelacker, Tolejko, Chatav, & McKelvie, 2006), and are less likely to suffer from depression (Whisman, 2001). These positive impacts are not trivial. Recent research (Holt-Lunstad, Smith, & Layton, 2010) shows that the quality of one's social relationships has an impact on physical health that exceeds the benefits of quitting smoking, exercising for cardiac rehabilitation, abstaining from excessive alcohol use, and taking drug therapy for high blood pressure. These benefits highlight the importance of the processes by which individuals form the interpersonal bonds that become significant in their lives.

All this is not to say that our romantic relationships are the site of continual happiness and pleasure. Certainly, the intensity of our romantic pairings brings the potential for conflict and tension, and, indeed, this paradox has been intensely scrutinized by scholars who look at the darker side of relationships, from obsessive relational intrusion to physical violence. And yet, once again, even after experiencing a destructive or dysfunctional romantic relationship, we go back, and seek the love and commitment that we find so life-enhancing.

This, then, is the focus of this book on the processes of romantic partnering. We seek to present both the history of romantic partnering and the current theory and research on the progression of romantic relationships from first meeting to the development or demise of commitment. This includes processes from first meeting to the last goodbye, examining the joy, stress, love, power struggles, intimacy, and aggression that characterize our romantic relationships.

This book represents an extensive revision and updating of the volume titled *Courtship*, first published in 1992 by Rodney Cate and Sally Lloyd. Those readers familiar with the previous edition will recognize some of the content from the 1992 book, and also the many changes and additions in the present volume. One important change is the title of the book, *The Developmental Course of Romantic Relationships*. This change was made quite purposefully, for a number of reasons. First, the term "courtship" increasingly feels rather passé, invoking an old-fashioned view of the "steps" that lead to heterosexual marriage. Although marriage is still a highly desired end-state for most Americans (Kreider, 2005), today, more than ever before, people engage their long-term romantic commitments in a variety of ways, including cohabitation and non-cohabiting long-term relationships, and through interactive technologies. The association of the term "courtship" almost exclusively with heterosexual marriage is additionally problematic, as it centers on the experience of heterosexual partners and ignores gay and lesbian partnerships. Since legal marriage is not available to all romantic partners in the U.S., we did not want to use a title that implied that the "proper end-state" for all romantic relationships is legal marriage. Indeed, one of the important goals of the present volume is to fully incorporate the rich literature on gay and lesbian romantic relationships, not as an afterthought or addendum, but as a central feature.

Changing the title and focus of the previous book also presented challenges in terms of nomenclature. Certainly, a term such as "non-marital" relationships would not work. We struggled with how to accurately describe the boundaries of the types of relationships that we describe in this volume. Our focus here is fourfold: (1) we wished to retain our previous focus on pre- and non-marital heterosexual relationships, (2) while adding an analysis of these processes in gay and lesbian couples, (3) focusing primarily on the period of emerging adulthood (adolescence through the mid- to late twenties), and (4) describing processes of intimate relationship development and decline. We eventually arrived at the terms "romantic relationships" and "romantic partnering"; the emphasis on "romance" is intended to capture the love and passion engendered by our developing intimate relationships.

There are many other additions and changes since the previous edition. Throughout the volume, all chapters have been updated with the findings from current research and theory. We have incorporated scholarship on the relationships of gay men and lesbians throughout, and added student-friendly features including key concepts and further reading. Two new chapters have been added—Chapter 4, "Romantic Relationship Initiation and Development," and Chapter 5, "Cohabitation"—and we significantly reconfigured the content on relational stability to encompass processes of relationship maintenance and dissolution.

The Layout of *The Developmental Course of Romantic Relationships*

Chapter 2, "The History of Romantic Partnering," places American partnering in historical context. This chapter emphasizes the ways in which this history is at its core a history of gender, sexuality, family, and economics. The chapter includes sections on the pre-industrial era; westward expansion and industrialization; the transition into the 20th century; the era of world wars; postwar changes; the gay, civil, and women's rights movements; and the transition to the new millennium. This chapter is intended to situate the research presented throughout the rest of the book by exploring the changes and continuities that form the social and structural underpinnings of contemporary romantic relationships.

Chapter 3, "Theories and Models of Partnering," presents the various models and theories of partnering that have guided research over the past 50 years. This chapter first discusses early models of partnering that were relatively simple and focused on determining compatibility with potential partners. Next, the chapter presents contemporary theories, including social exchange, attachment, uncertainty reduction, dialectics, gender/feminist, and evolutionary. Finally, an overarching model is presented: the social ecological model of partnering.

Chapter 4, "Romantic Relationship Initiation and Development," centers on how individuals go about initiating a relationship and moving it to higher levels of intimacy and commitment. This discussion first describes how the structure of society narrows the pool of potential partners that are available. Next, a four-stage model of the initiation process is described. Finally, we describe the factors that lead to higher levels of commitment to the relationship.

Chapter 5, "Cohabitation," examines cohabitation as an emerging phase in the progression to commitment. Initially, discussion focuses on the increase in rates of cohabitation in the U.S. and other countries, as well as the factors influencing the increase. Next, we examine both the transition from dating to cohabitation and transition from cohabitation to marriage. Finally, we examine how participation in cohabitation is related to the quality of committed partnerships.

In Chapter 6, "The Stability of Romantic Relationships: Processes of Maintenance and Dissolution," research is examined on two developmental aspects of romantic relationships: maintenance and dissolution. We first discuss the research literature that examines the individual, relationship, and external factors that are predictive of relationship maintenance. The latter half of the chapter focuses on two aspects of relationship breakup. First, discussion centers on the process of romantic relationship dissolution. Research is presented on: (a) factors that predict dissolution; (b) communication of the desire to leave the relationship; and (c) events that precipitate breakup. Next, discussion focuses on the emotional aftermath of breakups, with an emphasis on distress and adaptation.

Chapter 7, "Violence in Romantic Relationships," addresses the issue of intimate partner violence in the romantic relationships of emerging adults. The chapter discusses physical, sexual, and psychological aggression, and outlines the incidence, correlates, and effects of these types of violence. A discussion of stalking concludes the chapter.

Chapter 8, "Future Directions in Relationship Research," addresses the implications of changes in partnering practices for the study of romantic partnerships. The chapter begins with a brief discussion of contemporary partnering practices that are already bringing about changes in the ways we think about finding partners, dating, commitment, and breaking up. Next, methodologies are discussed that have enriched our ability to study romantic relationships, followed by a discussion of what we see as the major arenas for advancing theory and research in the future, including life course perspectives, the social construction of gender, and intersections of race, class, sexuality and gender, and universal properties of romantic relationships.

Throughout this volume, we have attempted to emphasize the amazing complexity not only of our romantic partnerships, but also of the theory and research that has been developed to help us understand relational processes. We ultimately seek to advance an understanding of romantic relationship development and decline that incorporates careful attention to so many levels of analysis, from microprocesses of communication and relational maintenance, to the interplay of gender, sexuality, and race, to the fundamental influence of changes in societal structures, economies, and technologies.

2

THE HISTORY OF ROMANTIC PARTNERING

This chapter traces the historical roots of contemporary romantic partnership practices in the United States. Fortunately, since the late 1980s several notable historical works have been published including D'Emilio and Freedman's *Intimate Matters: A History of Sexuality in America* (1988), Takaki's *A Different Mirror: A History of Multicultural America* (1993) and Coontz's *Marriage: A History* (2005). These works, along with feminist analyses of gender and sexuality, have created new models for situating our current customs, behaviors, and ideas about romantic partnering within the larger context of history, including the legal, structural, and social supports/constraints surrounding intimate behavior. Additionally, they point out the myriad ways in which race, class, gender and sexuality are simultaneously regulated (Andersen & Witham, 2011).

This chapter explicitly rests on the thesis that the history of romantic relationships is at its core a history of sexuality, gender, and family. Indeed, heterosexual marriage has strong roots in the regulation of "moral" sexual behavior, and in the assurance of paternity (D'Emilio & Freedman, 1988). These roots are intertwined with a discourse of heteronormativity, which emphasizes the attraction and bonding of different sexes, the "naturalness" of heterosexual desire, heterosexuality as a standard sexual practice, and binaries of natural versus unnatural sexuality, and genuine versus pseudo families (Oswald, Blume, & Marks, 2005). As a result, both the past and present contexts of romantic relationships are intimately tied to notions of heterosexuality as both a legal and social organizer for couple and family life (D'Emilio & Freedman, 1988; Oswald, Kuvalanka, Blume, & Berkowitz, 2009). Changes in ideas about sexuality, namely, the movement from a dominant view of sex as primarily for procreation to a view of sexuality as enhancing emotional intimacy and physical pleasure, fundamentally changed patterns of romantic partnering over time (D'Emilio & Freedman, 1988).

This chapter is organized around periods of history utilized by D'Emilio and Freedman (1988), Rothman (1984), and Bailey (1988). They divide their discussions of courtship, marriage, and sexuality into the pre-industrial era (roughly early settlement through the early 1800s); the westward expansion of the country and industrialization (early 1800s to reconstruction); the transition into 20th century customs and mores (1880s to the 1920s); the era of world wars (1920s through 1945); the postwar era and the anomaly of the 1950s; the gay, civil, and women's rights movements (1960s through 1980s); and the transition to the 21st century (1990s through the present). Within each of these historical periods, we discuss the customs surrounding the development of romantic relationships, how these customs varied depending on one's class, gender, race, and sexuality, and how they changed over time.

Early Settlement and the Pre-Industrial Era

D'Emilio and Freedman (1988) document the wealth of diversity among Native American tribes in patterns of sexual expression and pair bonding. In contrast to the European colonists, "most native peoples did not associate either nudity or sexuality with sin" (p. 7). Children were granted freedom to explore their sexuality with both same- and different-sex partners, men were allowed to live and dress as women (and, in some tribes, women lived and dressed as men); sexuality outside a committed relationship was accepted, as were polygamy and homosexuality. Marital discord was addressed by dissolving the union and forming a new bond with a different partner, without social stigma. Sexual conflict and prostitution were relatively unknown, due to different ideas about gender, property, and sexuality (D'Emilio & Freedman, 1988, p. 8). Indeed, many Native tribes (for example, the Cherokee and the Seneca) gave women high status and equality, and were both matrilineal and matrilocal (Jensen, 1994; Perdue, 1994).

Within many Native cultures, there was room for multiple explorations of gender and sexuality. Although given the derogatory term "*berdache*" by French explorers, Native tribes made room for male and female transgender people, emphasizing their "two-spirit" natures (Rupp, 2001). Rupp notes that "the male transgendered role could be found in over a hundred American Indian tribes, the female in about thirty" (p. 291).

In contrast, European settlers brought to the colonies many ideas about sexuality and marriage that were deeply rooted in the Protestant Reformation, which emphasized that sexuality was reserved for marriage and reproduction (D'Emilio & Freedman, 1988). As a result, European settlers were quick to emphasize the differences between their customs/mores and those of Native peoples, labeling the latter as savage and uncivilized, and their sexuality and relationship patterns as sinful and lacking self-control (D'Emilio & Freedman, 1988; Takaki, 1993). Although some of the traditional courtship customs of European society were changed, settlers who immigrated to the colonies did retain the emphasis on the importance of affection in marriage, the husband as the patriarch who ruled the home, and the nuclear family as a discrete and independent unit (D'Emilio & Freedman, 1988). Indeed, popular notions to the contrary, Tibbits' (1965) analysis of census data shows that the incidence of extended families in America was never large.

Furthermore, the demands of life in the new frontier worked against the tradition of long heterosexual courtships and chaperones. The need for workers meant that women could not be "relegated to inertia," as her European sisters were; her labor was necessary to the continuation of the community (Murstein, 1976). In some communities, the need for population was so great that bachelors were harassed, being fined for their singleness or run out of town. Marriage was clearly encouraged, and singleness was seen as a sign of sloth (D'Emilio, 1999; Murstein, 1974).

Many scholars note that the American system of heterosexual courtship for European Americans of the middle and upper classes contained elements of a participant-run system from its earliest days (Coontz, 2005; D'Emilio & Freedman, 1988; Gadlin, 1977; Rothman, 1984). Young people were granted autonomy in their choice of a mate; parents exerted control largely through determining the timing of the marriage by withholding inheritance of land or the release of a son's labor (Glenn & Coleman, 1988; Greven, 1970; Rothman, 1984). The choice of a mate was based on reason, and perhaps the single most important criterion for marriage readiness was the ability of the man to support a wife and family (Gadlin, 1977; Rothman, 1984). Still, love was not entirely absent; for example, both the Puritans and the Quakers believed in the importance of affection to marital harmony (Coontz, 1988; Rothman, 1984). By the early 1800s, the definition of love went beyond reason to include openness, candor, and sincerity; still, romantic love was not valued, as it was viewed as immature and unreliable (Rothman, 1984).

Young European settlers met in church, the neighborhood, and at home; few were strangers, because they had grown up together. The intertwined lives of young men and women were an American phenomenon, and different-sex socializing was integrated into everyday life (Demos, 1986; Rothman, 1984). Young people interacted in mixed-sex groups; however, couples could spend time alone and were relatively free to determine the nature of their premarital interactions (Furstenberg, 1966), as parents made little effort to oversee heterosexual courtship. In fact, Rothman (1984) noted that parents would give a young couple privacy when a suitor came to call by going out for a walk or going to bed, and in some communities, practices such as bundling (sleeping together fully clothed, and bundled together) were common.

Sexual passion, however, was to be contained, and in New England, in particular, it was harshly sanctioned when it occurred outside heterosexual marriage (D'Emilio & Freedman, 1988; Rothman, 1984). Still, couples were given the privacy necessary for the expression of physical affection, and Rothman notes that couples did not always suppress their sexual desires; the premarital conception rate hit an all-time high of 30% in the 1770s. Premarital pregnancy was a sign of weakness rather than immorality, but if the couple married, especially well before the child was born, few sanctions were brought to bear (Coontz, 2005; D'Emilio & Freedman, 1988).

The views of heterosexual sex outside of marriage and the sexuality of women began to change at the end of the 18th century. Earlier sexual freedom was replaced with an emphasis on self-control and chastity, for women in particular (Coontz, 1988; D'Emilio & Freedman, 1988). The ministerial view of women as passionless gained momentum (Murstein, 1974) and premarital pregnancy was now viewed as a sign of female impurity (Rothman, 1984). Yet, the boundaries of sexual interaction were still loosely drawn. Improper behavior of the man was likely to draw nothing more than a scolding, and both flirting and sexual playfulness were still common (Rothman, 1984). Courting couples in the early 19th century responded to the dilemma of proper sexual restraint with the invention of petting, that is, sexual expression short of coitus (Rothman, 1984).

In the colonies and the early years of the republic, there was no sharp demarcation between home and commerce. This situation resulted in a relatively interdependent set of roles for men and women; labor was sex-typed but not rigidly divided into separate spheres (Coontz, 1988; D'Emilio, 1999; Gadlin, 1977). Women enjoyed relatively greater participation in business and home manufacturing in the 1700s and early 1800s than in the remainder of the 19th century, giving them a central role in the economy of the household (Margolis, 1984), although the structure of male–female relationships was still largely patriarchal (Coontz, 2005).

Unfortunately, there is almost no documentation of same-sex romantic relationships during this historical period beyond discussions of "sexual devi-ance." D'Emilio and Freedman (1988, 2002) discuss the multiple ways in which European-American communities regulated such deviance during the colonial years; indeed they note that "an accurate portrayal of sexuality in the colonial era both incorporates and challenges the puritanical stereo-type" (2002, p. 142). The colonists were very concerned about, and closely monitored, the sexual behavior of the community; men were sanctioned for sodomy and rape, and women for adultery, fornication, and bearing a bastard child. Public humiliation, whippings, jail, fines, and even death (for sodomy, buggery, and bestiality) all served as reminders that deviance was not toler-ated, and sexuality belonged within heterosexual marriage. Ultimately, "colo-nial society had no permanent cultural category for those who engaged in sexual relations with members of their own gender"; such transgressions were punished as "unnatural sexual acts" (1988, p. 31).

Scholars disagree on the extent of the historical record of gay and lesbian relationships. Shifting terms of reference for a lover (such as "friend," "brother," or "sister"), as well as fluid views of sexuality, usually mask same-sex desire and relationships (Goode & Wagner, 1999; Smith, 2000). Goode and

Wagner note that, in early America, "homosexuality" was not viewed as an identity, but rather as a "weakness or inclination" to sin. Additionally, as sex was constructed as reproductive in nature, and individuals were deeply embedded in heterosexual families and communities, there was "no hope for a life apart . . . an identity, a way of being" (p. 34). Thus, gay and lesbian relationships were rendered invisible during this era.

On the other hand, courtship and marriage were not permitted for all heterosexuals in the developing United States, as both race and class intersect here. The partnering and sexual practices of Native Americans were viewed as immoral, some immigrant men were prohibited from marrying lest they form permanent homes in the United States, and interracial relationships were taboo (D'Emilio & Freedman, 1988; Franklin, 2010, Takaki, 1993). White and Black indentured servants, and Black slaves, were not allowed to marry, and sexual exploitation of female indentured servants and slaves was common (D'Emilio & Freedman, 1988; Takaki, 1993).

The family lives of Black slaves were influenced by both legal mandates and sex ratios. Initially, more African men than women were brought to America, making the formation of families difficult. Due to the influence of African culture, and encouraged by the slave owners, slaves accepted both premarital intercourse and polygamy (D'Emilio & Freedman, 1988). The bringing together of Africans and Europeans in the new world brought about the possibility of interracial relationships; for example, Takaki (1993) notes accounts of White and Black indentured servants running away together, and being harshly sanctioned for their sexual interaction. And, when there was a very low ratio of women to men, White men sometimes took a Black mate (D'Emilio & Freedman, 1988). After slavery became entrenched in the late 1700s, marriage between Blacks and Whites was legally banned in the South (D'Emilio & Freedman, 1988). Free Blacks who lived in the North experienced prevalent racism, and interracial marriage laws were passed to ensure the purity of the White race (Takaki, 1993).

Over time, family formation among Black slaves changed, due to a more even sex ratio, higher birth rates, and lower mortality rates. Slaves formed stable, monogamous relationships, although these were not always co-residential due to the selling of a partner, or to the small numbers of slaves on non-plantation farms (Coontz, 2010; D'Emilio & Freedman, 1988). Ideas of family and kin were expansive, and not restricted to blood ties, setting the stage for the community and fictive kin ties seen in today's African American families (D'Emilio, 2002).

Similar to the Europeans' views of Native American sexuality and family patterns, the colonists also constructed the sexuality and family lives of African slaves as aggressive, bestial, and savage, using this in part as justification of domination and enslavement of African peoples. Although White men could have casual encounters with female slaves without sanction, harsh and lethal punishment was wrought on Black men who dared to have sex with White women, reinforcing systems of racial dominance (D'Emilio & Freedman, 1988; Takaki, 1993). As Coontz so eloquently puts it, "concerns about racial/sexual hierarchies created high levels of sexual hypocrisy" (2010, p. 36).

A final note of interest from this historical era concerns the legal regulation of marriage for European-Americans. Coontz (2010) notes that between the American Revolution and the Civil War, ideas about what constituted a "marriage" were not entirely steeped in legalities. Instead, "if a couple acted as if they were married, they were treated as such" (p. 40), and cohabitation accompanied by community acceptance was sufficient to constitute a legal marriage. It was not until the post-Civil War era that informal or common-law marriages were declared invalid, and marriage rights were heavily legislated.

Westward Expansion and Industrialization

Over the course of the 19th century, several major changes occurred in marital and family life that were to have a profound impact on romantic relationships. Black couples who had been precluded from marriage under slavery were allowed to marry with the advent of emancipation. Both Black and White heterosexual couples began to exercise more control over their fertility and the close connection between sex and reproduction began to erode; sexuality was increasingly linked with love and intimacy; and gender was constructed in more rigid and separate terms (Coontz, 2010; D'Emilio & Freedman, 1988). These changes resulted from economic and geographic growth, such as westward expansion and the displacement of Native peoples, industrialization, increased immigration, the growth of towns, and the "market revolution" spurred by the production of cotton and textiles (D'Emilio & Freedman, 1988; Takaki, 1993). Rather than relying on small close-knit communities, Americans increasingly relied on the family for social stability. And, as men left the home to participate in the market economy, women remained in the home, imbued with the task of the moral purity of the family (D'Emilio & Freedman, 1988). The era of separate spheres for middle- and upper-class European-Americans, with complementary yet natural differences between the sexes, and the separation of work and home, had arrived (Coontz, 2005).

Ironically, new expectations for communication and sentimentality in marriage arose at the very time that men and women were entering these separate spheres (Coontz, 1988). Romantic love began to flourish in all areas except among the Whites on the plantations of the South and increasingly was viewed as the only acceptable basis for marriage (Coontz, 2005; D'Emilio & Freedman, 1998; Lystra, 1989; Rothman, 1984). Romantic love contained elements of passion as well as mutuality, emotional intimacy, communion, sympathy, candor, and mystery (Lystra, 1989; Rothman, 1984). Still, women had to remain realistic about marriage and romantic love, as they needed to marry in order to survive economically, and men were not encouraged to marry until they were able to provide a home and income (Coontz, 2005).

Romantic love also entailed sexual passion and expression (Lystra, 1989); however, because standards for premarital sexual behavior were tightening, sexual intercourse for middle-class White couples was clearly reserved for marriage, and the premarital conception rate fell (D'Emilio & Freedman, 1988; Rothman, 1984). The range of acceptable sexual behavior became more constrained over the 19th century so that petting became unacceptable behavior (Coontz, 2005). Young women were given the responsibility of controlling affectionate expression, and a "unique middle-class identity based partly on male self-control but especially on female virtue" was ushered in as a core feature of a new emphasis on female purity, passionlessness, and moral superiority (Coontz, 2005, p. 159). In contrast to this middle-class ideal, the poor and working classes were blamed for the presence of "fallen women" and loose sexual morals, and women who did not have access to the middle-class ideal of home and full-time domesticity were seen as "moral degenerates" (Coontz, 2005, p. 169).

This changing view of men and women was to have a pervasive effect on American heterosexual courtship and marriage (Rothman, 1984). "Separate spheres," as an ideology, emphasized the immutable differences between the sexes from the mundane to the spiritual. A woman's nature was virtuous and angelic; she was capable of calming the wild nature of a man and leading him to a path of virtue (Coontz, 1988). Her domesticity was prized, whereas his ability to support his family was his most important goal. Rather than the interdependent relationship of husband and wife of rural colonial times, the mid-19th century was marked by separation of the sexes (Coontz, 2005; D'Emilio, 1999; D'Emilio & Freedman, 1988; Gadlin, 1977). The cult of domesticity sanctified the home and gave European-American women a revered place of their own; ironically, it also reduced their economic power, as it took away their roles as co-producer of the family's subsistence (Coontz, 2005). However, this ideology of separate spheres did not extend to all; White middle-class mothers were supported in their "cult of domesticity" through the domestic and factory labor of working-class, poor, and slave women and children (Coontz, 2010).

The separation of the spheres of middle-class men and women served to limit the ability of middle-class White adolescents to get to know each other (Rothman, 1984). Whereas before puberty boys and girls shared everyday life, after puberty young girls entered the "female world" and prepared for future housewifery (Demos, 1986). Among middle- and upper-class White families in the northern states, when a relationship was begun, the couple was afforded a great deal of time together in private, often in the home of the girl, and couples were still relatively autonomous in their choice of mate (D'Emilio &

Freedman, 1988). In the southern states, among the plantation class, White courtship was more restricted, female sexual purity was heavily regulated, men were allowed great sexual privilege, and economic considerations were a priority in the choice of a mate (D'Emilio & Freedman, 1998). Ironically, the emphasis on female chastity and purity made sexual intimacy in marriage difficult for many women (Coontz, 2005). In both the North and the South, over the course of the 19th century, heterosexual courtship became more formalized and the customs of the formal announcement of the engagement and exchanging of engagement rings or other tokens of commitment began (Murstein, 1974; Rothman, 1984). This was also the beginning of the public wedding ceremony with a white dress (the latter inspired by Queen Victoria), symbolizing the purity of the bride (Coontz, 2005; Rothman, 1984).

Urban, White, working-class young adults conducted their courtships in public. D'Emilio and Freedman (1988) note that, by working in urban factories, or as seamstresses, young adults were freed from family and small-town scrutiny and obligation. They would walk out together, flirt, spend time in parks, at beaches, and in dance halls, and pair up into couples. And, until mid-century, premarital sex was accepted for working-class engaged couples.

Immigration of Europeans to the eastern half of the country increased from the 1830s through the beginning of the next century, and of Chinese to the western states with the advent of the Gold Rush and the building of the railroads. Each new immigrant group brought their marriage customs and kinship patterns with them; however, as they were the "other" and were cast as less-than and sexually depraved (to support the notion of White moral and sexual superiority), their customs were devalued (Coontz, 2005; D'Emilio, 2002; D'Emilio & Freedman, 1998; Takaki, 1993). European immigrants often settled together in cities and formed tight-knit, neighborhood-based communities, where the youth were watched over by family and neighbors alike. The emphasis was on courtship and marriage within one's immigrant group (Coontz, 2010; Takaki, 1993).

In the West, courtship and marriage among the Chinese were effectively prevented through exclusion laws that precluded citizenship, granted permission to enter the country only to men, and, by 1881, excluded Chinese immigrants altogether. These policies were designed to encourage the Chinese to return to China rather than establish families in the United States (Takaki, 1993). Still, Chinese women did immigrate to the United States in small numbers by the end of the century. Early on, they were forced into brothels or sold as brides; later on, through arranged marriages that emphasized parental control and economic considerations, they became integral workers in the economy of cities such as San Francisco (Barsanti, 2005; Cott, 2000). As it became permissible for Chinese women to emigrate by century's end, Chinese men would send for brides from China, engaging the services of a matchmaker to ensure a good match (Riley, 1996).

The sexuality and romantic relationships of Native Americans, Blacks, and Mexicans continued to be constructed in negative terms (savage, promiscuous, inferior, syphilitic), as White concerns about the purity of the White race continued (D'Emilio & Freedman, 1988). The federal government enacted social control over marriage practices by demanding that former slaves, ex-polygamists, and Native Americans adhere to monogamy as a condition of being granted citizenship (Cott, 2000; Perdue, 1994). These depictions and laws failed to acknowledge the unique family and sexual patterns that evolved in non-White groups in response to the larger social forces of immigration, slavery, manifest destiny, and religion (D'Emilio & Freedman, 1988).

In the West and Southwest, family customs evolved from Spanish and Native American practices, and were also influenced by Catholicism. Spanish couples courted in public, meeting at fiestas and fandangos, and sensuality was openly expressed; still, economic considerations and parental arrangement of matches rather than romance took precedence in marriage choices. Women were allowed to be passionate (although the double standard was maintained); when premarital conception occurred, families insisted on marriage, and family honor was prized (D'Emilio & Freedman, 1989; Riley, 1996). "Free unions" were accepted, and occurred when there was no access to a priest or to a legal marriage (D'Emilio & Freedman, 1988, p. 89). Prior to the Mexican-American War, Mexican women in the West were allowed to own and inherit property (well before European women in the East were able to do so), which gave them more power in mate choice and family decisions. Yet these legal rights eroded from mid-century on with the formation of the western states and the influx of European settlers (Barsanti, 2005).

Many Native American courtship practices were continued in the West throughout the 19th century. These included courtship walks (two circles, one of single men, one of single women) that allowed available partners to be perused, the presentation of gifts to the parents of the woman, and the exchange of tokens (such as venison and corn) to symbolize the ability to provide for one another. Some tribes, such as the Salishan, emphasized that young girls were to remain relatively secluded and closely supervised until they were married; most villages or camps encouraged within-group mate choice (Riley, 1996). As Whites conquered more and more of the Southwest, active programs to wipe out Indian and Spanish cultures ensued, and the sexual values of the European Protestant middle classes were imposed (Cott, 2000; D'Emilio & Freedman, 1988).

Constructions of Black unrestrained sexuality continued; in the South, this was cast in terms of inherent characteristics, and in the North, as a product of the institution of slavery, which denied the right to marry (thus eliminating the regulatory aspects of a legal union). Slaves emphasized the formation of stable and monogamous relationships, although they had to constantly

13

balance their customs and desires with the wills of their masters (D'Emilio & Freedman, 1988). Initial meetings between potential partners usually occurred during church services, dances, and holiday events; corn shuckings and candy pulls were also social events that fostered male–female interaction (D'Emilio & Freedman, 1988; Griffen, 2005). Men would compete for the attention of a woman, using verbal wit to show their prowess (Griffen, 2005). Courtships could last as long as a year, and consisted of a series of supervised visits that took place on the plantation of the woman; however, much of the courting relationship was intermittent and infrequent (D'Emilio & Freedman, 1988; Griffen, 2005; Parent & Wallace, 1993). Masters still retained control, as permission was needed to marry or to court someone from a different planation. Still, slave mothers in particular controlled the courtships of their daughters, working to delay childbearing by emphasizing the ages of 20 or 21 as the right time to begin courting (Parent & Wallace, 1993). Slaves developed marriage rituals, including "jumping the broom," and incorporated aspects of Christian ceremonies into these rituals. Courtship and marriage were based on mutual attraction, emotional ties, love, and pragmatic concerns. Under the strictures of slavery there was no need to establish the "legitimacy" of children, or property rights, so premarital sex was accepted, as were children who were born outside a committed union (Cott, 2000; D'Emilio & Freedman, 1988).

Emancipation fundamentally changed courtship and marriage for Black Americans, who now were granted the legal right to marry (in some areas, slave marriages were automatically validated), and the ability to reunite with family members who had been dispersed. Former slaves eagerly married in great numbers, and Black and White clergy alike emphasized premarital chastity and monogamy as markers of progress and respectability (D'Emilio & Freedman, 1988; Franklin, 2010). Whereas permission of the master controlled partnering during slavery, after emancipation Blacks emphasized parental consent and supervision (Griffen, 2005; Parent & Wallace, 1993). Blacks in the South continued to engage in premarital intercourse, and children born outside of wedlock were accepted as full members of the community (D'Emilio & Freedman, 1988).

At the same time, "the dismantling of slavery initiated a new and terrifying era in southern race relations in which sexuality became one of the central means of reasserting white social control over blacks" (D'Emilio & Freedman, 1988, p. 104). The purported lusting of Black men after White women was used to justify lynching and murder, and Black women were raped and sexually assaulted by Whites without sanction. The fear of mixing the races, and the dilution of the purity of the White race, fostered both new laws to prevent miscegenation and an elaborate system of social segregation that would ensure sexual segregation.

D'Emilio and Freedman (1998) place these concerns over interracial sex into a larger picture of the social dynamics of the 19th century. The White middle class used ideals of female purity, male self-control, and family stability, and notions of the depraved sexual and family lives of non-Whites, as means to justify the conquest of and denial of full citizenship to "others." In this context, other racial groups maintained their older traditions of sexuality and family. Equally threatening to White middle-class culture was the development of commercial sexual outlets and the movement of sexuality into the public sphere.

Although sexual expression between members of the same sex was viewed as immoral and unnatural, in the 19th century such intimate same-sex relationships were flourishing. Intense, passionate friendships with members of the same sex were common, and such quasi-romantic friendships were accepted (Coontz, 2005; Faderman, 2000; Rupp, 1989; Smith-Rosenberg, 1985; Vicinus, 2004). Because middle-class women so highly valued the separate feminine sphere, they were especially encouraged to develop intimate friendships, along with expressions of "passionate longings for emotional, spiritual and physical intimacy" (D'Emilio & Freedman, 1988, p. 121). Many scholars believe that such passionate same-sex friendships for women and men alike included genital sexual expression, although there are few historical references to such interaction. The surviving letters and poems of middle-class women do express longing, romance, and physical intimacy between female friends, but whether these refer to normative Victorian female friendship practices (which were physically close but not sexual) or mask lesbian romantic relationships is under debate (D'Emilio & Freedman, 1988; Goode & Wagner, 1999; Rupp, 1989). Still, over the course of the century, new opportunities did arise for same-sex sexual interaction. White men working in cities had opportunities, because family control was absent and anonymity was possible. There is also documentation of male same-sex unions and relationships among the cowboys of the West, and among soldiers. For women of the working class, forming a same-sex union meant dressing and passing as a man, in order to earn wages and to marry one's same-sex partner (D'Emilio, 1999; D'Emilio & Freedman, 1988).

Transition to the 20th Century

By the 1890s, several profound changes would affect American's ideas about sex, love, and romantic relationships. Whereas during industrialization sex and marriage were intimately linked together, by the end of the 19th century opportunities for sexual interaction increased with the development of the commercial sex industry (D'Emilio & Freedman, 1988). Simultaneously, the seeds of women's equality and economic independence were sprouting, as White women gained legal rights, and both Black and White women demanded suffrage, were granted access to high-school and college educations, reduced their fertility, and entered the paid labor force (Coontz, 2005; Demos, 1986).

Still, the theme of heterosexual men and women as creatures with different natures persisted among middle-class White couples through the late 19th century, but with an added twist. Now, rather than being possessed of wild spirits, men were viewed as depraved; their immorality became a grave problem (Rothman, 1984). Men had to learn to control their animal passions, which could only be accomplished through women's modesty. Yet, although modest, women were still seen as needing protection due to their perceived physical and intellectual inferiority (Smith-Rosenberg, 1985). When young men and women were together, the propriety of the times increasingly demanded that they keep their distance, because the purity of the young woman had to be guarded; simultaneously, romantic love became ever more romantic, and was increasingly viewed as the best vehicle for stability in marriage (Coontz, 2005; Rothman, 1984).

Middle- and upper-class Black women followed the White middle-class values of the times, as evidenced in the Women's Clubs of the late 19th and early 20th centuries (Franklin, 2010). Black club women in the North were activists and reformers who sought to uplift Black women by bringing in new images of respectability. The ideology of patriarchy did not hold sway, however, as the emphasis was on Black women as community leaders and as equal to Black men. Within the Black community, there was more acceptance of women's leadership, activism, and intelligence, and well-educated Black men highly valued marriage to well-educated Black women. A "Black Woman's Era" was ushered in by the turn of the century; Black women attained higher levels of education, constituted 43% of Black professionals, and in many public spheres challenged Black men's authority (Franklin, 2010). Black women of the upper and middle classes placed great stock in romantic love as the basis of marriage; as the daughters of ex-slaves, they "treasured their right to select their mates, to court, and to marry" (Alexander, 2004, p. 17). Rituals developed around "the courtship season," including an emphasis on only receiving the attentions of respectable and Christian men who were well educated. Many times, these romances were conducted via correspondence, including the exchange of letters, poems, and love tokens (locks of hair and photographs; Alexander, 2004).

The customs of courtship among the White upper classes became increasingly formal, and chaperones became a common fixture (Riley, 1996; Rothman, 1984). A young man and young woman had to be formally introduced before they were allowed to speak to each other. In the early stages of courtship, long rides and late hours were frowned upon; instead, most courting activities took place in the girl's home (Waller, 1951). If a relationship lasted too long or became too intimate, it was supposed to result in an engagement. After an engagement, the couple was given more privacy and time alone; however, women's chastity was still highly valued (Bailey, 1988).

The elaborate system of calling was not feasible for the less wealthy, however. Families living in one or two rooms did not have the space available for partnering in the home, so working-class youth courted in public (Bailey, 1988). In addition, increasing urbanization meant that many young people were on their own, working in the cities (Coontz, 1988). Because rules of propriety dictated that a young woman could not have a gentleman in her apartment, boarding house, or dorm room, courting activities had to take place in the public domain (Bailey, 1988). Eventually, the wealthy saw the less formal system of courtship in public as something to emulate, and the fun and excitement of "dating" became an upper-class phenomenon as well (Bailey, 1988; Coontz, 2005).

"Going somewhere" became the activity of heterosexual courtship and the pastime of working-class youth by the turn of the 20th century (Rothman, 1984). In earlier times, young people had gone alone to dances, or stayed out late without adult supervision; however, these activities took place within a system of informal community control (Koller, 1951). Now the system of informal controls was loosening, as partnering moved into the dance halls, cabarets, and amusement parks (Bailey, 1988; D'Emilio & Freedman, 1988). The custom of "treating" (the male partner buying refreshments, theater tickets, etc.) began, although the expectation was that working-class girls would exchange sexual favors for such treats (Peiss, 2004). Interestingly, the very term "date" has its origins in prostitution, although in the early years of the 20th century this word origin became obscured (Bailey, 2004). Additionally, the movement of courtship from the home to the public sphere afforded less privacy and time to get to know one another, and, although the cabaret allowed for more sexual experimentation, it did not allow for emotional intimacy (Rothman, 1984).

The separate spheres that dominated much of the 19th century began to erode by century's end, fueled by the increased numbers of adolescents who continued schooling through high school, the eradication of child labor, the growing role for European-American women in the public sphere, the women's rights movement, and the continuing development of economic opportunities for men and single women (Coontz, 2010). It was still up to the woman to keep sexual behavior in check, however, and sexual restraint was valued (Coontz, 2005; Rothman, 1984). The link between sex and marriage was still present, and sexual fulfillment was seen as an important component of a happy marriage and the development of the bond between man and wife. At the same time, sexual expression expanded beyond marriage, particularly as sexuality became a private rather than a communal concern, the link between sex and procreation was severed, and methods of preventing conception became more available. Indeed, the emergence of a birth control movement was a sign of a huge shift in views about female sexuality, from one of passionlessness to one where female sexual expression was accepted (Coontz, 2005; D'Emilio & Freedman, 1988).

17

Customs of immigrant courtship were shifting in this era, as well. In the West, Japanese immigrants developed a system of "picture brides" that allowed men to send for a wife. This practice utilized the Japanese tradition of engaging a matchmaker through the use of photos accompanied by information on the woman's family genealogy, health, and finances (Riley, 1996). Though their numbers were small, Japanese immigration spurred more anti-Asian sentiment and fears about interracial unions; as a result, in the early 1900s the "gentlemen's agreement" between the Japanese and U.S. governments was forged to effectively exclude Japanese immigration. This agreement did allow a very small number of Japanese men already in the U.S. to bring in Japanese brides (Cott, 2000). And, in the eastern U.S., social reformers heartily disapproved of immigrant marriages arranged by the larger family, and instead emphasized the importance of adopting the "love match" as a marker of assimilation and moral adaptation (Cott, 2000).

By the end of the 19th century, the opportunities for same-sex love and sex had expanded, as a result of the possibility to live apart from the community of the family of origin, the accessibility of wage labor allowed economic independence, and, for middle-class White women, growing enrollment in college (D'Emilio, 1999). Female same-sex relationships that were intensely passionate developed among college-going women, and a disproportionate number of college-educated women at the turn of the century never entered into a heterosexual marriage (D'Emilio, 1999). These female partnerships, sometimes termed "Boston marriages," would encompass living and traveling together, sharing holidays and family traditions, and even sleeping in the same bed (D'Emilio & Freedman, 1988).

Same-sex desire and eroticism were becoming more available, as a result of the growth of both large cities and a capitalist economy that allowed the freedom to develop a distinct sexual identity (D'Emilio, 2002). Meeting places for men developed where sexual "deviance" was tolerated, including restaurants, bathhouses, drag balls, YMCAs, clubs, bars, and resorts, allowing for the expression of same-sex attraction (D'Emilio, 1999). Women could form same-sex relationships in large cities that had furnished-room districts. Yet, these spaces and same-sex relationships remained hidden, as punishment and ostracism meant that same-sex desire had to remain a secret (D'Emilio & Freedman, 1988). And, even as the possibilities for same-sex romantic relationships increased, they were defined as abnormal and diseased by the leading sexologists of the era, making what had been previously viewed as innocent same-sex passionate friendships into a mental illness (D'Emilio & Freedman, 1988; Innes, 2000). The term "homosexual" was increasingly used, and same-sex sexual expression was transferred from a discrete behavior to "a description of the person, encompassing emotions, dress, mannerisms, behavior and even physical traits," leading eventually to the creation of a sexual minority (D'Emilio & Rothman, 1988, p. 226).

The Era of World Wars

By 1920, dating was the centerpiece of 20th century American heterosexual partnering. Dating involved informal, unchaperoned male–female interaction with no specific commitment (Murstein, 1974). The rules of dating were established by the peer group rather than the community at large (Modell, 1983). Bailey (1988) attributed the rise of dating in the first part of the 20th century to both the creation of adolescence as a distinct period of the life cycle and to the emergence of mass culture. The former trend allowed the selection of a mate to be delayed, and the latter trend provided a uniform set of rules of etiquette to be followed. Other scholars cite the shift from rural to urban society, the emancipation of women, the emphasis on companionate marriage, widespread ownership of cars, the creation of youth culture in high schools, the emergence of motion pictures, and the decrease in community oversight as forces that brought dating into being (Burgess, Wallin, & Schultz, 1954; D'Emilio & Freedman, 1988; Lynd & Lynd, 1937; Murstein, 1974).

Dating was to quickly become the major recreational pastime of youth (Waller, 1951). Although courtship had always had an economic basis (e.g., a man's readiness to marry was contingent on his ability to support a family), dating made a man's access to a woman contingent on money in a very direct way. Dating also changed the balance of power. When courtship was centered in the home, the woman was more in control, but as courtship shifted to the public sphere and the need for money arose, control also shifted to the man (Bailey, 1988). Perhaps the best example of this economic basis of European-American courtship comes from Waller's (1937) classic study of the "rating and dating" complex. By the time of Waller's study, dating was no longer about "love"; it was about competition and consumption (Bailey, 1988).

The most popular pastimes on dates were dancing and going to the movies (Lynd & Lynd, 1937; Rothman, 1984). Dancing transitioned at this time from a group to a couple activity, and allowed the excitement of physical closeness without the dangers of sex (Modell, 1983; Rothman, 1984). Another powerful influence on dating was the automobile, as it allowed both privacy and intimacy, and the practice of "petting" became more common (Lynd & Lynd, 1937).

It should be noted that the system of heterosexual dating was somewhat independent of the system of heterosexual courting for marriage (Rothman, 1984). Dating became a vehicle for getting to know someone before settling into an exclusive pairing (Burgess et al., 1954). Dating and courtship also had different objectives: dating focused on success and increasing one's popularity without becoming emotionally involved, whereas courtship focused on finding a mate who exhibited the traits of emotional maturity, honesty, genuineness, and a desire for family life (Waller, 1951). Dating left off and courtship began when a young woman and a young man began keeping "steady company"; a graduated series of dates was considered the first step into a serious romance (Modell, 1983). By the 1930s, "steady" relationships had developed as a stage between the casualness of dating and the commitment to marry (Modell, 1983).

Still, the heterosexual dating patterns described above were not really available to all adolescents, as they required income and access to entertainment that were only available to White youth of the urban and suburban middle class. Poor Black youth of the rural South maintained earlier patterns of meeting at church, picnics, or working in the fields; sex play and premarital intercourse were not sharply sanctioned. Middle- and upper-class Black youth, in contrast, were more restricted in their behavior, as parents emphasized respectability and a strict moral code that was seen as a critical component of social mobility. White rural youth lacked access to cars, and parents were able to more closely monitor their behavior in these smaller communities. White working-class youth who worked in cities had the ability to meet each other in dance halls, bowling alleys, and taverns, and were more likely to engage in premarital intercourse as a result of their new freedoms (D'Emilio & Freedman, 1988).

Beginning in the 1910s and continuing through the 1930s, several great migrations occurred that would change the fabric of the urban East and Midwest. Cuban and Puerto Rican migration to New York was fueled by poverty and unemployment, as was African-American migration from the South to the urban North (Opie, 2008). Like their White counterparts, Latino and Black youth met in the dance and music halls, as well as eateries, of urban areas. The emphasis on marrying members of one's own race eventually gave way to the melding of Latino and Black cultures and intermarriage (Opie, 2008).

Portions of the 19th century conception of male and female sexuality continued into the 20th century. Men were presumed to be interested in sex, and women were expected to control sex in the relationship by saying "no" (Bailey, 1988). Sexual expression was liberalizing, however, as the culture of adolescence brought with it new norms of liberal sexual behavior (Bailey, 1988). Caplow, Bahr, Chadwick, Hill, and Williamson (1982) remarked that the 1920s represented a period of sexual and social revolution unmatched until the late 1960s; sex was the dominant theme of movies and literature, the code of behavior for women liberalized, and the incidence of premarital intercourse was on the rise. Sexual norms and behavior patterns that had previously been associated with White and Black working-class youth increasingly were appropriated by the middle class, forming the sexual revolutions of the 1920s. Sexual experimentation before marriage became more common, and sexual pleasure and eroticism were increasingly viewed as important aspects of personal happiness. All of these changes were intertwined with increased legal rights for women, and the growing availability of contraceptives (D'Emilio & Freedman, 1988).

Despite liberalization, a double standard of sexual behavior blamed women for sexual transgressions and even rape (Bailey, 1988). Unless a woman was truly pure, she was considered cheap, and fair game; the good girl versus bad girl dichotomy abounded (Modell, 1983). Such a depiction of the sexual natures of men and women failed to recognize the increasing pressure placed on women to repay the debt engendered by a man's spending money on a date (Bailey, 1988). Despite the pressure, most of the women who had premarital sex had intercourse only with the man they were engaged to marry; whereas 87% of women born before 1890 were virgins at marriage, only 30% of those born after 1910 waited until marriage. The comparable figures for men were 49% and 14% virgins at marriage for the pre-1890 and post-1910 birth cohorts (Terman, 1938). Although virginity was still desirable in a bride, it was no longer a requirement, and "going all the way" was permissible in the context of an engagement (D'Emilio & Freedman, 1988; Rothman, 1984).

Romantic love was considered the only basis of marriage, and there was an increasing emphasis on the couple relationship, with higher expectations for emotional closeness (Coontz, 1988). Still, sex roles in the 1920s and 1930s were clearly organized around separate spheres for men and women (Lynd & Lynd, 1937). The roots of equality for women were firmly in place, however, as enfranchisement, legal rights, and greater freedom in divorce developed during the first three decades of the 20th century (Kelley, 1969). However, this emancipation did not include "freedom to pursue a career"; from 1920 to 1930 there was only a 1% rise in female employment (Margolis, 1984).

The rating and dating scene was disrupted by the Great Depression and the Second World War. College enrollments declined, as did the influence of fraternities, and women entered the labor force with a vengeance (Margolis, 1984; Rothman, 1984). Dating became a less elaborate affair, and heterosexual courtship was put on hold for many college-age youth, although younger adolescents continued with the social patterns of the 1930s (Bailey, 1988; D'Emilio & Freedman, 1988; Lynd & Lynd, 1937; Rothman, 1984). At the same time, when the Second World War began, opportunities for sexual interaction and economic autonomy increased, as young men joined the services and young women moved to cities for wartime employment (D'Emilio & Freedman, 1988). The changes in the world at large were to have a profound impact on the heterosexual courtship system after the war.

The era of world wars was also an era of increased development of gay and lesbian relationships and communities. During the 1920s and 1930s, gay and lesbian communities evolved, although in different manners based on race and class. For working-class individuals, especially in immigrant communities, a gay lifestyle was difficult to pursue given close-knit ties within these neighborhoods. On the other hand, urban Black working-class communities were relatively tolerant of homosexuality (D'Emilio, 1999; Leonard, 2011). Some White working-class women "crossed," that is, dressed and worked as men, and married other women. There were also working-class lesbian communities that developed around bars in large cities (Kennedy & Davis, 1993). Among middle-class Whites, there were friendship networks of "women-committed women" who were working in settlement houses or in women's movements; these women usually had enough financial independence and social status to be able to live together without men (Rupp, 1989). Still, these communities were difficult to find, and unstable (D'Emilio, 1999). Although the 1920s and 1930s brought more explicit references to homosexuality into plays, movies, literature, songs, and popular culture, psychiatry continued to label homosexuality as deviant. Ultimately, the liberalization of heterosexual sexual interaction was not accompanied by positive attitudes toward homosexuality, as earlier moves to demonize and pathologize homosexual desire continued (D'Emilio & Freedman, 1988).

Even though the military labeled homosexuality as deviant (and used the new tests of mental health to screen out gays and lesbians), the Second World War created new opportunities for same-sex desire and the development of gay identity. The movement of men into the military, and women into the cities and factories, created spaces to be away from the scrutiny of family and neighbors, and to be together with large numbers of one's gender. D'Emilio and Freedman note that, "for a generation of young Americans, the war created a setting in which to experience same-sex love, affection, and sexuality, and to participate in the group life of gay men and women . . . a dramatic . . . alternative to the years of isolation and searching for others that had characterized gay life in the previous half century" (1988, p. 289). Gays and lesbians continued to form communities after the war, and created spaces and institutions that supported their sexual identities, such as gay bars and bathhouses, and lesbian clubs and friendship networks (D'Emilio & Freedman, 1988).

Black heterosexuality continued to be demonized. D'Emilio and Freedman (1988) note that, as Blacks migrated to the North during the 1920s through the 1940s, "northern white society reshaped the sexual mythology of the South to its own ends" (p. 295). Whites were attracted to the vibrant nightlife of the urban ghettos, and places such as Harlem, which were experiencing a Black renaissance, became spaces for White voyeurism. And, due to the harsh economic times, Black women were forced into prostitution, for which they were arrested at significantly higher rates than their White counterparts. Black men, too, were constructed in negative terms, as sexual aggressors and rapists. These trends all contributed to the continued construction of Black sexuality as wild and animalistic, the Black family as pathological, and Black sexuality as something to be controlled. Indeed, the birth control movement was ironically supported by southern states, which increasingly provided state funding as part of a program to limit the fertility of Black women (despite the fact that Black women's fertility had been lower than that of White women for quite some time; D'Emilio & Freedman, 1988).

The Second World War catalyzed changes for immigrants, as well. Longstanding ideas about Asian immigration had begun to break down, although anti-Asian sentiment reached new heights with the internment of Japanese Americans. Chinese exclusion laws were repealed, and Chinese American men demanded the immigration of their Chinese wives. The War Brides and Soldiers Brides Acts also served to liberalize the rules for American men who married European and Japanese women during the war and occupation. And, the first challenge to interracial marriage bans was successfully argued in the California Supreme Court in 1948 (Cott, 2000).

Postwar Changes

One of the most notable heterosexual demographic trends of the 20th century was the drop in the age at first marriage and the increase in the marriage rate during the late 1940s and early 1950s. By 1950, the age at marriage was at its lowest point for the 20th century: 22 years for men and 20 years for women (Mintz & Kellogg, 1988). Whether fueled by a desire for stability after years of upheaval, the much-publicized "man shortage," or a desire of youth to assert their independence (Bailey, 1988; Modell, 1989), the increasingly younger age at marriage had important effects on heterosexual courtship and dating. Dating activities were starting at an earlier age: by junior high school, group dating was common, in which a group of boys met up with a group of girls and subsequently paired off (Rothman, 1984). These youth began dating in earnest in high school (over three-quarters of youth reported dating during high school; Burgess, Wallin, & Schultz, 1954), with "going steady" as the new centerpiece of the heterosexual dating system (Kelley, 1969). Going steady brought a whole new set of rituals, including tokens of commitment (such as a class ring), a specified number of telephone calls and dates each week, and the implication of greater sexual intimacy (Bailey, 1988). Although youth were likely to go steady several times by the end of high school, going steady often entailed strong affection and love for the partner (Burgess et al., 1954; Rothman, 1984). Popularity for heterosexual girls now rested on their ability to attract a "steady." Unfortunately, such popularity often meant early marriage and low educational attainment for women (Modell, 1989). Those youth who did not go on to college married soon after graduation (Rothman, 1984), after a partnership of one to two years in length (Burgess et al., 1954). For college women, "landing a man" by senior year was an openly acknowledged goal (Bailey, 1988).

Parental reaction to going steady was not positive, especially as parents feared a resulting increase in premarital sexual behavior. Simultaneously, the emphasis on early marriage was seen as a "moral" way of dealing with the issue of youth sexuality (Bailey, 1988), and masked the continuing 20th century trend of sexual permissiveness among youth. The "good girl" engaged in every form of petting except intercourse, or at least that is all she admitted to with her peer group (Rubin, 1976). The incidence of premarital intercourse for both men and women, however, was still about the same as it had been during the 1920s (Caplow et al., 1982). Burges, Wallin, and Schultz (1954), in their study of engaged couples, reported premarital intercourse rates of 67% for men and 46% for women; Ehrmann's (1959) study of dating couples demonstrated similar rates for men only: 62% for men and 15% for women. A woman was still most likely to engage in intercourse only with the man she intended to marry. Indeed, the likelihood of intercourse occurring during an engagement was directly proportional to the length of that engagement (Burgess et al., 1954), and the sanctions among Whites for bearing a child out of wedlock were still very high (Coontz, 2005).

The double standard still held strong sway: men were expected to push for greater sexual interaction, and women were expected to put the brakes on. The main change from the 1920s was that the double standard referred more to petting, whereas by the 1950s it was all about intercourse. A gap was developing between men and women, with the link between sex and love/commitment being much stronger for women, and fewer negative consequences of engaging in intercourse with multiple partners for men (D'Emilio & Freedman, 1988). It is important to note, though, the ways in which class differences played into this heterosexual double standard. Both White and Black middle-class men could engage in intercourse with working-class women and maintain their belief in the importance of chastity among their middle-class female peers (D'Emilio & Freedman, 1988).

Love was still the primary basis for heterosexual marriage. Marriage was seen as the most important source of happiness and fulfillment; among Whites, single men and women were to be pitied because they could not achieve a state of happiness without a spouse (Mintz & Kellogg, 1988; Stein, 1976). Couples emphasized compatibility, common interests, and love as reasons for the selection of their mates (Burgess et al., 1954); the companionate marriage with complementary roles of provider and homemaker was the ideal (Coontz, 2005; Mintz & Kellogg, 1988). As Coontz (2005) notes, the 1950s became the apex of "traditional marriage"—a pattern of male-provider, love-based marriage that had been tinkered with and changed over the preceding 200 years.

The emphasis on masculinity and femininity also changed during the postwar period. Advances in the understanding of prenatal development helped foster the idea that gender identity was a fragile entity (Bailey, 1988). Coupled with this was a fear that the "provider role" of men was being undermined by the wartime influx of women into industry (Margolis, 1984). This fear resulted in a postwar campaign to help men rediscover their masculinity, largely through an emphasis on increased femininity in women and a return to the cult of domesticity (Bailey, 1988). The formula for marital bliss among Whites was a return to the passive female (Lundberg & Farnham, 1947). In courtship this meant that women had to demonstrate their frailties: their need to be protected, and their inferior mental capacity. The new etiquette of courtship further reinforced a man's right to be dominant and made female submissiveness a requirement in a date (Bailey, 1988).

Among Blacks, however, romantic relationships and marriages had always been more equal (Franklin, 2010). The strong emphasis on Black women's education and employment that had begun at the end of the 19th century continued. For example, by 1960, over 60% of Black professionals were women, in contrast to 37% of White professionals (Franklin, 2010). As a result, Black middle-class marriage was constructed in terms of gender equality long before this was the case for White couples. Patterns were different still for Black couples who were working class and poor (D'Emilio & Freedman, 1988). Because premarital sex and out-of-wedlock births were accepted in the Black community, the pressure for early marriage was reduced. And widespread unemployment, coupled with reduced educational and job opportunities, made the ability to support a separate household very difficult for Black men. As a result, women continued to rely on their own kin for support, and their heterosexual romantic relationships "were embedded in a complex network of extended family kinship ties" (D'Emilio & Freedman, 1988, p. 273).

Although there was clear evidence that Black families had many strengths, including strong ties to community and kin, Blacks nevertheless continued to be labeled as promiscuous and immoral. Programs to limit the fertility of Blacks (and the poor, and other racial ethnic minorities) continued, including forced sterilizations (Davis, 2006; D'Emilio & Freedman, 1988). The sexuality of Blacks increasingly became the counterpoint between what was permissible and immoral (White heterosexuality; Black sexuality) (D'Emilio & Freedman, 1988).

Despite the strong emphasis on the "traditional" family, with its laser-sharp focus on heterosexuality, male breadwinner, and female domestic goddess, there was growing evidence of same-sex desire and intimacy during the era. Kinsey's studies of male sexual behavior, conducted in the 1940s, documented as never before the widespread extent of homosexual behavior and relationships. Over one-third of the men studied by Kinsey acknowledged having had homosexual sex, and 4% stated they were exclusively homosexual (D'Emilio & Freedman, 1988). Stable gay communities and subcultures continued to develop, particularly in cities, expanding the opportunity to develop gay identities and relationships (D'Emilio, 1999). The ability to pursue same-sex desire was still related to economics, however. There were more gay men than lesbians in same-sex relationships, due to the greater labor force participation of men; and a greater proportion of lesbians were seen among college-educated women, reflecting their ability to support themselves (D'Emilio, 1999).

Unfortunately, during the 1950s, the postwar backlash against communism, along with the fears of the Cold War, latched onto homosexuals as scapegoats. Gays and lesbians were labeled as both perverts and risks to national security, and the gay communities that had just started to become visible were vulnerable to attack. Masculinity itself was cast as ultra-heterosexual and straight. At the same time, the postwar backlash sparked the development of organized responses by gays and lesbians (such as the Mattachine Society) that became the first gay rights organizations (D'Emilio & Freedman, 1988; Johnson, 2003).

Ultimately, then, the diverse patterns of romantic relationships and sexual expression among non-Whites and gays and lesbians were not acknowledged or recognized in the larger culture of postwar America. Instead, during the "long decade of traditional marriage," a dominant discourse emerged about a singular form of "normalcy"—the heterosexual male breadwinner, married couple with children (Coontz, 2005, p. 230). Despite growing evidence to the contrary, the social construction of these traditional heterosexual relationships was one of unending happiness and romance. And yet, the 1950s, coupled with the decades before it, set the stage for vast changes in our ideas about romance, sexual expression, marriage, and gender (Coontz, 2005; D'Emilio & Freedman, 1988).

The Era of Change: Civil, Women's, and Gay Rights

All was not well in the White, middle-class, idealized family of the 1950s. Coontz (1988) notes that the 1950s ideals about "the family" blatantly ignored the realities of family life for Black, Hispanic, gay, lesbian, and poor Americans, who lived in a context of discrimination and/or poverty that meant that the male breadwinner family was never a viable option. From the civil rights movements of the 1950s and 1960s, to the women's liberation movement and the Gay Liberation Front, the civil rights and social desires of racial minorities, women, and gays/lesbians were pushed to the forefront in ways heretofore unseen (Coontz, 2010; D'Emilio & Freedman, 1988). Simultaneously, the resurgence of youth culture and the generation gap encouraged young people to define themselves in a manner distinct from that of their parents (Mintz & Kellogg, 1988). Youth as a life stage was extended in both directions, as sexual maturation occurred earlier, and the increasing emphasis on educational attainment extended the upper bound of youth (McCary, 1973; Mintz & Kellogg, 1988).

The civil rights movement challenged notions of innate Black inferiority, including the pathologizing of the Black family and intimate relationships.

The movement brought to light not only the deep prejudices of many White Americans against Blacks (and indeed all racial minorities); it also created a space where young people organized together for social change.

Both the women's movement and the burgeoning gay rights movement challenged deeply held ideas about sexuality. Rather than an instinct or drive, sexuality was recast as a "vehicle for domination which, in complex ways, kept certain social groups in a subordinate place in society" (D'Emilio & Freedman, 1988, p. 308). Activist women became vocal about the gender oppression and sexual harassment they experienced in the civil rights and antiwar movements, and began forming women's groups in the 1960s. The women's movement also brought to the forefront the concerns of lesbians (although there were many tensions between straight and gay women in the movement), contributing to the nascent gay rights movement, which had erupted into national consciousness with the Stonewall riots of 1969. These movements together began to reshape the social construction of sexuality within romantic relationships and social/legal institutions alike, and, in particular, the "naturalness" and "immutability" of heterosexuality (D'Emilio & Freedman, 1988). Thus, the civil rights, youth, women's, and gay rights movements together fundamentally challenged our ideas about gender, heterosexuality, and race, and profoundly affected the ways in which men and women approached and experienced romantic partnering.

D'Emilio and Freedman (1988) speak to the contradictory forces that were at play mid-century. Certainly, there was a continuing movement of sexuality out of the realm of the private, and into the public sphere (through literature, movies, pornography, media) that kept non-marital heterosexual sex constantly on display. Simultaneously, there was a movement among White middle-class Americans to keep sexuality contained, coupled with the rejection and demonizing of the sexuality of Black urban communities, and homosexuals. Clear lines were drawn that demarcated what was good versus bad sexuality.

One of the most influential changes in dating and courtship was the result of what Coontz (1992) terms "the technological revolution in reproduction" (p. 191), that is, the development of safe and reliable birth control that effectively separated sex from procreation. Although this revolution occurred throughout the 20th century, the advent of the birth control pill during the 1960s is of particular note, as it placed control over conception firmly in women's hands. Significant changes in the incidence of non-marital intercourse, especially for women, occurred during this period. By 1980, upwards of 80% of male and 65% of female heterosexual college freshmen reported non-marital sexual experience (Robinson & Jedlicka, 1982). Moreover, the timing of intercourse changed: whereas in the 1950s White women were likely to have premarital sex during engagement, by the 1970s they were more likely to engage in sexual intercourse while going steady (Ehrmann, 1959;

Wolfe, 1981). Heated media attention to the contrary, sexuality among youth was not promiscuous, but rather was limited to a few partners (Caplow et al., 1982).

The increased equality of women had pervasive effects upon many aspects of heterosexual dating and courtship. Between 1960 and 1972, the proportion of women attending college increased threefold (Glick, 1975); by the early 1980s, the number of women in college equaled the number of men for the first time. The trend of greater college attendance for both men and women through the 1970s, the increased emphasis on careers for women, and the growing "singles" culture of urban areas, encouraged the delay of the age at first marriage (D'Emilio & Freedman, 1988; Surra, 1990). By 1988, the age at first marriage was 25.9 years for men and 23.6 years for women, the highest it had been since the turn of the century (Surra, 1990).

Dating and going steady were still central features of the heterosexual courtship system; however, White adolescents of the 1970s did not date as often, and they began to date at an older age (the average age for women was 13 in 1958 and 14 in 1978). Rice (1990) noted that dating in the 1970s and 1980s changed in three important ways: there was greater opportunity for informal different-sex interaction, dating became less formal than in previous generations, and there was no longer a set progression of stages from first meeting to marriage. Although by no means egalitarian, dating (and marriage) were nevertheless moving away from a strictly patriarchal ideology.

Changes in sexual behavior and delay of marriage were accompanied by a new stage in the heterosexual courtship system: cohabitation. Although cohabitation was first studied as a lifestyle of college youth (Macklin, 1972), later studies demonstrated that more than 50% of all young adults had cohabited at some point before age 30 (Bumpass & Hsien-Hen, 2000). Interestingly, at the same time there was a seemingly contradictory trend towards more young people ages 18 to 35 living at home with their parents (Coontz, 1988).

The 1950s vision of the perfect relationship had changed by the late 1960s. Now the emphasis was on totally open communication, self-fulfillment, creative and unique forms of interaction, and relationships as inherently changeable (Kidd, 1975). Thus the 1960s and 1970s were characterized by a profound shift in values and behavior for heterosexual romantic relationships. Ironically, whereas the new values emphasized self-fulfillment, they simultaneously focused on marriage as a source of intense emotional intimacy and companionship (Mintz & Kellogg, 1988). Ultimately, however, couples still married for the same reasons their parents did: love and emotional commitment. In fact, over time the importance of love in mate selection increased such that "the degree of emotional satisfaction ... demanded from husband–wife ... relations in the 20th century would have astounded previous generations" (Coontz, 1988, p. 356).

By the mid-1960s, the civil rights movement had reached its height, and voting rights and other civil rights legislation for Black Americans was enacted. The movement also brought to light the extent of government complicity with negative constructions of minorities, such as the forced sterilization of Black, Native American, and Puerto Rican women, and sparked deep protest over the control of the sexuality and reproduction of minorities (Davis, 2006). But, in the midst of these struggles and new-found rights, the Moynihan Report was released, and once again Black romantic relationships and sexuality were constructed as pathological (D'Emilio & Freedman, 1988). Although the report acknowledged the stability and strength of Black middle-class families, it painted a portrait of Black poor families that remains ensconced in our national discourse today, one that blames Black families for their poverty, and uses terms such as "a tangle of pathology" to emphasize the depth of the problem. And, sadly, the purported rise in unwed births among Black women was based on inaccurate data, while simultaneously taking our gaze away from the fact that White unwed births were on the rise (D'Emilio & Freedman, 1988).

Black families continued the trends of romantic partnering seen in earlier times. The gender gap in education persisted, with more Black women completing college and entering professions (Franklin, 2010). The "marriage squeeze" continued, which marked the lower marriage rate for Black women resulting from a decrease in eligible partners (a phenomenon that remains true today for both middle- and low-income Black Americans; Franklin, 2010). Cohabitation rates and non-marital births remained higher for Blacks than for Whites (D'Emilio & Freedman, 1988).

Profound changes were also occurring in gay and lesbian romantic relationships. The early gay rights organizations formed to protest the witch hunts of the McCarthy era began to take bolder steps in the 1960s, challenging laws and policies that subordinated gays and lesbians. Emboldened by the examples of Black power, radical feminism, and the counterculture of the New Left, gay activists began to launch their movement for equality (D'Emilio & Freedman, 1988). They critiqued the ways in which rigid gender roles and the supremacy of the nuclear family created compulsory heterosexuality, and advocated for a view of homosexuality as a normal capacity in all people (Rich, 1980). Gay pride, publicly coming out, and self-acceptance were central themes, and contributed to the development of gay identities and relationships, as well as the demand for public acceptance. Gay organizations proliferated, and new gay institutions were formed, including churches, travel agencies, media, community centers, and health clinics. Progress was also made in the legal sphere as the states began to take sodomy laws off their books, and the American Psychiatric Association took homosexuality out of the DSM (D'Emilio & Freedman, 1988).

Gay rights movements often incorporated intersections of race; for example, Wat (2002) documents the development of gay Asian activism and communities in Los Angeles, and Ramírez (2003) provides a history of the Gay Latino Alliance in San Francisco. At the same time, the gay rights and civil rights movements experienced many tensions; for example, Black civil rights leaders emphasized that the previous acceptance of Black homosexuality among the working class would have to be replaced with a strong emphasis on heterosexuality if social acceptability and racial equality were to be achieved (Leonard, 2011).

The Closing of the 20th Century

The last two decades of the 20th century witnessed a continuation of the trends of greater equality for women, racial-ethnic minorities, and gays/lesbians. Additionally, academic researchers paid more and more attention to their romantic and sexual lives, creating expanded understandings of the differences and similarities between and within groups. Scholars of color, including Andrew Billingsley (1968) and Harriette Pipes McAdoo (1981), catalyzed scholarship on the myriad strengths of ethnic families and romantic relationships. Blumstein and Schwartz's (1983) study of American couples examined men and women, gay and straight, and found both commonalities and differences. McWhirter and Mattison published *The Male Couple* in 1984, describing romantic relationship development and maintenance among gay men; and Anne Peplau (1982) published an early review of research on gay couples.

And yet, the 1980s brought political changes once again, as debates about sex, race, gay rights, and reproductive rights were increasingly polarized. A New Right conservative movement emerged, one that was deeply linked to both religion and politics (D'Emilio & Freedman, 1988). This polarization was accompanied by inklings of a return to a more conservative system of heterosexual romantic partnering in some quarters. Although the women's movement emphasized the alternatives available to women, the ideology of the importance of having a mate for women had not diminished a great deal; indeed, a backlash against feminism and reproductive rights was beginning to erupt (Faludi, 1991). A perusal of the popular literature for women during this time shows a strong emphasis on "finding and keeping a man," often through the traditional wiles of femininity. In the early 1980s the "man shortage" created a nationwide furor (Salholz et al., 1986), and sent the message that women could have education or marriage, but not both. The vision of the perfect relationship emphasized the importance of balancing togetherness and individuality, other-orientation and self-fulfillment, and communicating openly while protecting the partner's feelings (Mintz & Kellogg, 1988). Concern over sexually transmitted diseases such as AIDS and herpes caused a harkening back to monogamous sexual relationships for straights and gays alike (D'Emilio & Freedman, 1988; Mintz & Kellogg, 1988). The battle for civil rights for gays ventured into the demand for marriage rights, engendering cries once again that homosexuality was unnatural and likely to bring about the demise of the traditional family (D'Emilio, 1999). Pro-life movements gained ground in the fight to repeal abortion rights, and public funding for contraception for poor women (Gordon, 2002).

Thus, reforms aimed at creating equality for women, and for gays and lesbians, continued to experience well-organized resistance, and racial ethnic minorities saw earlier gains slowed in the wake of the backlash against affirmative action. And yet, the fundamental challenging of the immutable link between biological sex, gender, and sexuality would not be undone. Indeed, D'Emilio and Freedman (1988) remark on the two centuries of changes to romantic partnering that were culminating by the end of the 20th century: American society had become deeply sexualized, with a consumer culture that made sex both public and profitable; households were smaller and yet more diverse, fundamentally changing in composition over the life cycle; most Americans came to believe that sexual fulfillment was a necessary component of adult life and personal meaning; and the idea that a stable and monogamous heterosexual marriage was the only place to find such fulfillment had long since been abandoned.

Romantic Partnering in the New Millennium

Since the turn of the millennium, romantic partnering has continued to undergo the rapid changes set into action in the latter part of the 20th century. Marriage, although still highly valued, is occurring later in life; the median age at first marriage is approximately 28.3 years for men and 25.8 for women (U.S. Centers for Disease Control and Prevention, 2012). In conjunction with the rise in age at first marriage, rates of premarital sex have increased such that an estimated 80–90% of unmarried people in the United States report having sex by age 20 (Laumann, Gagnon, Michael, & Michaels, 1994). In fact, the average age of first sexual intercourse is 16.9 years of age for boys and 17.4 years of age for girls (Mosher, Chandra, & Jones, 2005). The new millennium also brought increased attention to issues of gender, sexual orientation, and race.

Equality across gender continues to be a major influence on the romantic partnering process. Gender distribution in the workforce approaches equilibrium with women accounting for about 46.9% of paid employees (Bureau of Labor Statistics, 2012). Despite a nearly equal proportion of men and women in the workforce, women still make approximately 18% less money than men, illustrating the persistence of the gender wage gap (Bureau of Labor Statistics, 2012).

In addition to the movement toward equality across gender, the new millennium brought a legal movement toward equal rights for gay and lesbian couples. Recent estimates show that approximately 9 million Americans, or approximately 4% of the population, identify as gay, lesbian, or bisexual (James, 2011). Despite these figures, it was not until 2004, in Massachusetts, that same-sex couples were able to legally marry in any of the United States. As of January 2013, nine more states/districts allow same-sex couples to marry (Connecticut, Iowa, Maine, Maryland, New Hampshire, New York, Vermont, Washington, and Washington, DC). An additional ten states provide legal recognition of civil unions or domestic partnerships (Rhode Island, Delaware, New Jersey, Illinois, Wisconsin, Colorado, Nevada, California, Oregon, and Hawaii).

Race also continues to play a role in the romantic partnering process. Although nearly 98% of couples in the United States are of the same race, more than 1 million couples are interracial (Fields & Casper, 2001). Of these interracial relationships, more than 25% are between Whites and Blacks. Despite the increased prevalence of interracial relationships, acceptance of these relationships has been slow to follow (McNamara, Tempenis, & Walton, 1999). Many have speculated that the reason for the low rates of acceptance of interracial relationships is that they are perceived to experience more difficulties due to cultural or ethnic differences (Gaines & Ickes, 1997). Recent research, however, has shown that individuals in interracial relationships are just as likely to experience relationship satisfaction as those in intraracial relationships (Troy, Lewis-Smith, & Laurenceau, 2006).

This constellation of findings on the changing demographic composition of romantic partnerships, in addition to the emergence of higher levels of equality across gender, sexual orientation, and ethnicity, illustrate the complex nature of romantic partnerships. Furthermore, a number of historical changes and trends will continue to play an important role in the development of romantic relationships, including: rising rates of heterosexual cohabitation, continuing changes in the expression of heterosexual sex, rising rates of out-of-wedlock births, increases in the number of children being born to or adopted by gay parents, the gay marriage movement, and the explosion of Internet-mediated relationships.

The past two decades have seen considerable changes in the frequency of non-marital cohabitation and sexuality. During the 2000s, more than half of all heterosexual couples reported living together before marriage (Coontz, 2005). Many have suggested that the increase in non-marital cohabitation signals the continued movement to less traditional relational values. Further evidence of this movement can be seen in the changes in sexual behavior in young couples. Although the past two decades brought a revival (for some) of virginal pledges to abstain from non-marital sexual intercourse, many teenagers and young couples substitute other sexual behaviors, such as oral sex, which has continued to increase in recent decades (Coontz, 2005). Ostensibly, this increase in oral sex stems from the view that vaginal intercourse is the only behavior that results in the loss of one's virginity. The past two decades also brought increased attention to what some scholars refer to as the "hook up culture," that is, a single sexual encounter with no expectations for the future (Bogle, 2008). Although some researchers argue that hooking up has replaced dating as the primary means of intimate interaction on college campuses (Bradshaw, Kahn, & Saville, 2010), others document that casual sex is not on the rise among youth (Armstrong, Hamilton, & England, 2010).

Perhaps the most striking change in partnering during the past two decades was the emergence of the Internet. Unlike past technological "breakthroughs" like the telephone, the Internet allows users to interact with each other through multiple means (visual, auditory) simultaneously (Bargh & McKenna, 2004). In addition to communication functions, the Internet also serves as a source of a seemingly infinite amount of information. It is currently estimated that approximately two billion people use the Internet, which is nearly double the number who used the Internet even two years ago (Ogolsky, Niehuis, & Ridley, 2009). Given the vast number of individuals who are on the Internet, the ability of individuals to meet, interact, and maintain relationships using technology has increased dramatically in the past decade (Bargh & McKenna, 2004).

Summary

Throughout the history of romantic partnering in America, there are themes of both continuity and change. Change occurred in many ways. Control over the activities of heterosexual courtship went from female to male to semi-egalitarian, the spaces for courtship changed "from front porch to backseat" (the title of Beth Bailey's 1988 book), romantic partnering increasingly required access to monetary resources, and sexual interaction became disconnected from procreation and formal marriage. The gatekeepers of heterosexual courtship also changed from informal community control to parental oversight to the participants themselves.

There were significant changes in possibilities and visibility of romantic relationships for same-sex partners, as well. Whereas the early days of European settlement were marked by no possibility for or recognition of same-sex desire, by the turn of the 20th century, gay and lesbian communities were beginning to form. Through mid-century and into the gay liberation movement of the 1960s, the space and opportunity to form gay and lesbian romantic relationships increased exponentially, and has resulted today in a robust debate over gay marriage and changes in many states to legally recognize gay and lesbian romantic commitment.

Similarly, the romantic relationships of racial and ethnic minorities experienced great changes. We have come far from the eradication of Native

33

partnering practices, the legal prevention of marriage of enslaved African Americans, and the Chinese exclusion laws. We are in the midst of a time when Native, Black, Latino, and Asian Americans have created unique patterns that blend culture and courtship, as well as a time when interracial relationships are widely (though not universally) accepted.

These changes all reflect the myriad ways in which gender, sexuality, race, economics, and families are linked together in our histories. The history of romantic partnering is marked by fundamental changes in ideas about the differences between men and women, the superiority of Europeans over racial/ethnic minorities, and the immorality of same-sex desire. We have traversed many boundaries, including community regulation of intimate relationships, parental efforts to control courtship, the creation of urban spaces for single working men and women, a change to greater equality between men and women, an increase in cohabitation, and the development of gay and lesbian communities. Along the way, changes in our economic structure, and our increased life span, have catalyzed changes in our communities and personal lives. What began as a system of choosing partners from those you had grown up with and worked beside has evolved into 21st century practices of dating, cohabitation, and matchmaking services.

And yet, there is great continuity in the practices of American romantic partnering over time. American youth have always enjoyed relative autonomy in choosing their romantic partners. And love and sexual interaction have been important components of the partnering process for all groups of people, across racial groups and sexualities. Like Coontz (2010), we imagine that the intimate partnerships of the future will continue to emphasize love and sexual passion as the centerpieces of our romantic ties to one another.

Key Concepts

African Americans (pp. 9–10, 12–14, 15–16, 20, 22–23, 25, 26–27, 27)
Asian Americans (pp. 12, 23, 30)
Black Americans, see African Americans
Cohabitation (pp. 28, 32)
Dating (pp. 17, 19–20, 23, 28)
Economics of courtship (pp. 8, 9, 21–22, 25–26, 31)
Gay male relationships, see Same-sex relationships
Gender roles (pp. 8, 11, 16, 20, 21, 23, 25, 27–28, 30–32)
Going steady (pp. 23–24, 28)
Heteronormativity (pp. 5, 26, 27)
Hooking up (p. 33)
Immigrant communities (pp. 12, 18, 21, 23)
Internet (p. 33)
Interracial relationships (pp. 9, 14–15, 32)

Additional Readings

Bailey, B. L. (1988). *From front porch to back seat: Courtship in twentieth-century America.* Baltimore, MD: Johns Hopkins University Press.

Coontz, S. (2005). *Marriage, a history: From obedience to intimacy or how love conquered marriage.* New York, NY: Viking.

D'Emilio, J., & Freedman, E. (1988). *Intimate matters: A history of sexuality in America.* New York, NY: Harper & Row.

Mintz, S., & Kellogg, S. (1988). *Domestic revolutions: A social history of American family life.* New York, NY: Free Press.

Takaki, R. (1993). *A different mirror: A history of multicultural America.* Boston, MA: Little Brown & Co.

3

THEORIES AND MODELS OF ROMANTIC PARTNERING

As we discussed the history of romantic partnering in Chapter 2, we emphasized the myriad ways that partnering processes are embedded within historical, economic, and political contexts. And yet romantic partnering is at its very core a process of individual attraction and choice, and dyadic interaction. In order to explain how partners come together, a host of theoretical models have been developed over time. The present chapter traces the development of the major theories and models proposed to explain the development of romantic relationships, from compatibility models to stage theories to the current emphasis on interpersonal process.

Early Models

Compatibility Models

Interest in the heterosexual partnering process as a subject for systematic study and theoretical development began in the 1940s. As might be expected, most early research was not guided by formal theory. The earliest theoretical developments centered on models of heterosexual compatibility (Cate & Lloyd, 1988). In fact, notions of compatibility are implicit in much current thinking about the partnering process. Early models focused on the role of complementarity or similarity in values, attitudes, roles, and social background in producing compatibility and stable heterosexual partnerships.

Complementarity Needs Model

One of the earliest formal compatibility models of heterosexual mate selection is a more complex version of the layperson's postulate that "opposites attract." Winch's (1955a) complementary needs theory assumed that individuals have certain psychological needs and that people seek marital partners who can fulfill or "complement" those needs. Supposedly, compatibility is induced by Partner B either enacting behaviors that satisfy a need in Partner A, or Partner B avoiding certain behaviors that would conflict with Partner A. In other words, complementarity can exist when one partner has a high need in one personality area, with the other partner having a low need in that same area (e.g., one partner having a high need for submissiveness and the other having a low need for submissiveness). On the other hand, complementarity can exist when different needs are gratified within the couple (e.g., one partner having a need to be dominant and the other having a need to be submissive). Winch (Winch, 1955b; Winch, Ktsanes, & Ktsanes, 1954) reported support for this theory through the results of two studies that used psychoanalytic assessments of needs interviews, as well as the answers of interviewees to projective testing. Unfortunately, although the idea of "complementary needs" has great appeal in folk wisdom, there was a lack of empirical support for the theory. The findings of Winch's studies have received serious criticism on the basis of faulty conceptualization and interpretation, as well as a lack of replication (see Murstein, 1976; Seyfried, 1977; and Tharp, 1963, for comprehensive critiques of the theory).

Similarity Models

In contrast to the complementarity model, the similarity model holds that heterosexual mate selection operates according to the lay hypothesis that "birds of a feather flock together." In other words, the theory holds that individuals select marital partners on the basis of whether they are similar to each other on an array of attributes. Empirical evidence appears to support this model, in that both premarital and marital partners have been found to be similar in attitudes and values (Burgess & Wallin, 1953; Schellenberg, 1960), personality (Antill, 1983), physical attractiveness (Price & Vandenberg, 1979), and several demographic characteristics (age, religion, race, ethnicity, etc.; Hendrick, 1981; Hill, Rubin, & Peplau, 1976). As with complementarity models, similarity models have received criticism. The fact that individuals tend to interact with people living close to them and are likely to be socially similar limits opportunity to select others who are not similar to themselves, thus shedding doubt on whether similarity plays a direct role in the actual decision-making process (Kerckhoff, 1974). In other words, because we live near and are likely to interact with those who are already very similar (in terms of race, education, age, etc.), our chances of meeting a similar other are heightened by mere proximity, rather than systematic choice. In addition, some empirical evidence suggests that the observed similarity in values and world-views of couples evolves over time through their interaction together, rather than being used as an initial selection factor (Stephen, 1985). Other empirical evidence shows that similarity does not distinguish between couples who break up and those who stay together (Hill et al., 1976).

Stage Models

These models of complementarity and similarity led researchers to search for explanations for these contradictory findings. One potential explanation for the contradiction was that complementarity and similarity operated at different stages of heterosexual relationship development (Kerckhoff & Davis, 1962; Murstein, 1970). For example, Murstein's (1970) S-V-R model posited that people first select partners on the basis of physical attraction. At the next stage, people were supposedly seeking partners with whom they had complementary values. Finally, people ostensibly sought others with whom they perceived a compatible role fit.

McWhirter and Mattison (1984) developed a stage model for the development of gay male relationships, based on a sample of 156 male couples. Their theory posited that developing male couples go through a stage of blending (characterized by high sexual passion, limerence, and equalizing of the partnership), followed by stages of nesting (including a compatibility testing phase), maintaining, building, releasing, and renewing.

Despite their intuitive appeal, however, stage models were severely criticized on grounds of faulty conceptualization and their lack of empirical support (Rubin & Levinger, 1974), and fell out of favor within the research literature. Indeed, the idea that all couples go through the same set of stages as they form their romantic relationships simply failed to capture both differences across couples and the complexity of relationship formation.

Contemporary Models and Theories

Dissatisfaction with stage models resulted in relationship researchers exploring other perspectives that might better account for the path to commitment and a long-term romantic partnership. These early conceptualizations were focused on explaining the processes that influenced the movement to heterosexual marriage. Surra, Gray, Boettcher, Cottle, and West (2006) point out that this focus on studying movement to heterosexual marriage has declined because theorists in both psychology and sociology (Berscheid, 1995; Blumstein & Kollock, 1988; Hinde, 1987, 1996) have suggested that researchers should shift their emphasis from studying particular types of relationships (e.g., marriage) to consideration of factors that are salient across several types of relationships (i.e., universal processes). Current research shows that there has been a dramatic shift from studies focused on movement to marriage to those that examine processes (e.g., love, commitment) that are applicable to a wide range of relationship types (Surra et al., 2006). Some approaches have emphasized specific relationship processes (e.g., social exchange, attachment, uncertainty reduction, dialectics) to explain romantic relationship development and maintenance. Others speak to larger processes, such as the intersection of gender, and evolutionary forces. Perhaps the most comprehensive model is the social ecological model (i.e., interpersonal process model) that has been proposed to account for myriad aspects of the development of romantic partnerships.

It should be noted that the study of universal processes has largely been applied to heterosexual couples. Still, there is room for this perspective to be expanded to the study of gay and lesbian couples. Indeed, using extensive longitudinal studies, Kurdek (2004) has documented the many ways in which gay and lesbian cohabiting couples are similar to heterosexual married couples in love, relationship quality, and relationship stability.

Social Exchange Theories

Social exchange theories have been widely applied to the study of relationship development, primarily in heterosexual couples (Homans, 1961). The most basic assumption of these theories is that people seek partners who will provide more rewards than costs (Thibaut & Kelley, 1959). Rewards are those concrete (e.g., social support) and intangible (e.g., happiness at being in a relationship) things exchanged between partners that are perceived to be pleasurable. Costs are those concrete (e.g., arguments, monetary sacrifices) and intangible things (e.g., loss of freedom, worry about partner's fidelity) exchanged between partners that are perceived as punishing or undesirable. Kelley and Thibaut (1978) elaborated this basic view of social exchange into a theory of *interdependence*. Interdependence theory provides a straightforward and parsimonious explanation of its central construct, dependency. Dependency is defined by the degree to which people depend on their relationships for their valued *outcomes* (rewards minus costs). Dependency is engendered as a result of *satisfaction* and *comparison level for alternatives*. Satisfaction (i.e., positive affect) in romantic relationships is fostered when relationship outcomes (rewards minus costs) in the relationship are greater than the level of outcomes that people are accustomed to receiving from their past and present relationships (the comparison level: CL). This is expressed as:

Satisfaction = Outcomes − CL

The other determinant of dependence in a relationship is the comparison level for alternatives (CL-Alt), which is the attractiveness of outcomes available from other relationships or situations. *Dependence* in a relationship is higher to the extent that outcomes exceed the comparison level for alternatives. Thus, dependence is greater when satisfaction is high and the comparison level for alternatives is low.

Rusbult (e.g., Rusbult, 1980; Rusbult, Coolsen, Kirchner, & Clarke, 2006) extended interdependence theory with the development of the *investment model*. This model posits that satisfaction and the quality of alternatives alone cannot sufficiently explain dependence. Rusbult reasoned that, because some relationships persist despite low relational satisfaction or an abundance of quality alternatives, other factors also must contribute to dependence. This reasoning resulted in Rusbult and colleagues (2006) proposing that investment into the relationship also should increase *dependence* on a relationship. Investments can be direct (e.g., partner support, effort, time) or indirect (e.g., children, friends). Investments increase dependence because they raise the costs of ending the relationship (Rusbult et al., 2006).

The significance of increasing levels of dependence is that it fosters *commitment* to the relationship. Commitment is identified as intent to persist, as well as feelings of attachment to the relationship (Rusbult, 1980; Rusbult et al., 2006). Thus, the investment model can be illustrated by the following:

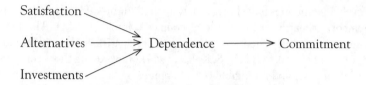

The investment model has been widely studied since its first introduction in the early 1980s. Le and Agnew (2003) conducted a meta-analysis of 52 studies on the investment model, which found that relationship satisfaction, quality of alternatives, and investments were strongly associated with commitment to relationships (across samples of dating, cohabitating, married, heterosexual, and same-sex couples). Another study (Bui, Peplau, & Hill, 1996) found that components of the investment model predicted relationship stability over a 15-year period. This is particularly strong evidence, because it allows one to make causal inferences about the association of the investment model components (satisfaction, quality of alternatives, investments) and later relationship stability and commitment.

An additional extension of social exchange is *equity* theory, which has been studied in both same- and different-sex couples (Cate, Lloyd, & Henton, 1985; Scheurs & Buunk, 1996). Equity theory suggests that individuals in relationships are also concerned with issues of justice or fairness. In equity theory, satisfaction is posited to be highest when the ratio of outcomes to contributions (e.g., time, effort, money, emotional support) for each partner in a relationship is equal. For example, if Partner A is receiving eight outcomes and making two contributions to the relationship and Partner B is receiving four outcomes and making one contribution, the relationship is said to be equitable. This can be expressed as follows:

Partner A		Partner B
$\dfrac{8 \text{ outcomes}}{2 \text{ contributions}}$	=	$\dfrac{4 \text{ outcomes}}{1 \text{ contribution}}$

Each partner is receiving a ratio of four outcomes for each contribution that they make to the relationship (e.g., A: 8 / 2 = 4; B: 4 / 1 = 4).

An example of an inequitable relationship can be expressed as:

Partner A		Partner B
$\dfrac{8 \text{ outcomes}}{1 \text{ contribution}}$	=	$\dfrac{4 \text{ outcomes}}{1 \text{ contribution}}$

In the above case, Partner A is receiving eight outcomes for every one contribution, whereas Partner B is receiving only four outcomes for every one contribution. In this inequitable relationship, Partner A is said to be overbenefited because A is getting twice as many outcomes as B for the same number of contributions, whereas B is said to be underbenefited, because B receives only half the number of outcomes for every one unit of contribution. According to equity theory, people who perceive their relationships to be equitable will have the highest satisfaction, followed by those who are overbenefited, with those who are underbenefited having the least satisfaction. The theory proposes that people who are in inequitable relationships will engage in strategies designed to reduce the inequity (Sprecher & Schwartz, 1996). For example, persons who feel underbenefited can reduce their contributions to the relationship in order to restore equity. Or, equity could be restored by decreasing the partner's outcomes through being less cooperative or pleasant in interactions.

Social exchange theories are not without drawbacks (Bradbury & Karney, 2010). Several theorists argue that the assumption that rationality governs relationships is untenable. Such rationality implies that humans are highly cognitively aware and able to make rapid and accurate assessments of costs and rewards. Other criticisms focus on the lack of specificity about relational processes. For example, the process by which partners move from a state of satisfaction to one of dissatisfaction is not clearly delineated (Bradbury & Karney, 2010). Despite these shortcomings, social exchange theories continue to be used by many researchers to explain relationship development.

Adult Attachment Theory

Since the late 1980s, proponents of adult attachment theory have generated an overwhelming amount of research. Adult attachment theory is an extension of Bowlby's (1969) theorizing about attachment in infants. Bowlby proposed that infants possess an innate predisposition to reduce distress through seeking proximity to their caretakers when they feel threatened. When proximity seeking is met by responsive and sensitive caretakers, feelings of *security* are increased. When proximity seeking is met by insensitive and unresponsive caretakers, feelings of *insecurity* are increased. As people interact with

41

ıregivers over time, they begin to develop internal *working models* of how ꞈlationships with caretakers operate. Hazan and Shaver (1987) have applied similar reasoning to adult romantic relationships.

Adult attachment theory suggests that the underlying dimensions of security/insecurity are *anxiety* and *avoidance* (Brennan, Clark, & Shaver, 1998). These two dimensions can be used to classify individuals into four attachment styles or types (Bartholomew & Horowitz, 1991). However, Shaver and Mikulincer (2006) have proposed a more parsimonious typing. This classification proposes three attachment types: (1) secure (low on both anxiety and avoidance), (2) anxious (high on anxiety), and (3) avoidant (high on avoidance). Secure individuals feel they deserve to be loved, are comfortable with closeness, and believe that relationships are rewarding. Anxious individuals worry about the availability of a partner to fulfill their needs and question the extent to which they deserve love. Avoidant individuals are prone to distrust their partner and try to remain independent and distant from their partners. We use these categories in the remainder of this discussion.

Shaver and Mikulincer (2006) suggest that having a secure versus anxious or avoidant orientation influences the strategies people use during different temporal points in relationship development. The following discussion addresses the first two phases.

Initial Phase

During the initial phase, people's interpersonal predispositions have relatively strong influence on individuals' strategies (Shaver & Mikulincer, 2006). Partners have little information about each other and must rely on their developmental tendencies in order to develop interpersonal strategies. Secure individuals will establish a positive, warm climate during interactions, present a balanced view of themselves, and engage in appropriate and responsive self-disclosure. In contrast, avoidant individuals will promote an emotionally detached climate, present an inflated view of self, and engage in low levels of self-disclosure. Anxious individuals set a negative tone, present themselves in a self-defeating manner, and engage in indiscriminate and premature disclosures.

Consolidation Phase

During the consolidation phase, individuals begin to concern themselves with establishing a more permanent bond based on mutual goals, support, nurturance, intimacy, and need satisfaction (Shaver & Mikulincer, 2006). Secure individuals will develop positive, optimistic beliefs about the relationship, make positive appraisals of the partner, and develop a strong commitment. In addition, secure people will be comfortable both giving and receiving social support from the partner. Avoidant individuals will develop dysfunctional, distrustful beliefs and negative views of the partner and relationship, and a weak, negative commitment. In addition, avoidant people will be reluctant to either provide or receive support from the partner. Anxious individuals will develop dysfunctional, pessimistic beliefs and negative, destructive appraisals of the partner and relationship, and doubts about the partner's commitment. Anxious individuals also may be reluctant to seek support or be overbearing in seeking support. They may provide support in a compulsive, intrusive way.

The empirical work on attachment is extensive and largely supportive of the basic tenets of the theory (see Mikulincer & Shaver, 2010). On the other hand, certain flaws in the theory have been noted. First, issues with the measurement of attachment have been noted. Studies have shown that attachment measures are unstable over time (e.g., Baldwin & Fehr, 1995). Other studies suggest that most people are found to be secure in their orientations, which raises the question of why so many relationships terminate (Bradbury & Karney, 2010). Adult attachment theory also views relationship outcomes as largely a product of individual differences. Consequently, little attention is paid to interpersonal dynamics or contextual influences on developing relationships.

Uncertainty Reduction Theory

Uncertainty reduction theory (URT) focuses on the process by which individuals attempt to understand behavior (Berger & Calabrese, 1975). The underlying premise of the theory is that people are motivated to reduce uncertainty by being able to predict future outcomes and explain past outcomes (Berger & Bradac, 1982). Uncertainty in relationships occurs at the beginning of all relationships when individuals are not able to explain or predict the behaviors of their partner. Uncertainty is especially problematic when individuals are unclear about their partners' perceptions of their relationship (Parks & Adelman, 1983). According to URT, uncertainty is high early in relationships when individuals know very little about each other, but decreases over time as relationships develop (Berger & Calabrese, 1975). Individuals who experience uncertainty are motivated to reduce these feelings to the degree to which they perceive the possibility of future interaction. That is, if individual P believes that he/she will continue to interact with and potentially begin a relationship with individual O, individual P is likely to attempt to gain as much information about O as possible to minimize uncertainty in future interactions. This desire is heightened when individual P perceives that individual O has the potential to control rewards and costs of future interaction (Berger & Calabrese, 1975). Given the high levels of uncertainty at the beginning of relationships, URT proposes that individuals use communication as a means of acquiring information in potential relationships. In the original paper describing URT, Berger and Calabrese (1975) postulate that communication decreases uncertainty in relationships by producing increases in expressiveness, intimacy, liking, and allowing individuals to observe potential similarities in personal traits, values, interests, and social networks. Moreover, as uncertainty decreases, individuals are less likely to engage in information-seeking behaviors and show a decreased need for reciprocity in levels of communicative disclosure.

Past research on URT has identified a number of predictors of uncertainty. Specifically, higher levels of uncertainty are related to higher global uncertainty (Douglas, 1991), low social network involvement (Parks & Adelman, 1983), and higher levels of anxiety (Gudykunst, 1985). Current relational research using URT has proposed an extension of the theory known as the relationship turbulence model (Solomon & Knobloch, 2001) . According to the model, there are three potential sources of uncertainty within the relational context: self uncertainty, partner uncertainty, and relationship uncertainty (Solomon & Knobloch, 2001). Self uncertainty occurs when individuals have questions about their own commitment to a relationship, partner uncertainty involves questions about a partner's commitment to a relationship, and relationship uncertainty involves a mutual questioning of the dyad as a unit (Knobloch & Solomon, 2002).

According to the relationship turbulence model, uncertainty in relationships is problematic because it interferes with an individual's ability to process information accurately (Solomon & Knobloch, 2001). Specifically, uncertainty is problematic during periods of transition because it heightens individuals' reactions to the relational events that they are experiencing (Knobloch & Solomon, 2005). Individuals then begin to question their relationships, which casts doubts on the future of the relationship. Such doubts result in negative attributions about surprising events and often result in perceptions that exaggerate the potential threat of these events (Knobloch, 2007).

Past research on the relationship turbulence model has shown that individuals who are experiencing periods of uncertainty perceive less support in their social networks (Knobloch & Donovan-Kicken, 2006), perceive relational conversations more negatively (Theiss, Knobloch, Checton, & Magsamen-Conrad, 2009), and report high levels of jealousy (Theiss & Solomon, 2006a). In addition, other research has shown that, early in relationships, couples are more likely to attend to their partners' relationship maintenance in order to reduce feelings of uncertainty (Ogolsky, 2009).

Much work has supported the utility of URT in predicting early relationship development, especially during relationship initiation, which is a time in which uncertainty is high. One major critique of the theory, however, is that it does not explain relationship development in more established relationships void of uncertainty. Moreover, the theory does not postulate how relationship uncertainty governs behavior during relationship transitions such as the transition to marriage or parenthood. An additional critique of URT is its view that uncertainty in relationships is inherently problematic. Although the costly nature of uncertainty has been well documented (Parks & Adelman, 1983), some theorize that uncertainty may help facilitate relationship development by heightening feelings of excitement and attraction (Knobloch & Miller, 2008). As such, rather than being motivated to reduce uncertainty (the central tenet of URT), individuals may be motivated to increase or preserve uncertainty in order to extend positive feelings.

Dialectical Theory

The relational dialectics model emphasizes change rather than stability. Romantic partners may develop love and commitment at different rates, and their relationships experience ups and downs, and contradictions that create tension (Baxter & Montgomery, 1996). These tensions, termed *dialectics*, put relationships in a constant state of change as each arises. According to the theory, there are three core dialectics that capture the push and pull of relationships: integration–separation, stability–change, and expression–privacy (Baxter, 1993). For example, a relationship might begin as intensely integrated, with partners doing everything together; over time, though, this relationship might move toward separation as partners reintegrate with family and friends, or seek personal space. Therefore, the dialectics approach illustrates the continual push and pull between the two poles.

The core dialectics can be divided into both internal and external dimensions. Internal dialectics represent tensions experienced between the partners; these tensions are termed autonomy–connection, openness–closedness, and predictability–novelty. External dialectics represent the tensions that exist between partners and the external environment, whether extended family, friends, or society; these tensions are termed inclusion–seclusion, conventionality–uniqueness, and revelation–concealment (Guerrero, Andersen, & Afifi, 2007).

Research examining relationship dialectics has shown that tensions exist in romantic relationships, and that individuals manage these tensions through the use of strategies such as separation (favoring one side or the other), neutralization (avoiding both poles and balancing in the middle), and reframing (adjusting one's perception of the dialectic as complementary rather than tension-filled). Moreover, the use of effective strategies for coping with dialectical tensions is associated with relationship satisfaction (Baxter, 1990).

Although the relational dialectics approach has received empirical support, and has been used to delineate key relational processes from privacy regulation

45

(Altman, Vinsel, & Brown, 1981) to violence and control (Olson, Fine, & Lloyd, 2005), there is still some question about whether it is a true theory. Proponents of this approach argue that it is a theory because it presents a set of key concepts and propositions, but not a deductive theory meant for prediction. Instead, the dialectic approach is a "sensitizing theory" (p. 17) due to its heuristic value in the way that it illustrates the experience of relating (Baxter, 2004).

Gender and Feminist Theories

Gender and feminist theories have been utilized both to understand how men and women interact in relationships, and to situate romantic relationships within their larger social-structural contexts. Lloyd (2009) identifies five key tools of analysis within feminist perspectives on relationships: gender and sexuality as social constructions, intersectionality, power dynamics, historic and sociocultural contextualizing, and the diversity of romantic relationships.

Gender and feminist perspectives theorize *gender and sexuality as social constructions* that embody culturally specific ideas about femininity, masculinity, heterosexuality, and homosexuality; in this view, gender and sexuality shape our ideas and enactment of what it means to be male and female, gay and straight (Baber & Allen, 1992; Oswald et al., 2005; Wood, 1995). Gender is a social status that organizes many aspects of our close relationships, as it is enacted continuously in our family relationships (often described as "doing gender"; West & Zimmerman, 1987). Such a conceptualization stands in contrast with a biological definition of gender, and with gender-role perspectives (gender as a role with a well-articulated set of socialized behaviors and attitudes). Feminist perspectives also deconstruct sexuality, with an emphasis on challenging binaries, for example, the construction of heterosexuality as "normal," and gay, lesbian, bi-and trans-sexualities as "deviant or pathological." In addition, these perspectives urge scholars to examine ways in which our ideologies about romantic relationships are tightly intertwined with notions of heterosexuality, masculinity, and femininity (Oswald et al., 2005).

Intersectionality emphasizes the ways in which the interplay of social locations (such as race, class, gender, sexuality, nation) influences the identities, privileges, and oppressions of individuals and their close relationships (Allen, Lloyd, & Few, 2009). For example, the intersection of race and gender shapes both the stereotypes of Asian women's romantic relationships and the choices they have in responding to stressors; the intersection of homophobia, race, and gender fundamentally shapes how Black lesbian romantic relationships are viewed by outsiders and experienced by the partners themselves (Lloyd, 2009).

46

Scholars who emphasize gender and feminist theories also bring to the forefront the ways in which *power* operates within our romantic relationships and social contexts, by highlighting the ways that men and women, gay, bi, straight, and trans, are granted different access to material and social resources (Allen & Walker, 2000; Wood, 1995). Structural inequities play out in a variety of ways, including a view of inequality as an expected outcome of natural gender differences, the demonization of non-heterosexual relationships, and the devaluation of women's care work and work in the paid labor force. These power processes are not always overt; for example, they may be concealed within a romanticized discourse of equality that masks male domination of heterosexual relationships (Lloyd & Emery, 2000).

Feminist perspectives push scholars to go beyond the individual and relational levels to consider the influence of larger *sociohistorical contexts* (Lloyd, 2009). As the previous chapter demonstrates, the history of U.S. heterosexual romantic relationships includes a strong emphasis on couple choice, romantic heterosexual love as the basis for legal marriage, separate spheres for men and women, differential access to economic resources, and the importance of sexual satisfaction. Gay and lesbian relationship history documents the ways that the disengagement of sexuality from procreation, and the development of urbanization and industrialization, opened up spaces for both gay identity and same-sex relationships.

Finally, gender and feminist scholars embrace the *diversity of romantic relationships*, and challenge the idea that heterosexual romantic relationships are universal across time and culture (Allen et al., 2009). Indeed, feminist scholars were among the first to study same-sex romantic relationships, in particular bringing a strengths perspective that is also rooted within an understanding of the unique context of gay and lesbian relationships in a largely heterosexual world. Ultimately, gender and feminist theories have been used to understand same-sex and different-sex relationships alike.

Evolutionary Psychological Theory

Considerable research began in the 1970s and 1980s to address how evolutionary processes were involved in heterosexual mating. A basic assumption of evolutionary psychological theory is that any universal psychological process that exists in humans today is a result of that same process being reproductively advantageous to humans in ancestral times (Buss, 1998). However, these adaptive processes likely were not identical in ancestral men and women (Trivers, 1972). Women in primeval times spent a disproportionate amount of time and energy caring for their offspring relative to men, and, as a consequence, women were reproductively disadvantaged and thus more cognizant of the need for resources. This need required that women focus their mating efforts on finding men who could provide sufficient resources or provide protection, thus increasing their reproductive ability. On the other hand, men's reproductive success was maximized by mating with as many healthy, fertile women as possible. This required that men mate with women who showed signs of health, such as certain body types. Over the centuries, these sex-related preferences led to virtually universal tendencies in humans.

According to Buss (1998), over evolutionary time, men and women have developed both short-term and long-term mating strategies to maximize the probability that they will be reproductively successful in various contexts. The psychological underpinnings of these strategies differ considerably for men and women. For short-term mating, women seek to acquire many mates for protection, high-quality genes, and gaining increased resources. Men engaging in multiple short-term matings would increase their chances of reproductive success. For long-term strategies, men look for signs of fertility (physical appearance, body shape) and sexual fidelity. Women prefer men who possess greater resources and willingness to commit those resources to her and her offspring. Acquiring these preferences increases reproductive success.

In order to attract and keep a suitable long-term partner, evolutionary theorists suggest that people will employ certain mating tactics to maximize the stability of those relationships (Buss, 1998). For example, women seeking a long-term relationship may communicate their willingness to be sexually faithful because they know men seeking long-term relationships desire that in a partner. On the other hand, a woman may communicate that other available women are promiscuous and not suitable for a man who wants a long-term relationship. A man seeking a long-term partner, however, may talk to a desired partner about the likelihood that his resources will greatly increase over time, thus suggesting his ability to provide for a partner and children in the long run. Alternatively, he may talk about rivals being unwilling to commit to a long-term relationship. When such tactics are successful, the likelihood that the relationship will move to a deeper commitment is enhanced.

There are numerous studies that support evolutionary ideas (Buss & Schmitt, 1993; Clark & Hatfield, 1989 ; Thiessen, 1994); however, the evolutionary model also has several weaknesses. This model suggests that contemporary partnering processes reflect behaviors that have evolved over long periods of time. Out of necessity, these assertions about ancestral times are speculative (Eagly, 1997) because it is very difficult for scientists to determine accurately whether or not the relationship patterns that exist currently are due to evolution or to social and economic influences. Indeed, Eagly and Wood (1991), in a reanalysis of data reported in Buss (1989), demonstrate that there is cross-cultural variation in mate selection that supports a social-structural rather than an evolutionary model. Eagly and Wood further critique evolutionary theory for the ways in which it reifies traditional hetero-sexual gender constructions. Finally, evolutionary researchers have largely neglected to address how ongoing relationships develop over time (Bradbury & Karney, 2010).

Social Ecological Models

Many of the theories discussed so far have assumed that romantic relationships can be understood from knowing the personal qualities of the individuals involved or how the couple members act toward each other. Those theories largely ignore how the external environment influences the nature of romantic relationships. Several social ecological models have been proposed to take into account these external factors, including the interpersonal process (Cate & Lloyd, 1992), social ecology of committed unions (Huston, 2000), and close relationships (Kelley et al., 1983) models. These models share several common features.

The social ecological models discussed here posit that the interaction between individuals in the relationship is of primary importance in shaping the pattern of development to increasing levels of commitment (cf. Duck & Sants, 1983). Interaction can be described as "two chains of events, one for P, and another for O, that are causally interconnected" (Kelley et al., 1983, p. 27). These individual (P, O) chains consist of actions, thoughts, and affective events that are causally connected to each other, while the two chains are also causally interconnected. For example, a fictional couple, Chris and Alex, are discussing where to go on their vacation. Chris suggests that they go somewhere close to the ocean (an action). Alex reacts by remembering that they went to the ocean last year and had a miserable time (a thought). Alex's thought creates anxious feelings about the same happening again (an affective event). Alex expresses reservations about going to the ocean (an action). Chris thinks Alex is placing too much emphasis on last year's trip (a thought) and becomes irritated with Alex (an affective event). Alex responds negatively (an action), while Chris responds, and so on. This interaction "is well summarized by the term 'interdependence,' which refers to causal connections in both directions" between two partners (Kelley et al., 1983, p. 31). These interdependent chains make up the basic data of relationships from which researchers draw conclusions about the nature of romantic pairings. For example, if observation of Chris and Alex's interactions over time shows that Alex's actions are more influential than Chris's, Alex may be deemed to be the "dominant" partner in the relationship (Huston, 1983). Of course, "dominance" is only one of many properties of interdependence that can be deduced from examination of interconnected chains of events (e.g., love, commitment, conflict; Kelley et al., 1983).

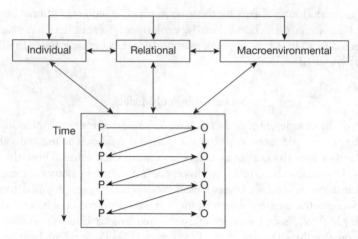

Figure 3.1 The Social Ecological Model

Social ecological models posit that the interactional context described above is causally connected to three other contexts: the *individual*, the *relational*, and the *macroenvironmental* (Kelley et al., 1983; see Figure 3.1).

The *individual* context is composed of relatively stable personal attributes, such as personality traits, attitudes, general beliefs, beliefs about the partner, and habits. These factors are assumed to influence the interaction between partners in relationships. For example, Chris's irritation with Alex's reservations about going to the ocean may arise from Chris's general propensity to negatively interpret others' opposition to his ideas. Or, Chris may be irritated because of a belief that Alex always opposes suggestions. Of course, both factors may simultaneously influence Chris's irritation. Figure 3.1 also illustrates the reciprocal association between the interactional and individual contexts. In other words, social ecological models assume that the interactional context can induce changes in the individual context, as well as the opposite causal direction. For example, if Chris encounters rejection of suggestions by Alex over time (i.e., the interactional context), it is plausible that Chris will form a belief that Alex generally opposes all suggestions (i.e., the individual context).

The *relational* context is composed of factors that can only be deduced from knowing each partner's status on a particular attribute (Kelley et al., 1983). For example, a couple where one partner is assertive and the other is passive are said to complement each other. Other relational constructs are attitude similarity, role complementarity, and division of labor. Some relational factors exist from the beginning of a relationship (e.g., each partner brings a set of attitudes to the relationship), which can be either similar or dissimilar. This pattern of similarity/dissimilarity of attitudes has implications for how couples function in the interactional context (e.g., dissimilarity in attitudes may lead to aversive interactions). The reverse causal connection can be illustrated by the emergence of an unbalanced power structure (e.g., the relational context) after many episodes where one partner makes all major decisions (the interactional context).

The *macroenvironmental* context includes aspects of the *social* and *physical* environment that are external to the relationship between partners (Kelley et al., 1983). Social ecological models assume that these environments influence the interactional context of romantic relationships. For example, Chris's irritation with Alex's opposition to Chris's vacation preferences (i.e., the interactional context) could partially stem from a stressful interaction with co-workers (i.e., the social environment) that continues to bother Chris at home. Or, Alex may be oppositional toward Chris because the rainy day has frustrated and thwarted Alex's plans for the day (i.e., the physical environment). On the other hand, the interactional context can induce change in the physical and social environments. The irritating exchange about vacation plans (i.e., the interactional context) between Chris and Alex may result in one or both of them avoiding each other (i.e., the physical environment) until their irritation fades. The macroenvironmental context includes a multitude of factors, from the historical context of our romantic relationships, to ways in which economic resources intersect with individual and dyadic interaction, to the interplay of racism, sexism, and homophobia.

Social ecological models are not based on specific theories (Huston, 2000). Such models are "intended to provide a conceptual blueprint, one that provides a sense of the types of questions that would be asked about marriage from an ecological perspective" (p. 299). Investigators can utilize different theories to examine the links between ecological contexts. One researcher might attempt to explain the link between the individual context and the interactional context by reference to personality factors, whereas another researcher may explain the link by reference to attachment orientations.

Summary

Theoretical views of romantic relationship development have evolved over time, with the development of models that reflect an increasing awareness that the partnering process is complex. The features of these models have also mirrored a change over time in partner selection that has moved from familial and societal control to personal control of choice. Early theories of relationship development focused on the compatibility between romantic partners. One compatibility theory was based on *complementarity* of personality traits (Winch, 1955a). For example, this theory posits that a dominant person would seek a partner who was submissive. Another prominent theory proposed that compatibility was maximized when romantic partners had *similarity* of attitudes and beliefs. These compatibility models were further developed into *stage* models. Stage models postulated an ordered sequence of factors (e.g., similarity in values, complementarity, and role compatibility) that operate during the process of partnering and propel people to marriage. These models were deemed inadequate on the basis of conceptual and methodological problems, as well as a lack of replication.

More recently, theories of partnering have been developed that are based on more general theories of social behavior. *Social exchange theories* propose that the partnering process is driven by people's desire to maximize their rewards and minimize their costs. The *investment model of social exchange* proposes that the development of commitment is higher when satisfaction with the relationship is high, alternatives to the relationship are low, and investments into the relationship are high. An *equity model of social exchange* focuses on the fairness of exchange. This model posits that romantic partners will attempt to maintain a proportional equivalence of outcomes to inputs into the relationship. Those receiving the same proportion of outcomes to inputs are said to have an equitable relationship and should be highly satisfied. Those partners receiving proportionately less than they deserve are said to be underbenefited and the least satisfied. Those receiving proportionately more than they deserve are said to be overbenefited and have satisfaction levels between equitable and underbenefited partners.

Adult attachment theory proposes that people have interpersonal predispositions that develop during childhood due to interactions with caregivers. The predispositions (i.e., anxiety and avoidance) are used to create three types of attachment: secure, anxious, and avoidant. Secure individuals approach relationships in a positive, comfortable way that promotes successful relations. Anxious individuals present themselves to potential partners in a negative and self-defeating manner. Avoidant individuals approach relationships in an emotionally detached manner and develop pessimistic and negative beliefs about the relationship.

Uncertainty reduction theory (URT) was developed by interpersonal communication theorists. The theory posits that relationship development is motivated by the need to predict the partner's behavior. Uncertainty is reduced through communication processes. An extension of URT, the relational turbulence model, suggests that uncertainty that occurs during relational transitions sensitizes partners to events in the relationship. These events may induce doubts in the relationship and result in negative attributions that lead to relational concerns.

Dialectic perspectives emphasize the inherent tensions that our romantic relationships embody. These tensions, termed dialectics, put relationships in a constant state of change as each arises. Three core dialectics capture the push and pull of relationships: integration–separation, stability–change, and expression–privacy. The core dialectics can be divided into both internal and external dimensions: internal dialectics represent tensions experienced between the partners; and external dialectics represent the tensions that exist between partners and the external environment, whether extended family, friends, or society. Individuals manage these tensions through the use of strategies such as separation, neutralization, and reframing.

Gender and feminist perspectives emphasize perhaps the broadest factors as they affect romantic relationships. These perspectives examine the social construction of both gender and sexuality, and challenge a strictly biological view of the differences between men and women, and heterosexuals and homosexuals. They also emphasize an examination of the intersections of gender and sexuality with race, culture, and class; the analysis of social-structural and interpersonal power dynamics; the importance of examining our romantic relationships across history and social context; and the diversity of romantic relationships, including same-sex and different-sex pairings.

In contrast, *evolutionary theory* posits that behavior in relationships is a result of strategies implemented in ancestral times that increased people's success in reproduction. Women were reproductively successful when they mated with men who had material and physical resources needed to sustain the life of offspring. Men were reproductively successful when they mated with as many women as possible. Consequently, over evolutionary time, men more than women evolved preferences for those with physical attributes indicative of ability to reproduce, whereas women more than men evolved a preference for partners with resources.

Finally, *social ecological models* of partnering have been developed. These models posit that partners' behavioral interactions help drive the development of romantic relationships. At the same time, these models acknowledge that the causes of partner choice can exist at several levels (i.e., individual, relational, social environment, and physical environment).

Key Concepts

Anxious attachment (pp. 42–43, 52)
Avoidant attachment (pp. 42–43, 52)
Commitment (pp. 38, 40, 43–44, 52)
Compatibility models (pp. 36, 52)
Complementary needs (pp. 36–37)
Dialectical tensions (p. 45)
Dialectics (pp. 45, 52–53)
Equity (pp. 40–41, 52)
Evolutionary psychology (pp. 47–49, 53)
Feminist perspectives (pp. 46–47, 53)
Gender perspectives (pp. 46–47, 53)
Intersectionality (pp. 46, 54)

Additional Readings

Boss, P., Doherty, W., LaRossa, R., Schumm, W., & Steinmetz, S. (1993). *Sourcebook of family theories and methods: A contextual approach*. New York, NY: Plenum.

Guerrero, L. K., Andersen, P. A., & Afifi, W. A. (2007). *Close encounters: Communication in relationships*, 2nd ed. Los Angeles CA: Sage.

Kelley, H. H., Berscheid, E., Christensen, A., Harvey, J. H., Huston, T. L., Levinger, G., McClintock, E., Peplau, L. A., & Peterson, D. R. (1983). *Close relationships*. New York, NY: W. H. Freeman.

White, J., & Klein, D. (2002). *Family theories*. Thousand Oak, CA: Sage.

4

ROMANTIC RELATIONSHIP INITIATION AND DEVELOPMENT

People typically enjoy hearing about how people met their partners and how their relationships progressed to intimacy and commitment (Custer, Holmberg, Blair, & Orbuch, 2008). Listeners are often amazed at the apparent role of serendipity in bringing two people together. Are the beginnings and progression of personal relationships totally up to chance? Unfortunately for relationship researchers, there is most likely considerable randomness in the initial stages of relationship development. However, there is extensive research on the process of early relationship formation (see Sprecher, Wenzel, & Harvey, 2008). In this chapter, we discuss (a) social structural factors that narrow the field of potential partners, (b) a model of relationship initiation, (c) the role of Internet dating sites in initiating relationships, (d) the development of intimacy and commitment, and (e) a social ecological perspective on relationship development.

Structural Factors in the Partnering Process

In Chapter 2, contemporary partnering was portrayed as largely participant-run. This relative freedom to select a partner of one's own choosing does not imply that there are no limitations on this choice. However, the likelihood of meeting a particular person is relatively circumscribed in most societies. In this section, three such factors are discussed: residential proximity, the heterosexual sex ratio, and the availability of same-sex partners.

Residential Proximity

It is not surprising that people must have contact with each other in order to develop a relationship. The most common way to meet a potential partner is to physically meet another person, although an increasing number of contacts with others occur via some type of mediated communication (e.g., Internet; Sprecher, Schwartz, Harvey, & Hatfield, 2008). Research has consistently shown that people tend to befriend and partner with people who reside geographically close to them (Bossard, 1932; Tsai, 2006). For example, Cadiz Menne and Sinnett (1971) found that the probability of becoming friends with another student in the same residence hall was related to how close their rooms were to each other: the closer their rooms were, the greater the probability that they would become friends. Proximity not only enhances the likelihood of making friends, but is related to whom we marry. In a study of marriage records, Bossard (1932) found that about 50% of married couples resided within 20 blocks of each other at the time of their marriages. Today, living in a nearby neighborhood may not be as important as working in the same vicinity, or attending college together. So, it is clear that living close to each other, or working together, sets the stage for a relationship to begin. However, one characteristic of neighborhoods (and other places where people congregate) is that people tend to live and interact with those who are similar to themselves (Kalmijn & Flap, 2001). Neighborhoods consist of people of similar social classes; schools consist of people of similar education; and workplaces consist of people with similar occupations (Erbe, 1975). Indeed, sometimes people purposefully choose neighborhoods based on their characteristics, for they will bring them together with similar others. This has particularly been the case for many years for gay and lesbian individuals; there are many rich histories of gay and lesbian neighborhoods across the country that provide ample evidence of purposeful choice of neighborhoods, and how this choice brings gays and lesbians into romantic relationships (Chauncey, 1994; D'Emilio, 2002; Kennedy & Davis, 1993). The end result of this segregation of people is that our pool of prospective acquaintances and potential partners is narrowed considerably by the time that we first make contact, and as a result most people end up with demographically similar partners. Same- and different-sex couples do differ in their levels of demographic similarity, however, with heterosexual and lesbian couples showing more demographic homogamy than do gay male couples (Kurdek & Schmitt, 1987).

Sex Ratios

Sex ratios represent the proportion of men to women in a specific social group, and are important for understanding heterosexual romantic partnering. These ratios are typically calculated as the number of men divided by the number of women; the higher the ratio, the more men outnumber women in that group. For example, a 2:1 ratio signifies that there are twice as many men as women in a particular social group, and a 1:2 ratio indicates that there are twice as many women as men in the group. This ratio is important because it is associated with social phenomena pertinent to partner selection; for example, the sex ratio is associated with the "marriage squeeze" for African American women. For various reasons, the number of marriageable partners for African American women is reduced relative to those of other ethnicities (Kiecolt & Fossett, 1997). This results in lower marriage rates for African American women in comparison to Whites and Hispanics (South & Lloyd, 1992). The sex ratio is also related to other aspects of partner selection. For example, the higher the number of men to women in a society, the more men will lower their standards for what they want in a mate (Stone, Shackelford, & Buss, 2007). In addition, high male-to-female sex ratios have been associated with lower divorce rates (Pederson, 1991).

Same-Sex Partner Availability

Unfortunately, demographers have not examined same-sex relationships with the same level of scrutiny that has been devoted to heterosexual couples. So, although there is not documented evidence, we think the availability of potential same-sex partners would operate in similar ways as does the sex ratio. Certainly, D'Emilio and Freedman (1988) carefully document the ways in which urbanization and the development of a market economy fostered the development of gay and lesbian communities. These communities in turn allowed for the identification of potential partners, and fostered the development of gay and lesbian romantic relationships. Thus, we would hypothesize that a greater availability of gays and lesbians in a community would foster the development of more same-sex romantic relationships. And, analogous to the ways that sex ratios operate, same-sex romantic relationship stability would be associated with lower availability of alternate partners.

A Model of Relationship Beginnings

Most (if not all) people have been in situations where they have to decide how to approach another individual. In many of those situations there is a socially agreed upon script of how to approach. Salespeople know that when they approach customers they should present themselves in a friendly manner, and then offer their help in making purchasing decisions. Unfortunately, the manner of approach toward a potential partner is not so clearly prescribed. Consequently, the decision to approach a specific other can be fraught with uncertainty, anxiety, and fear (Downey & Feldman, 1996). Is there one "right" way to initiate a relationship? Probably not, but social scientists have suggested several models of relationship initiation (Davis, 1973; Duck, 1985; Knapp, 1984). In this section, we discuss a conceptual model of relationship initiation developed by Bredow, Cate, and Huston (2008). This conceptual model is primarily based on research done with heterosexual individuals. However, we believe that the model is substantially applicable to gay and lesbian relationships.

This relationship initiation model (Bredow et al., 2008) is an elaboration of Davis's (1973) earlier model of first encounters. The model postulates four stages of relationship formation. Although the stages are presented sequentially, people may recycle to earlier stages and repeat the process. We discuss the model using the following fictional first meeting:

> Amy has decided to have her bag lunch outside in the plaza of her office building. There are several options: She can sit by herself, eat with a group of female coworkers, or sit near a man who is eating alone and reading *Variety*. Amy notes that the guy is "hot," and that he looks "so good" in his business suit. Would he be open to talking with her? Amy takes the seat across from the man. She notices that his posture changes subtly toward her. She sees that he is not wearing a wedding band. Amy says, "It's such a nice day, I couldn't resist having lunch outside." He smiles, and replies, "It couldn't be nicer. It's supposed to be like this for the next week or so." Amy notices his smile, and then says, "I see you're reading *Variety*. What type of entertainment do you like?" He responds, "I love music, especially musical theater! In fact, I just saw *Mama Mia* last night. Have you seen it?" Amy says that she has. They soon discover that they share a taste for jazz and bluesy rock-and-roll. Finally, Amy says, "By the way, my name is Amy." He responds, "I'm Michael." Before she returns to work. Amy asks, "Would you like to have lunch again tomorrow?" Michael replies, "That would be great. I'll see you at noon"
>
> (Bredow et al., 2008, p. 4).

Stage 1—Appraisal of Initial Attraction

At this stage, a would-be initiator determines whether a potential partner possesses qualities that they find attractive. In the fictional scenario, Amy is attracted to Michael's "hotness" and how good he looks in his suit. Physical appearance has consistently been shown to be attractive to both men and women (Sprecher, 1989). However, the importance of physical attractiveness will vary depending on people's motives in relationships. For example, the relative importance of physical appearance in the attraction process has been shown to vary depending on whether an initiator is seeking a short-term versus a long-term partner (Fletcher, Tither, O'Loughlin, Friesen, & Overall, 2004). When seeking a long-term versus a short-term partner, both men and women devalue physical appearance over other attributes (Li & Kenrick, 2006). Although our fictional Amy is attracted to Michael's good looks, her desire for a marriage partner may also make other attributes (e.g., being in a business suit) salient to her decision to make an approach.

Whereas many attributes pertinent to one's goals are manifestly evident in an initial encounter, would-be initiators are not always aware of potential partners' relevant attributes. Physiological states can influence our appraisals of potential partners. In a classic study (Dutton & Aron, 1974), an increased level of emotional arousal was found to enhance attraction to a potential partner. Additionally, for women, their menstrual cycle may play a subtle role in the attraction process. A recent study (Little, Penton-Voak, Burt, & Perrett, 2002) showed that women in the fertile phase of their menstrual cycle rated masculine faces as more attractive than feminized male faces versus when they were in the infertile phase.

Stage 2—Decision to Make an Overture

During the second stage, a would-be initiator must decide whether to approach a potential partner (Bredow et al., 2008). This decision might be easily determined through assessment of one's attraction to a potential partner. However, it is evident that people quite often do not approach someone to whom they are attracted. In addition to attraction, the decision to approach is also influenced by initiators' assessment of the likelihood that a potential partner is going to reciprocate their attraction. Expressed mathematically, the decision to approach is the product of the initiator's attraction multiplied by the perceived probability of the proposed partner's reciprocation of attraction. Consequently, a would-be initiator could be highly attracted to a potential partner, yet not make an approach, because the initiator thinks the potential partner is unlikely to reciprocate the attraction. A decision to approach is most likely when an initiator is highly attracted to a potential partner and believes that partner is highly likely to reciprocate the attraction. Shanteau and Nagy (1979) have shown empirical support for this multiplicative decision rule.

How do initiators gain information about a potential partner's interest in exploring a relationship? For initiators, the initial task is to determine whether a potential partner is available for a relationship (Bredow et al., 2008). For example, Amy notices that Michael does not have a wedding band, suggesting possible availability. Next, after assessing availability, would-be initiators look for indicators that the potential partner might reciprocate their attraction. Potential partners may signal interest in the initiator by using non-verbal means such as smiling, making sustained eye contact, or other signals. In our fictional scenario, Michael adjusts his posture toward Amy and smiles at her when she sits down across from her. Finally, when initiators discover common interests (e.g., Amy noticing Michael reading *Variety*), it can lead to an assumption that a potential partner may be receptive to an overture.

Initiators' personal characteristics can influence their estimates of the likelihood that a potential partner would return their attraction. Even when both attraction and the probability of acceptance are high, some people will decide not to approach a potential partner. People who are high on attachment anxiety (see earlier discussion of attachment theory in Chapter 3) will be pessimistic about a positive response from a potential partner. Many others are predisposed to fear rejection and believe that others will not be receptive to an approach (Downey, Freitas, Michaelis, & Khouri, 1998).

Stage 3—Strategic Self-Presentation

If a decision is made to approach a potential partner, initiators must next formulate a strategy of self-presentation that will be attractive to a potential partner. In initial encounters people often struggle with wanting a potential partner to recognize their true selves, while at the same time wanting to be liked (Baumeister, 1998). Especially when pursuing long-term relationships, people would prefer to openly express themselves, be liked for their positive characteristics, and be forgiven for their shortcomings (Swann, Griffin, Predmore, & Gaines, 1987). Such an encounter is most likely to occur, however, when attraction for the other is high and the probability of acceptance by the potential partner is also high. For example, imagine that our fictional Amy has heard from co-workers that Michael has been observing her from afar and is attracted to her, as well as looking for a long-term partner. Under these conditions, Amy should feel comfortable being herself without the need to bring attention to her positive qualities. In the event that Michael also was informed by an insider that Amy finds him "hot" and wants a long-term relationship, the likelihood of a mutually self-expressive conversation is high. Empirical work (Figley, 1974, 1979) has shown that when people are highly attracted to a potential partner and also confident of the other's willingness to reciprocate the attraction, they are more likely to present their true selves.

For many (if not most) first encounters, initiators have little information about whether a potential partner will reciprocate their attraction. Consequently, initiators often must present themselves in a strategic fashion in order to ingratiate themselves to the other. This can be a daunting task, because ingratiation tactics are most effective when they are perceived by the recipient as genuine. People can attempt to pique a potential partner's interest through three means: (a) they can attempt to appear likable, (b) they can try to appear capable, and (c) they can endeavor to appear morally virtuous. One particularly effective way to induce liking on the part of the potential partner is through flattery (Gordon, 1996), although it must be perceived as credible (Vonk, 2002). Calling attention to one's capabilities and virtues also can be effective at attracting interest from a prospect. Use of these strategies, however, comes with some social risk. Drawing attention to one's positive attributes at times may be interpreted as bragging. In fact, obvious self-promotion often backfires (Gordon, 1996). Similar risks can occur with promoting one's virtues. It is possible that self-promotion of one's virtues may be seen by potential partners as pompous.

Stage 4—Build-up of Rapport

After an approach is made, the next task in an encounter is to begin developing rapport between the initiator and potential partner. This process involves an initiator using a verbal opener, building affinity, and scheduling a second encounter (if both people agree). The function of an opening line is to induce the prospective partner to continue the encounter. Many people are confident in doing this and will open a conversation without much thought, whereas others who fear rejection may never get to this point (Downey et al., 1998). What opening lines are most effective for heterosexual attraction? The effectiveness of openers differs by sex of the initiator. For men, the most effective openers are those that are confident, direct, or innocuous (Clark, Shaver, & Abrahams, 1999; Cunningham, 1989). In other words, openers that do not come across as "lines" are the ones perceived as most effective. Most openers work equally well for women.

When an opener is successful, the presumption is that there is at least a modicum of attraction between the individuals. This mutual attraction can trigger a cycle of interactions between the two would-be partners that aids in establishing rapport. For example, Snyder, Tanke, and Berscheid (1977) found that, when initiators are attracted to a potential partner, they enact behaviors that elicit attraction from the other, thus further building their affinity. When men were told that a woman they were conversing with on the phone was physically attractive, they were more outgoing and warm than when told the woman was unattractive. In return, these supposedly attractive women also were more outgoing and warm than women thought to be unattractive. In other words, we "get" back what we "give." A similar process takes place with mutual self-disclosure between would-be partners (see Derlega, Winstead, & Greene, 2008). Emotional self-disclosure is a particularly skilled way to induce rapport between individuals (see more extended discussion of self-disclosure in the next section).

Some individuals are unable to build sufficient rapport in an initial encounter, which may lessen the likelihood of moving to subsequent encounters. For example, people who fear rejection in general tend to communicate with potential partners in ways that elicit dysfunctional communication from the recipient (Downey et al., 1998). When those high in anxious attachment are attracted to a potential partner, they are less likely to effectively communicate their interest, thus hampering the build-up of rapport (Vorauer, Cameron, Holmes, & Pearce, 2003).

One important area for future research centers around understanding relationship beginnings for gay and lesbian partnerships. Although Bredow and colleagues' (2008) model may be applicable to same-sex relationships, it was developed based on research on heterosexual couples. Indeed, there has been only limited examination of the processes of initially meeting and forming a relationship with a same-sex partner. Peplau and Fingerhut (2007) note that gay and lesbian partners show some similarities to heterosexuals in the ways they meet potential partners: meeting through friends, work colleagues, the Internet, and in bars and other social settings. Gay men indicate that physical attraction is important in these initial encounters, whereas lesbians note that personality is of primary importance. And the "scripts" for a first encounter may be somewhat conventional.

Peplau and Fingerhut (2007) do highlight the unique context of same-sex romantic relationships, and their work is important in creating nuanced models of their initial relationship development. In particular, the boundaries between friendship and romance are more fluid, and same-sex relationships may evolve from one to the other and back again. For example, many lesbians note that their romantic relationships began as friendships, evolved to dating, and then became sexual; in addition, gays and lesbians are likely to remain friends with their ex-partners (Peplau & Fingerhut, 2007). It remains to be seen whether a model such as the one developed by Bredow and colleagues (2008) is useful in understanding how gay and lesbian relationships move from friendship to romance.

The Role of Internet Dating Sites in Initiating Relationships

The majority of romantic relationships continue to be formed through face-to-face meetings of partners. On the other hand, the most striking change in romantic partnering during the past two decades is the emergence of the Internet as a means for finding a partner. Both different-sex and same-sex romantic partners are using the Internet to meet, interact, and maintain their relationships. The existing body of research on Internet-mediated relationships illustrates that individuals are more likely to use the Internet to maintain existing relationships than to initiate new unions; Boase (2008) estimates that fewer than 10% of romantic relationships are formed online.

In addition to social networking sites, the Internet has become a veritable marketplace for matchmakers. Dating sites like eHarmony.com and Match.com have become increasingly profitable in the new millennium. Although only about 15% of young adults report knowing someone who met through a dating service (Sprecher et al., 2008), the collective membership of eHarmony.com and Match.com is over 60 million (eHarmony.com, 2012; Match.com, 2012). Matchmaking websites allow members to create profiles, as well as browse the profiles of other users to look for potential partners. Some sites also offer computerized assistance that compares profiles of users to identify potential compatibility. In addition to general matchmaking sites, a number of niche sites have begun to emerge that narrow the population based upon a trait of interest. For example, individuals can pursue a Jewish partner on Jdate. com or an African American partner at Blacksingles.com. There are numerous sites dedicated to finding same-sex partners such as Gaydating.com. Recently, eHarmony.com launched its own niche sites based upon age, race, religion, and sexual orientation. Although the number of "success stories" represents a small proportion of the couples (e.g., eHarmony.com claims that it accounts for 5% of all marriages; eHarmony.com, 2012), virtual matchmaking sites have changed the landscape of available partners (Sprecher et al., 2008).

In conjunction with the pervasiveness of online dating websites, researchers have begun to ask important questions about the function and quality of matchmaking sites. The largest review of online dating sites to date examined the differences between online and offline dating and whether online dating facilitates higher-quality relationships (Finkel, Eastwick, Karney, Reis, & Sprecher, 2012). These researchers showed that online dating sites have fundamentally changed romantic partnering by altering both the process of meeting and assessing compatibility by bombarding potential mates with a broad range of information at one time. In effect, such a large quantity of information provides partners with the feeling that they know a lot about a potential partner before they meet. In addition to showing that there were substantial differences between online and offline dating, Finkel and colleagues (2012) presented mixed results regarding the quality of relationships produced online. In particular, their review showed that online dating sites provide opportunities for people to meet others that they may have never interacted with because of the large number of potential partners. However, this study questioned whether computer matchmaking resulted in more quality pairings than those formed in person. The study found that no credible scientific evidence exists to support the superiority of computer matching over standard face-to-face methods of selection.

The Development of Intimacy and Commitment

The majority of first encounters likely do not continue to subsequent meetings. Some are never intended to go past the first meeting. Others are not continued because interest is not sparked in either of the potential partners. Some end with a rebuff on the part of the would-be partner. Those destined to be long-term pairings will progress along a path to intimacy and commitment, properties that have been shown to be central to the experience of love in relationships (Sternberg, 1986). In the following discussion, we first examine the role of the social ecological context in the development of romantic relationships. Second, we discuss how intimacy and commitment grow as relationships develop.

Social Network Influences

When romantic relationships progress past the initial encounter, additional factors exert influence on intimacy and commitment processes. Several studies have addressed the ability of network support to predict commitment and relationship stability in romantic relationships. Typically, network support is assessed by asking individual partners (a) how much they generally perceive that family and friends are supportive of their romantic relationships (e.g., Sprecher & Felmlee, 1992) or (b) an aggregation of how much specific network members are supportive of their relationships (e.g., Etcheverry & Agnew, 2004). As expected, studies have shown for heterosexual couples that the greater the network support of the couple, the greater the likelihood that the relationship will persist (e.g., Felmlee, 2001; Sprecher & Felmlee, 1992) and the higher the commitment level (Cox, Wexler, Rusbult, & Gaines, 1997). Other studies (e.g., Felmlee, 2001; Felmlee, Sprecher, & Bassin, 1990) have shown that network support accounts for unique variance in relationship stability over and above relationship variables. A meta-analysis by Le and colleagues (2010) has revealed a moderate association of network support with romantic relationship stability; the strength of this association was similar to those found for relationship factors.

For gay and lesbian couples, networks may be even more important. Weston (1991) notes that same-sex couples are often embedded in a mutual friend network that provides support for their relationships; they term these "families of choice." Elizur and Mintzer (2003), in a study of gay male couples, found that the support of friends was consistently related to attachment security, relationship quality, and self-acceptance. They situate their findings in the context of dealing with prevalent heterosexism, which makes the development of a strong friend support network especially important for same-sex couples.

Intimacy

Relationship scientists have conceptualized the development of intimacy as a process of mutual self-disclosure between partners. One of the earliest conceptualizations of this process is the *social penetration model* (Altman & Taylor, 1973). According to this model, initial disclosures between partners are relatively superficial (a *depth* dimension) and limited to only a few topics (a *breadth* dimension). For example, early in the acquaintance process, interacting partners exchange limited information on hometowns, educational background, and other superficial topics. These disclosures are typically reciprocated with others of similar depth and breadth. When mutual disclosures are perceived as rewarding, partners engage in further disclosures that increase in depth and breadth. As depth and breadth increase, closeness and intimacy grow. However, the growth of intimacy is accompanied by a lessening of strict reciprocity of disclosures. For example, when Amy and Michael's relationship becomes more intimate, Amy's disclosure that she is still saddened by her parents' divorce does not elicit an immediate intimate disclosure by Michael. Trust has likely developed in the relationship, thus negating the need to have an immediate reciprocal disclosure (Derlega, Wilson, & Chaikin, 1976).

Elaborations of the above model have been suggested (Reis & Patrick, 1996; Reis & Shaver, 1988). These elaborations are designed to specify more closely the mechanisms that might explain the association between mutual self-disclosure and increasing intimacy. The *interpersonal process model of intimacy* focuses not only on disclosures between partners, but also on the responsiveness of each person to the other's disclosures. Feelings of intimacy are engendered to the extent that the discloser perceives the partner's response to be validating, understanding, and caring (Reis & Shaver, 1988). For example, imagine that Chris discloses to Alex that he feels unappreciated by his boss because a co-worker was promoted to a higher position. When Alex responds that he has been in a similar situation, felt unappreciated, and is willing to help Chris work through his bad feelings, Chris is likely to feel validated, understood, and cared for, thus increasing levels of intimacy.

Commitment

As intimacy grows, so does commitment (Agnew, Van Lange, Rusbult, & Langston, 1998; Robinson & Blanton, 1993). Commitment is "the degree to which an individual experiences long-term orientation toward a relationship, including intent to persist and feelings of psychological attachment" (Rusbult, Wieselquist, Foster, & Witcher, 1999, p. 433).

As discussed in Chapter 3, within the Investment Model, commitment level is determined by three factors: *satisfaction, quality of alternatives,* and *investment size* (Rusbult et al., 1999). These three factors directly strengthen the intent to persist in a relationship, but also promote other positive behaviors that assist in maintaining the relationship (Kurdek, 1995; Rusbult et al., 1999). These positive *maintenance* behaviors are purported to be a result of the *transformation of motivation* that occurs as commitment increases (Rusbult et al., 1999). Simply stated, transformation of motivation results when one or both relationship partners are willing to put aside self-interest and sacrifice for the sake of the partner or the relationship. For example, imagine a committed couple who is deciding which movie to see on the weekend. Michael really wants to see *Rock of Ages,* but knows that Amy would prefer to see *Prometheus.* Michael agrees to see *Prometheus,* thus transforming from a self-interested motive to a motive that may promote the relationship.

The transformation from self-interest to favoring the partner or relationship can come about through either cognitive/affective or automatic processes (Rusbult et al., 1999). Our example above illustrates a cognitive process of transformation. On the other hand, the transformation could be virtually automatic if the partners have encountered such situations many times before and found that these situations produce high outcomes for the partner or relationship.

Rusbult and colleagues (1999) have identified five pro-relationship maintenance behaviors that result from high commitment, although many likely exist. Research has supported the positive association of these maintenance behaviors with the level of commitment (Rusbult et al., 1999). *Accommodative behavior* is the tendency to react to negative behavior by one's partner in a manner that avoids reciprocating with negative acts and instead responding in a positive way. Thus, when our fictional Michael criticizes Amy for being chronically late to meet him, she refrains from pointing out one of his shortcomings and instead comments about how much fun she expects to have with Michael that day.

Willingness to sacrifice is an inclination to sacrifice one's personal interest for the good of the partner or the relationship (Rusbult et al., 1999). For example, assume that Beth and Kyra want to go to different musicals. Beth wants to see *Rent*, whereas Kyra has been looking forward to seeing *Ragtime* for weeks. Beth has seen *Ragtime*, but she forfeits seeing *Rent* for the purpose of pleasing Kyra and enhancing the relationship.

Most, if not all, committed people at times encounter alternatives to their partners that threaten the stability of their relationships. Committed individuals may counter this temptation through the *derogation of alternatives*. The derogation of alternatives is a cognitive mechanism by which people downplay the attractiveness of potential alternative relationships. Alex may have attractive alternatives, but he could tell himself that they also have several flaws. Or, he may play down the attractive attributes of potential partners.

Kurdek (2008a, 2008b) has developed an expansion of the Investment Model that incorporates personality factors (neuroticism and expressiveness), social support for the relationship, and effective arguing as additional predictors of commitment. He discovered support for this expanded model for both heterosexual (2008b) and gay and lesbian (2008a) couples.

Finally, people in romantic relationships often encounter uncertainties in their relationships. Indeed, some relationship theorists assert that relationship development is an uncertainty reduction process (Berger & Calabrese, 1975; see discussion of uncertainty reduction theory in Chapter 3). Highly committed individuals employ at least three social comparison processes to deal with these uncertainties (Rusbult et al., 1999). These comparison processes assist individuals in determining the appropriateness of their relationships. The process of *perceived superiority* involves perceiving one's own relationship as more positive (or less negative) than other relationships in general (Reis, Caprariello, & Velickovic., 2011). Thus, Chris may be irritated by Alex's tardiness in meeting him, but he rationalizes that most other relationships have more problems than do Alex and he. People can also utilize *excessive optimism* processes to deal with relationship uncertainties (Martz, Verette, Arriaga, Slovik., Cox, & Rusbult, 1998). Kyra may reason that the future of her relationship with Beth is far brighter than people in other relationships. Lastly, relationship anxieties and uncertainties can be dealt with through *unrealistic perceptions of control* (Martz et al., 1998), which is the belief that individuals have more power to control their own relationships than they actually do.

A Social Ecological Perspective on the Partnering Process

Our previous discussions have proposed general factors that promote commitment to relationships. One should not assume, however, that the progression to commitment is a homogeneous process. Social ecological models of relationship development acknowledge the complex processes that propel relationships toward commitment (see Chapter 3 for a discussion of this model). These complex processes can lead to different pathways to commitment, which have been explored by Cate, Huston, and Nesselroade (1986). This study was conducted with newlywed couples who were interviewed and asked to complete questionnaires about their relationships before marriage. The interviews focused on turning points where partners became more or less committed to marry and the reasons for these changes. The questionnaires asked about behaviors, feelings, and beliefs that characterized their relationship from "first date" to marriage in the partnering process. Analyses of the couples' responses to the interview and questionnaires revealed a picture of the development of commitment that was more complex than was suggested by earlier compatibility and stage models. Analysis of these data showed that there are three common pathways to commitment.

First, a *prolonged* pathway to commitment was identified that was characterized by numerous upturns and downturns over a relatively long period of time. Second, an *accelerated* pathway was found that moved smoothly and quickly to commitment. Finally, a *moderate* pathway was found that also had a smooth trajectory and moved at a relatively moderate rate to commitment. One might assume that these three pathways differ only in the smoothness and rapidity with which people move to commitment. However, further analyses of the information supplied by the participants showed that those from different pathways had unique experiences that characterized their trajectories to commitment. People in prolonged pathways reported more conflict and ambivalence (i.e., indicators of incompatibility) about staying in the relationship than those in the accelerated and moderate courtships. The turbulent nature of these prolonged pairings seems at odds with earlier models that viewed the movement to commitment as an orderly progression to marriage that focuses on assessing compatibility between partners. As suggested by the social ecological perspective, interactional factors (e.g., conflict) are not the only factors that may influence the movement to commitment. Those in prolonged pairings also differed from those in accelerated and moderate trajectories on factors in the social ecological environment, as they were younger than those from the other pathways and perceived that their parents were relatively less eager for them to marry. These findings suggest multiple reasons for the prolonged and turbulent nature of their trajectories to commitment. The turbulence of the trajectory may be due to the higher conflict (i.e., the interactional level), but could also be a result of parental reservations about their marrying (i.e., the social environment). The relatively longer trajectory could result from a combination of conflict, parental reservations, and being younger. Those in the other types of trajectories also showed interesting differences in factors that moved them toward commitment.

People in *accelerated* pairings reported lower conflict, love, and relationship maintenance (e.g., interactional activities) than those in the other trajectory types. These findings suggest a progression to commitment that is characterized by a relatively low level of involvement. Without considerable involvement, one is left to speculate about what moves these relationships rather rapidly to commitment. The answer may lie in factors not related to interaction between partners in this type of trajectory; in fact, people in this trajectory type were relatively older when they met their partners and perceived more approval from their parents to marry (e.g., social ecological). This could set the stage for a rapid progression to commitment.

People in *moderate* relationships progressed to commitment at a rate between the other two types. Like those in prolonged relationships, those in moderate pairings reported relatively high levels of love. Similar to those in accelerated relationships, those in moderate relationships experienced relatively less conflict. People in moderate relationships were relatively older when they met their partners compared to those in prolonged relationships. One might conclude that the relatively high love and low conflict characterizing the moderate pairings is indicative of compatible relationships.

This study examined various levels of causality, but did not establish definitive identification of causal factors in the variation of movement to commitment. Congruent with the social ecological perspective, however, the study did suggest that the interaction between partners (e.g., conflict), individual attributes (e.g., age at meeting partner), and factors external to the relationship (e.g., parental eagerness for people to marry) may act together to help shape the progression to commitment.

Summary

The initiation of a relationship can be viewed as a mysterious process that is fraught with chance happenings. However, social scientists have identified systematic processes that occur at the beginning a relationship. Society's structures play a role in narrowing the field of eligible of partners. Once the field is narrowed, initiation is theorized to proceed in a stepwise process. The first stage involves an evaluation of whether a potential partner is sufficiently attractive to warrant an approach. Next, a would-be initiator must decide whether to make an approach toward a potential partner. This decision is not based solely on the other's attractiveness, but involves an estimate of the likelihood that the potential partner would reciprocate a would-be initiator's attraction. The next stage requires that the initiator present in a manner that is attractive to the other. Finally, the initiator must begin to build rapport with the potential partner.

Once an approach is made and rapport begins to build, further interaction leads to the growth of intimacy and commitment. The support from social networks provides a context in which intimacy and commitment can grow. Intimacy initially grows through a series of self-disclosures between potential partners. Commitment also increases when people are (1) satisfied in their relationships, (2) perceive few alternatives to the relationship, and (3) invest considerable time, effort, and resources into their relationships. Commitment leads to the continued maintenance and stability of relationships by promoting enactment of behaviors such as (1) accommodative behavior; (2) willingness to sacrifice, (3) derogation of alternatives, (4) perceived superiority, (5) excessive optimism, and (6) unrealistic perceptions of control.

A social ecological perspective on relationship development posits that the progression to commitment may take several paths. One study from this perspective investigated how progression to commitment varied. Three common pathways were identified. First, a prolonged pathway was found. This pathway was characterized by a turbulent and slower progression to commitment with higher levels of conflict. Second, an accelerated pathway to commitment was uncovered. This pathway was marked by rapid movement to commitment. Love and conflict were both relatively low. Finally, a moderate pathway was found. This trajectory to commitment was characterized by relatively high levels of love and low levels of conflict. External factors also played a role in the progression to commitment in all three types of pathways.

Key Concepts

Accelerated relationship (pp. 68–69)
Accommodative behavior (pp. 66, 69)
Appraisal of initial attraction (pp. 58–59)
Build-up of rapport (p. 61)

Commitment (pp. 65–66, 69)
Decision to make an overture (pp. 59–60)
Derogation of alternatives (pp. 66, 69)
Excessive optimism (pp. 67, 69)
Fear of rejection (pp. 60, 61)
Intimacy (pp. 64–65, 69)
Investment model (pp. 65–66)
Investment size (p. 65)
Marriage squeeze (p. 56)
Moderate relationship (p. 68)
Mutual self-disclosure (pp. 61, 64–65)
Network support (p. 64)
Perceived superiority (pp. 67, 69)
Prolonged relationship (p. 68)
Quality of alternatives (p. 65)
Residential proximity (p. 55)
Satisfaction (p. 65)
Sex ratios (pp. 56–57)
Social penetration (pp. 64–65)
Strategic self-presentation (pp. 60–61)
Unrealistic perceptions of control (pp. 67, 69)
Willingness to sacrifice (pp. 66, 69)

Additional Readings

Bredow, C. A., Cate, R. M., & Huston, T. L. (2008). Have we met before? A conceptual model of first romantic encounters. In S. Sprecher, A. Wenzel., & J. Harvey (Eds.), *Handbook of relationship initiation* (pp. 3–28). New York, NY: Psychology Press.

Cate, R. M., Huston, T. L., & Nesselroade, J. R. (1986). Premarital relationships: Toward the identification of alternative pathways to marriage. *Journal of Social and Clinical Psychology, 4,* 3–22.

Kurdek, L.A. (2008a). A general model of relationship commitment: Evidence from same-sex partners. *Personal Relationships, 15,* 391–405.

Peplau, L. A., & Fingerhut, A. W. (2007). The close relationships of lesbians and gay men. *Annual Review of Psychology, 58,* 405–424.

Reis, H. T., & Shaver, P. (1988). Intimacy as an interpersonal process. In S. Duck (Ed.), *Handbook of personal relationships: Theory, research, and interventions* (pp. 367–389). Chichester, UK: Wiley.

Rusbult, C. E., Wieselquist, J., Foster, C. A., & Witcher, B. S. (1999). Commitment and trust in close relationships: An interdependence analysis. In J. M. Adams & W. H. Jones (Eds.), *Handbook on interpersonal commitment and relationship stability* (pp. 427–449). New York, NY: Kluwer Academic/Plenum.

Sprecher, S., Wenzel, A., & Harvey, J. (Eds.) (2008). *Handbook of relationship initiation.* New York, NY: Psychology Press.

5

COHABITATION

Perhaps nothing has changed the landscape of relationship development in recent decades as drastically as cohabitation outside of marriage. Although cohabitation has been normative among gay and lesbian couples for many decades, it has recently become a normative transition in the relationship development process for heterosexual couples as well. Participation in cohabitation, however, varies as a function of several factors, and the reasons for living together differ across individuals. In this chapter we discuss the rates of cohabitation, the movement from dating to cohabitation, and the reasons and consequences associated with the decision to cohabit. As we will discuss in the remainder of the chapter, research exploring cohabitation is difficult because of the diversity of decisions about whether or when to cohabit, as well as the specific arrangements that partners make following this decision. Most research relies on the partners to define whether they are cohabiting. As such, we discuss the research on cohabitation that focuses on romantic partnerships in which partners report a co-residential arrangement. In addition, we will discuss cohabitation for heterosexual as well as gay and lesbian couples.

Rates of Cohabitation

Although cohabitation has existed for hundreds of years in the United States, after marriage was heavily legislated in the mid-19th century, cohabitation was a relatively uncommon arrangement until the 1960s. Figure 5.1 shows the extent of heterosexual cohabitation in the United States over the past 40 years. From 1960 to 1997, the rates of cohabitation increased by more than 10 times and from 1997 to 2010 rates nearly doubled again (U.S. Bureau of the Census, 2010). In 2010, there were approximately 7.5 million heterosexual and 646,000 same-sex cohabitors in the United States. Currently, about 50% of all heterosexuals in the United States choose to live together in a romantic partnership and many more choose to cohabit after the dissolution of a past partnership (Bumpass & Hsien-Hen, 2000). For individuals who do not go to college, the rates are closer to 67% (Kennedy & Bumpass, 2008).

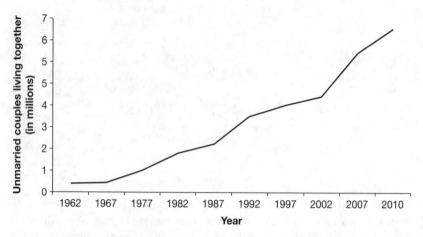

Figure 5.1 Number (in millions) of cohabitors in the United States
Source: U.S. Bureau of the Census, 2010.

Among same-sex individuals, approximately 68% of gay men and 94% of lesbian women cohabit at some point in time (Black, Gates, Sanders, & Taylor, 2000). These rates, however, underestimate the true incidence of cohabitation, due to weaknesses in measurement, definitional inconsistencies, and the fluidity of these kinds of unions (Manning & Smock, 2005). In fact, prior to 1990, the United States census did not identify unmarried partners (i.e., cohabitors) separately from roommates, which made population estimates quite difficult (U.S. Bureau of the Census, 2010). Since 1990, the United States census includes cohabitors under the category "unmarried partner," but such a term does not reflect the identity of many cohabiting couples and, in fact, excludes individuals for whom marriage is not currently an option. Many cohabitors simply refer to each other as "boyfriend/ girlfriend" or "fiancé/fiancée" if they are engaged, but it is uncommon for couples to describe themselves as cohabitors (Manning & Smock, 2005).

Cohabitation Rates by Culture

There are also moderate differences in cohabitation by ethnicity and country. Approximately two decades ago, African Americans had the highest rates of cohabitation. Currently, however, the rate of cohabitation among Whites in the United States has converged with that of African Americans (Bumpass & Hsien-Hen, 2000). The rate of cohabitation among Mexican Americans has been and continues to be slightly lower than the rate for Whites and African Americans (Rhoades, Petrella, Stanley, & Markman, 2007), and the rate for Asian Americans is lower than all other groups in the United States (Trask &

Koivunen, 2007). The rates of cohabitation internationally are also quite varied, but the dearth of cross-national data makes comparisons between countries quite difficult (Kiernan, 2004). The data that are available show that the percentage of couples who are currently cohabiting is highest in Sweden (28.4%), Denmark (24.4%), New Zealand (23.7%), and Norway (21.8%). For Canada (18.4%), France (17.2%), UK (15.4%), Australia (15.0%), and the Netherlands (13.3%), the percentage of all couples who are cohabiting falls between 10% and 20%. For the United States (7.6%), Italy (3.8%), and Spain (2.7%), the percentage of all couples who are currently cohabiting falls below 10% (Popenoe, 2008). Cherlin (2009) offers an explanation for the different rates of cohabitation between the United States and European countries, suggesting that Americans treat cohabitation (and marriage) more casually than Europeans. These differences stem from the conflicting values of individualism and desire for marriage. In other words, Americans emphasize the pursuit of emotional happiness and a strong sense of self, while embracing a strong desire to marry. The result of these conflicting values is that, unlike countries like Sweden, where cohabitation and marriage are virtually indistinguishable, Americans devalue cohabitation by treating it as a short-term arrangement. The outcome is that Americans cohabit and marry for the first time at younger ages than Europeans and, consequently, have relationships that are considerably more fragile. Americans also live with more partners, and those partnerships last for shorter periods of time than do the relationships of Europeans (Cherlin, 2009).

Reasons for the Increase in Heterosexual Cohabitation

As we discussed in Chapter 2, the 1960s and 1970s marked the first dramatic increase in heterosexual cohabitation rates in the United States. During that time period, two important changes, the liberalization of sexual attitudes and gender equality, were responsible for marked changes in developing relationships. The sexual revolution of the 1960s created an environment in which sex was more acceptable outside of marriage. This change was especially pronounced for women, who, until this time, had been pressured by the double standard to remain abstinent until engagement or marriage. The risk of pregnancy was also diminished by the widespread availability of safe and effective birth control. Now that sexual activity was more acceptable outside the marital context, young adults no longer needed to marry at such young ages.

In addition to the sexual revolution, heightened gender equality allowed more women into the workforce and into higher education. With increases in women in the workforce, many more women were enrolling in higher education to fulfill their personal aspirations and to compete for better jobs. In order to succeed on the job, women were delaying both marriage and childbirth at unprecedented rates. The result of the combination of sexual liberalization and gender equality in the workplace and higher education was an increase in cohabitation rates (Coontz, 2005).

Another outcome of gender equality was the rapid rise in the divorce rate. Women in the workplace were no longer dependent upon men to provide for them, which diminished the need to remain in unhealthy marriages. With the rise in the prevalence of divorce, people became fearful of having their marriages go sour and instead turned to cohabitation as a less risky alternative. Without the urgency to marry, individuals could take their time before settling down. As a result, the practice of cohabitation was normalized and attitudes toward cohabitation became more favorable—a trend that would continue into contemporary society (Coontz, 2005).

Contemporary Attitudes about Cohabitation

As recently as four decades ago, the majority of individuals in the United States had negative views about heterosexual cohabitation. Since then, however, young adults' attitudes toward cohabitation have become increasingly favorable. In fact, young adults age 18–23 have more favorable views of heterosexual cohabitation than their parents (Cunningham & Thornton, 2005). The majority of high-school seniors believe that it is a good idea to move in with a partner before getting married, to test compatibility. Nearly half of individuals in their twenties state that they would not marry someone until they had lived together (Popenoe, 2008). Individuals' views become even more favorable if they enter into a stable cohabiting relationship. Views of cohabitation become considerably less favorable, however, for individuals whose relationships dissolve after cohabitation (Cunningham & Thornton, 2005), which could be because these individuals attribute the failure of the relationship to their decision to cohabit. The meaning of marriage has also affected attitudes about cohabitation. Many young adults view heterosexual marriage as a less permanent commitment than it once was (Cunningham & Thornton, 2005). Instead, the acceptance of "serial monogamy," or a succession of marriages or long-term commitments, has increased. The result of this shift is a lack of clarity about potential benefits of legal marriage, resulting in generally favorable attitudes toward cohabitation. For individuals who make the decision to cohabit, however, their views on cohabitation depend upon whether they have positive or negative experiences while cohabiting.

Transition from Heterosexual Dating to Cohabitation

Given the diversity of pathways through relationship development, much attention has been paid to the transition from dating to living together.

The difficulty in theorizing a normative path from dating to formal commit-ment is that the decision to cohabit does not apply to all couples. Some couples choose to cohabit before marriage, whereas others choose to marry without prior cohabitation. Some treat cohabitation as an extension of dating, whereas others believe that it is an extension of marriage. This range of beliefs and experiences of cohabitation makes the task of studying this transition difficult, because researchers use many different methods of analy-sis, which can result in a lack of clarity across studies. To address this issue, Thornton, Axinn, and Xie (2007) propose five different perspectives that rep-resent characterizations of the role of cohabitation in the transition from dating to formal commitment or marriage: (1) singlehood and cohabitation as equivalent contrasts to marriage, (2) marriage and cohabitation as equivalent contrasts to being single, (3) marriage and cohabitation as independent alter-natives to being single, (4) marriage and cohabitation as a choice conditional on having a partner, and (5) cohabitation as part of the marriage process. Such a conceptualization allows researchers to explain the diversity of cohabi-tation experiences more consistently, and provides a framework for analyzing rates of entrance into each of these stages. We will briefly outline each below (see Thornton et al., 2007, for a comprehensive discussion).

According to the first perspective, there is only one transition and that is from unmarried to married. Marriage is seen as the ultimate goal and cohabitation is deemed equivalent to singlehood. This perspective maintains the legal distinction between marriage and all other statuses but is limited in its lack of attention to the similarities between cohabitation and marriage.

The second perspective suggests that sexual relations and residence are the distinctions of importance and separate singlehood from cohabitation and marriage. From this perspective, marriage is viewed as a legal process that provides a piece of paper recognizing the relationship but is otherwise equivalent to cohabitation. The transition between singlehood and living together is seen as the central transition point. This approach improves upon the first by highlighting the differences between cohabitation and singlehood but is limited in its attention to the legal distinctions between cohabitation and marriage.

The third perspective views cohabitation as a distinct category from singlehood or marriage. The departure from singlehood becomes a variable process in which individuals can move either to marriage or to cohabitation. The benefit of this approach is that it focuses on the important changes in contemporary relationship norms by attending to the distinctions between singlehood, marriage, and cohabitation. It is, however, still limited in that it does not attend to those individuals who transition their cohabiting unions to marriages.

From the fourth perspective discussed by Thornton and colleagues, couples engage in a two-step process in which they first decide to move from singlehood to a "coresidential arrangement" (p. 96). Then, they decide whether they will marry or cohabit without marriage and treat these as distinct from each other. The advantage to this conceptualization is that it provides credence to the idea that couples can make a choice between cohabitation and marriage when moving away from singlehood and that the choice implies the presence of a more serious relationship. The approach is limited, however, by the fact that it is unlikely that the decision-making process between singlehood and co-residence is as deliberate to the individuals making the decision. Instead, it is likely that individuals move from singlehood to co-residence in a less demarcated way.

From the fifth perspective, cohabitation is viewed as a step in the relationship development process that occurs between singlehood and marriage. Instead of being viewed as an alternative to singlehood or marriage, it is viewed as a transitional process between the two. Therefore, individuals first engage in a decision about whether to cohabit and later make the decision to marry.

Thornton and colleagues' discussion of the movement from dating to formal commitment illustrates the difficulty in creating a comprehensive theory of relationship development. The diversity of relationship paths indicates that cohabitation can be viewed as an alternative to marriage, an alternative to singlehood, or a phase in the romantic partnering process that is distinct from dating and marriage. Additionally, their conceptualizations only describe heterosexual cohabitation because of the focus on traditional marriage.

The existing data exploring the role of heterosexual cohabitation in the relationship development process are most in line with the view that cohabitation has evolved to become a status that is distinct from dating and marriage (Thornton et al., 2007). For young people, cohabitation is a transition period, or an extension of dating in adolescence or emerging adulthood. In fact, cohabitation rates increase dramatically in the late teens and early twenties and peak during the mid-twenties before decreasing (Thornton et al., 2007). Recent census data, however, highlight the diversity of cohabitors by illustrating that 45% of women and 39% of men who currently cohabit are under the age of 30, whereas 33% of women and 38% of men are older than 40 (Cherlin, 2010). These rates illustrate the fact that cohabitation occurs across the life span. In fact, about 55% of all marriages in the United States were preceded by a period of cohabitation, which is more than five times higher than the rate 20 years earlier.

Despite the prevalence of cohabitation, the duration of these relationships tends to be relatively short. The median length of a heterosexual cohabiting relationship in the United States is approximately 14 months, which is shorter than most other Western countries. In fact, fewer than 50% of cohabitating relationships in the United States last beyond one year, fewer than 30%

beyond two years, and fewer than 15% last longer than three years (Binstock & Thornton, 2003). Of heterosexual couples who stop cohabiting during the first year, about half go on to marry and half dissolve. After the second year of cohabitation, however, the majority marry (Binstock & Thornton, 2003). The results of these studies suggest that cohabitation is a relatively transitory relationship arrangement that is more likely to end in either a more formal commitment (e.g., marriage) or a breakup than to continue indefinitely.

Reasons for Cohabitation

Given that such a high percentage of couples choose to cohabit, what facilitates the decision to enter this kind of union? Research has identified several reasons for heterosexual cohabitation, including convenience, financial advantages, compatibility, family experiences, world-views, personal independence, and commitment.

Many partners believe that, because they spend so much time together, they view a single residence as a convenient choice to avoid frequent trips between residences. Research shows that individuals who rate convenience or spending time together as the primary reason for cohabitation also report higher levels of confidence and dedication to their relationships. Reasons of convenience are more commonly given by women than by men (Rhoades, Stanley, & Markman, 2009a).

Other individuals decide to reside with their romantic partners because of the financial advantages. For example, some individuals cannot or do not want to continue to pay for two residences and the other accompanying expenses. They believe that it is more cost-efficient to make only one rent or mortgage payment and need not possess twice the number of household contents. Studies suggest that those who make the decision to cohabit quickly tend to report reasons of convenience or financial gain (Joyner, 2009).

Compatibility testing is a third reason couples opt to cohabit. Individuals who provide this reason for cohabiting believe that the true test of the relationship is living together. Such a trial allows partners to see all facets of each other and to decide if they want to marry or continue the relationship indefinitely. They believe that this trial serves the purpose of compatibility testing. Research shows that those who report "testing" as their primary reason for cohabitation also report higher levels of depressive and anxiety symptoms, negative interaction with each other, psychological aggression, and lower levels of relationship confidence. The relationship trial reason is more commonly given by men than women (Rhoades et al., 2009a) and by individuals who do not yet have a clear intent to marry or formally commit to their partners (Thornton et al., 2007). Additionally, some of the individuals who report desiring cohabitation as a trial choose to do this because of a fear of divorce. These individuals may fear divorce and choose to cohabit rather than rush into marriage or formalized commitment. This fear is especially common among individuals who do not want to repeat their parents' divorce experience (Thornton et al., 2007).

Some couples choose to cohabit because they reject the traditional institution of marriage or, in the case of same-sex couples, are unable to marry by law in most states. These couples do not believe that "a piece of paper" is required to make their relationship deep and meaningful and therefore choose not to formally marry (Rhoades et al., 2009a).

In addition to these reasons to cohabit, a number of couples use their beliefs about cohabitation and marriage as the rationale for their choice. Specifically, some couples report that they chose to cohabit because there is less personal commitment and more independence than would be present in marriage or formalized commitment. Despite evidence to the contrary, others believe that cohabiting provides the context for more sexual satisfaction than dating, and that there is less need for sexual faithfulness when cohabiting as opposed to marriage (Thornton et al., 2007).

Perhaps as interesting and diverse as the reasons that couples choose to cohabit are the reasons that prevent couples from cohabiting. The most common reason that couples provide about why they chose not to cohabit is that cohabitation requires more commitment and sexual exclusivity than dating. This reason not to cohabit reflects the belief that cohabitation is an alternative to singlehood or dating that requires increased commitment to the relationship and sexual exclusivity. Many couples also report that there is heightened emotional or financial risk associated with the decision to move in together. Others make the decision not to cohabit based upon social or moral pressures that come from parents, peers, or religious beliefs. These couples choose not to cohabit because their parents or friends disapprove of living together outside of marriage, or they themselves believe it is morally wrong (Thornton et al., 2007).

Although research shows that couples provide many different reasons to explain their decisions to cohabit, it does not show the process of how these couples make the decision. For example, what pushes couples to decide that it is time to move in together, and what does this process look like? Manning and Smock (2005) sought to test this question through qualitative interviews of young adults who had been involved in heterosexual cohabiting relationships. Interestingly, they found that a majority of couples do not deliberately choose to enter into a cohabiting union. Instead, these individuals describe the choice to cohabit as something that more or less just happened, and often happened slowly. One of their interviews captures the essence of this slow transition: "there wasn't a definite date, he would stay one night a week, and then two nights, then . . . it got to a point where he just never left" (p. 994). This pattern of gradual movement from spending the night together to moving in together was a major theme across their interviews.

According to Manning and Smock's work, the lines between dating and cohabitation were not clearly defined for a large percentage of couples. In fact, only about 50% of partners reported the beginning of cohabitation in the same month as each other. Just fewer than 30% were discrepant by as many as three months. Fewer than 4.3% recalled the exact date and only 9.6% recalled the exact month. This inability to recall the origin of the cohabitation accurately may be due to the fact that many couples retain distinct residences for a period of time before completely moving in with the partner. This affords each partner the freedom to come and go as they please and minimizes boundaries to relationship dissolution. Manning and Smock suggest that, instead of viewing cohabitation as an overt choice, it be "reconceptualized as a 'sliding' or 'drifting' into and out of cohabitation" (p. 1000).

This idea of sliding vs. deciding was further developed by Rhoades and colleagues (2009a) in their study of relationship commitment among heterosexual couples. Essentially, individuals in relationships can make decisions about relationship development in one of two ways. They can either slide into each transition gradually without careful planning, or they can overtly decide to make the transition with more vigilance. According to their logic, the deciders are making a commitment to their relationship through the careful consideration of the future of their relationships. The sliders, however, are not making the same commitment. They are instead letting circumstances affect their entrance into this transition and may or may not have strong expectations about the future of the relationship. Moving in together imposes a constraint on couples that makes separating more difficult and undesirable. This is not a problem for couples who make a careful decision to cohabit; however, for those who slide into cohabitation, this constraint may keep them in the relationship simply because it is too inconvenient or difficult to dissolve it. In other words, cohabitation provides the relationship with inertia that keeps couples on the path toward commitment regardless of whether they want to remain in the relationship, which results in poorer relationship quality (Rhoades et al., 2009a).

Transition from Heterosexual Cohabitation to Marriage

Given the idea that cohabitation propels couples toward deeper levels of commitment, is it reasonable to assume that most heterosexual couples view cohabitation as a step toward marriage? And if so, how and when do they make this transition? The answers to these questions are somewhat complex. Data show that the proportion of cohabiting couples who eventually marry has decreased over time (Kennedy & Bumpass, 2008). Cohabitation, however, is not considered a true alternative to marriage by most heterosexual cohabitors in the United States, and a majority of individuals desire a more formalized context for raising children (Sassler, 2010). Some data on this topic show that, although most cohabiting partners intend to marry, the odds of marrying decrease each year that they postpone this decision (Manning & Smock, 2002) and, in fact, that the majority of cohabiting unions dissolve before marriage (Lichter, Qian, & Mellott, 2006). Other studies show that the decision to marry after cohabiting is strongest for partners who are most satisfied or desire children (Qu, Weston, & deVaus, 2009). Another predictor of marriage after cohabitation is partner agreement regarding the relationship. Specifically, couples who agree about their plans to get married before cohabitation are more likely to eventually marry than those who disagree (Sassler & McNally, 2003). The same is true regarding agreement about the division of labor (Sassler, 2010). Understanding the predictors of relationship success among cohabitors is extremely important, because of the wealth of information documenting the effects of living together on marital quality and success.

The Consequences of Cohabitation for Later Relationship Development

Many of the reasons that support individuals' decisions to cohabit suggest that these partners believe that cohabiting will improve the quality of their relationships and help them to prepare for an eventual marriage or formalized commitment. In actuality, most research suggests that the opposite is true. Heterosexual cohabitation has been linked to a number of problematic relationship characteristics and, perhaps most importantly, an increased risk of divorce later on (Dush, Cohan, & Amato, 2003; Stanley, Amato, Johnson, & Markman, 2006). This increased risk of divorce following cohabitation has been termed "the cohabitation effect" (Rhoades et al., 2006).

The cohabitation effect has been tested in many contexts and appears to be quite a robust finding. Premarital cohabitation has been shown to increase negative communication in later marriages (Stanley, Whitton, & Markman, 2004), lower marital satisfaction (Binstock & Thornton, 2003; Dush et al., 2003; Stanley et al., 2004), increase the number of depressive symptoms (Brown, 2000a), reduce commitment to the eventual spouse (Rhoades et al., 2006), decrease the perceived value of marriage (Axinn & Thornton, 1992), and increase the likelihood of divorce (Dush et al., 2003; Teachman, 2003; Stanley et al., 2006; Thornton et al., 2007). A recent meta-analysis of the published studies examining the cohabitation effect confirmed the deleterious effects of cohabitation on marital stability showing a significant negative relationship between cohabitation and both marital stability and quality (Jose, O'Leary, & Moyer, 2010).

It is unclear, however, what causes the cohabitation effect. It is possible that the types of people who choose to cohabit may differ in some systematic way that also affects marital outcomes (i.e., a selection bias). For example, individuals who choose to cohabit tend to have more liberal views, more sexual experience, lower income, and are less religious than individuals who choose not to cohabit (Smock, 2000). Individuals who have more liberal views, in particular, may be more accepting of the potential for divorce and may therefore see it as a viable option if their relationship should decline. On the other hand, it may be something about the experience of cohabitation that portends problematic outcomes. Research has shown that cohabitors tend to divide household tasks more equally than married couples and also have more similar incomes (Brines & Joyner, 1999). Maintaining equality over the long term may add additional stress to the relationship and become difficult to uphold over time as role conflicts emerge (Seltzer, 2000). At least one study shows that this effect is attributable, at least in part, to both selection and experience. Tach and Halpern-Meekin (2009) examined the effects of cohabitation on marital quality, with special attention paid to the role of childbirth, and found that the negative relationship between cohabitation and marital quality was largely driven by non-married parents who cohabit. That is, there is something about individuals who have a child outside the context of marriage that makes their relationships different than those who have children after marriage that is a function of the experience of non-marital childbirth, as well as personal characteristics that they bring to the relationship (Tach & Halpern-Meekin, 2009).

Another possible cause of the cohabitation effect lies within the relationship rather than the individual partners. Rhoades and colleagues (2009a) suggest that one reason why so many marriages that were preceded by cohabitation result in divorce is due to the inertia model that we discussed above. Their logic for this proposition stems from the idea that those who choose to cohabit to test the strength of their relationship are the most prone to later divorce and are therefore the individuals who should not be increasing their commitment to each other. As such, these "testers" choose cohabitation rather than marriage to give themselves the freedom to dissolve their relationship should it fail the test. In actuality, however, they constrain themselves on a path toward eventual marriage because of the added difficulty of breaking up after moving in together. In other words, although couples believe that cohabitation is a good way to test the relationship, cohabitation actually makes it more difficult to dissolve the relationship than dating without living together because of the added stress of relocation, division of belongings, and cutting ties with mutual friends, even if the relationship fails the original compatibility test. The ostensible result of this pattern is that cohabitation essentially keeps relationships of lower quality on the path toward marriage.

To test the inertia model, Rhoades and colleagues (2009a) examined the concept of commitment as it relates to the decision to cohabit. They posit that because the inertia model states that individuals who are less certain about their relationships (e.g., testers) are at a higher risk for problematic outcomes than individuals who have higher levels of clarity (e.g., those who are engaged prior to cohabitation) about the future of their relationship, that engagement should protect couples from the cohabitation effect. In fact, evidence from several studies supported this idea and showed that couples who cohabited before a formal engagement had lower levels of relationship quality than individuals who either did not cohabit before marriage or were engaged at the time of cohabitation (Kline et al., 2004; Rhoades et al., 2009a, 2009b; Stanley et al., 2004). In addition, cohabitors who choose a covenant marriage when they marry, which is a marriage with stricter criteria for beginning and ending the marriage (available in only four of the United States), are less likely to divorce than those who choose a traditional marriage (Brown, Sanchez, Nock, & Wright, 2006). Moreover, those who lack clear marriage plans at the onset of cohabitation are about 2.5 times more likely to dissolve than those with plans to marry (Brown, 2000b). The results of these studies suggest that formal commitment (i.e., covenant marriage or engagement) to the relationship creates a buffer from the cohabitation effect. It is believed that the primary explanation for this finding is that individuals who are engaged have already determined their marital fate. That is, they have committed themselves to their relationships and intend to remain in them. Instead of entering into cohabitation without expectations about the relationship's future and continuing a dating-like union, these couples are treating cohabitation as a marriage-like union.

Understanding the role of cohabitation in the success and failure of relationships has far-reaching implications for broader relationship and family issues. For example, recent estimates suggest that about 33% of all children of unwed parents are born to parents in a heterosexual cohabiting relationship, and more than 50% of all children born in the United States will live in a house headed by at least one unwed parent (Thornton et al., 2007). Moreover, approximately 22% of gay male couples and 34% of lesbian couples who live together are raising children, which represents roughly 250,000 children under the age of 18 (Peplau & Fingerhut, 2007). Having a child while cohabiting has been associated with a decrease in relationship quality in heterosexual (Doss, Rhoades, Stanley, & Markman, 2009) and same-sex (Goldberg & Sayer, 2006) couples, and cohabiting couples with low relationship quality are more than five times more likely to dissolve (Osborne, Manning, & Smock, 2007). Additionally, young adults' decisions about whether to cohabit versus marry are strongly associated with family-of-origin factors including socioeconomic status, parental marriage and childbirth experiences, religion, and family organization (see Thornton et al., 2007, for a review). Although the discussion of early childhood and adolescence is beyond the scope of this book, there is considerable evidence that the decision to cohabit has strong implications across the life course and across generations. Perhaps the most striking of these implications is the rise in the rate of serial cohabitation (Lichter, Turner, & Sassler, 2010).

The majority of this chapter has focused on single-instance cohabitation in which individuals cohabit with only one person whom they may or may not go on to marry. Recent attention has been paid to serial cohabitation, which entails having multiple cohabiting relationships in sequence. Serial cohabitation is unique from single-instance cohabitation because it represents a further disconnect between living together and formal commitment or marriage and, as such, may represent the emergence of a distinct phase of relationship development. Using a nationally representative sample of women, Lichter and colleagues (2010) found that serial cohabitation rates among heterosexual couples are rapidly increasing, more so than the rates of single-instance cohabitation. Serial cohabitation is most common among individuals with lower incomes and education and, most importantly, is associated with a greater risk of eventual divorce than single-instance cohabitation (Lichter et al., 2010). Serial cohabitors, however, are much less likely to marry their partners than single-instance cohabitors and this rate drops further with each additional co-residential relationship (Lichter & Qian, 2008). Although the body of research examining serial cohabitation is quite small, there appears to be evidence that more young people are choosing to cohabit with multiple partners outside of the context of marriage.

Same-Sex Cohabitation

In this chapter, where possible, we integrated findings from same-sex and heterosexual couples within each section. As is quite apparent after reading the chapter, however, there is a dearth of information detailing the experiences of cohabitation among same-sex couples. In this section we outline the major limitations in the literature on cohabitation and point to some important future directions.

We were unable to find any studies documenting the reasons that same-sex couples choose to cohabit. Given that same-sex couples are unable to legally marry in all but ten of the United States, these couples may report unique considerations when making the decision about whether to cohabit. Moreover, despite the relative prevalence of cohabitation among same-sex couples, there is very little research that explicitly examines attitudes toward cohabitation in this population. It is possible that same-sex couples view cohabitation more favorably than other individuals because they are unable to legally marry in most of the United States; however, without sufficient scientific attention, this question remains unanswered. Kurdek (2004) does provide consistent, longitudinal evidence that same-sex cohabiting couples are very similar to heterosexual married couples; his work implies that many same-sex couples who cohabit are in essence engaging in a "marital" relationship. Thus the dynamics of same-sex cohabitation may well be quite different than the dynamics of heterosexual cohabitation.

In our view, the most pressing unanswered question regarding cohabitation among same-sex couples is how they make the transition to cohabitation. Thornton and colleagues (2007) provided five perspectives that hypothesize this transition among heterosexual couples. Given their focus on heterosexual marriage, however, it is unclear if these perspectives apply to same-sex couples. In our view, applying such a model to same-sex couples raises a number of interesting possibilities that may have implications for the study of relationships. Specifically, if legal marriage is taken out of the equation as the end-state of a relationship, how does that change the definitions of commitment or stability? What are the potential milestones that would signify this commitment to others? Would relationship duration, a commitment ceremony, or having/adopting children be such milestones? These questions have the capacity to uncover important information about the role of cohabitation in relationship development for same- and different-sex couples alike.

Summary

Heterosexual cohabitation in the United States has increased tremendously over the past several decades to the highest levels in history. The emergence of high levels of cohabitation has resulted in rethinking the developmental course of relationships. Researchers have suggested that cohabitation may be an extension or alternative to dating, an alternative to marriage, or a distinct phase in the development of relationships. Much attention has also been paid to the reasons that couples choose to cohabit and the consequences of these choices. Partners choose to cohabit out of convenience, for financial benefit, as a trial marriage, or as a rejection of the institution of marriage. Others make the decision not to cohabit to avoid emotional or financial risk, to maintain independence, or for personal or familial moral objection.

The choice to cohabit by heterosexual couples has also been associated with a number of negative outcomes, including divorce. This set of negative outcomes is referred to as the cohabitation effect. Higher levels of commitment prior to cohabitation seem to mitigate the effects of cohabitation, but for those who move in together without clear intentions, the cohabitation effect appears to be quite robust.

Key Concepts

Cohabitation effect (pp. 80–82)
Co-residence (p. 76)
Formal commitment (pp. 75–77, 82–83)
Gender equality (pp. 73–74)

Additional Readings

Cherlin, A. (2009). *The marriage-go-round: The state of marriage and the family in America today*. New York, NY: Vintage Books.

Kurdek, L. A. (1998). Relationship outcomes and their predictors: Longitudinal evidence from heterosexual married, gay cohabiting, and lesbian cohabiting couples. *Journal of Marriage and Family, 60*, 553–568.

Kurdek, L. A. (2004). Are gay and lesbian courting couples *really* different from heterosexual married couples? *Journal of Marriage and Family, 66*, 880–900.

Stanley, S. (2010). Sliding vs. deciding. (Web log). Retrieved from http://www. slidingvsdeciding.blogspot.com/.

Thornton, A., Axinn, W., & Xie, Y. (2007). *Marriage and cohabitation*. Chicago, IL: University of Chicago Press.

Waite, L. (2000). *Ties that bind*. Hawthorne, NY: Aldine de Gruyter.

6

THE STABILITY OF
ROMANTIC RELATIONSHIPS
Processes of Maintenance and Dissolution

Thus far this book has focused on how romantic relationships begin and how they have changed historically. We now turn our attention to a very basic question: Why do some relationships work, whereas others do not? On the surface, the answer to this question seems like it should be straightforward given the fact that scholars have been studying relationships for several decades. This, however, is not the case. Despite the fact that relationship stability is one of the two most common outcome variables studied by relationship researchers (the other is satisfaction or quality), the actual meaning of the term "stability" is unclear. Most commonly, researchers conceptualize stability as a function of whether a relationship continues or dissolves. For example, in one of the early theories of stability, Lewis and Spanier (1979) posit that stability is simply a function of whether or not the relationship is intact. Unfortunately, such a definition positions relationship stability at the end of the relationship rather than viewing it as a dynamic process. That is, relationships may go through periods of growth and decline that would go unnoticed with a simple classification of intact versus dissolved. For example, Figure 6.1 illustrates trajectories of the chance of marriage over the course of four hypothetical romantic relationships (see Surra, Hughes, & Jacquet, 1999 for a discussion of the graphing procedure). If we assume that all of these relationships were still intact at the time of measurement, we would conclude that each of these relationships was stable according to the definition of stability above. Such a conclusion is problematic for two reasons. First, it is apparent from the graphs that the course of these relationships is obviously different, but a label of "stable" essentially equates them. Thus, predictors of dissolution emerging from these relationships may be inaccurate. Second, it is unknown whether these couples continue their relationships indefinitely or break up at a later time point, which further complicates the definition of stability in terms of dissolution.

Due to the lack of conceptual clarity resulting from the use of the term "stability," we suggest that the answer to the question posed above can be

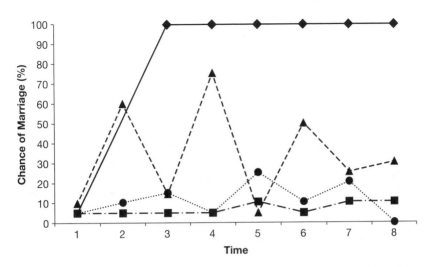

Figure 6.1 Change in chance of marriage for four hypothetical romantic relationships

answered more accurately by rethinking what is meant by stability. We contend that stability is not measured simply by considering whether a relationship is intact, but also by understanding the process of relationship maintenance, which refers to the efforts that partners put forth to facilitate the continuation of the relationship (Canary & Stafford, 1994). Such a conceptualization highlights the dynamic nature of relationships and allows for a focus on process rather than outcome. Therefore, understanding why relationships work requires a focus on the factors that facilitate relationship maintenance as well as those that predict dissolution. In adopting this approach, we begin the chapter with a discussion of the major models of relationship maintenance, turn to a presentation of the antecedents of persistence and dissolution, and conclude with the process and aftermath of relationship dissolution.

Relationship Maintenance

Defining relationship maintenance has been a source of difficulty for relationship researchers. Generally, the process of relationship maintenance encompasses cognitive and behavioral efforts that partners engage in to sustain their relationships or keep them satisfactory (Dindia & Canary, 1993). Some researchers have argued that relationship maintenance is a distinct phase that occurs between initiation and dissolution (Stafford, 1994), whereas others view it as an ongoing process by which partners attempt to keep relational properties (e.g., commitment, satisfaction) high (Canary & Dainton, 2006). As we discussed in the opening of this chapter, research examining relationship stability has important implications for the maintenance of relationships, yet these studies often do not use the term "maintenance." In this chapter, we adopt a broad view of relationship maintenance that encompasses research that explicitly examines maintenance processes as well as other processes that have implications for relationship longevity.

Models of Relationship Maintenance

Before discussing the primary models of relationship maintenance it is important to set the context for the development of these models. Researchers who study relationship maintenance generally take one of two perspectives when studying maintenance (Duck, 1988). The first is the *centripetal* perspective, which assumes that relationships are largely stable and must be torn apart by negative events or interactions. From this view, relationships are difficult to leave because of the presence of relational properties such as relational commitment as well as external barriers to dissolution. In contrast, the *centrifugal* view of relationships assumes that relationships are unstable and must be actively maintained in order to survive. Using the centrifugal view, people must invest a considerable amount of energy in their relationships, and relationship maintenance should be related to basic relational features that enhance satisfaction (Duck, 1988).

Centripetal Forces: Commitment

There is agreement that commitment to a relationship is strongly related to whether the relationship is maintained or dissolved (e.g., Kelley, 1979). Despite this agreement, there is considerably less consistency in how commitment is conceptualized. One key disagreement is how to define commitment. Some argue that commitment is the condition that causes relationships to persist over time (Johnson, 1991, 1999; Kelley, 1979), whereas others argue that the state of commitment involves more than relationship persistence (Rusbult, 1980, 1983). To complicate matters further, some researchers have argued that commitment is a global phenomenon (i.e., commitment is a single dimension; Rusbult, 1980, 1983), whereas others suggest that commitment is multifaceted (i.e., comprised of several different components; Johnson, 1991, 1999; Stanley & Markman, 1992). Currently, two conceptualizations of commitment dominate work in this area: the investment model (Rusbult, 1980, 1983) and the tripartite model (Johnson, 1991, 1999).

The investment model of commitment originated from interdependence theory (Kelley & Thibaut, 1978), which highlights the mutuality of partners' behavior in romantic relationships. As we discussed in Chapter 3, the investment model posits that an individual's desire to remain in a relationship is a function of relationship satisfaction (i.e., the positive versus negative outcomes experienced relative to what is expected), the perceived quality of alternatives to the current relationship (i.e., other partners or singlehood), and the investment size (i.e., the resources that stand to be lost if the relationship is terminated). Specifically, if satisfaction and investment size are high and perceived quality of alternatives is low, individuals experience commitment and are more likely to remain in their relationships (Rusbult, 1980). In addition, the level of commitment determines the degree to which maintenance occurs.

Relationship maintenance, according to the investment model, is a cognitive process (Rusbult, Drigotas, & Verette, 1994). Individuals maintain their relationships initially by deciding to remain in the relationship, which is an indicator of the level of commitment. In addition, as we discussed in Chapter 4, commitment promotes derogation of alternatives (i.e., the tendency to diminish the quality of other potential partners) and perceived relational superiority (i.e., the belief that one's relationship is better than other relationships). Committed partners also maintain their relationships with a willingness to sacrifice (i.e., foregoing personal interest for the betterment of the relationship) and increased accommodative behavior (i.e., compromise rather than retaliation; Van Lange, Rusbult, Drigotas, Arriaga, Witcher, & Cox, 1997).

Evidence in support of the investment model has been plentiful. Rusbult, Martz, and Agnew (1998) designed the Investment Model Scale to assess the components of the investment model and determined that their scale was a reliable and valid instrument for assessment of these components. Two recent meta-analyses also confirmed the utility of the Investment Model Scale in that satisfaction, alternatives, and investments account for 66% of the variance in relationship commitment (Le & Agnew, 2003), and commitment has a large, positive effect in predicting stability (Le, Dove, Agnew, Korn, & Mutso, 2010). In addition, there is consistent evidence for the utility of the investment model for gay and lesbian couples (Beals, Impett & Peplau, 2002; Kurdek, 1998, 2008a). Moreover, Rusbult (1987) presented a model that suggests that heterosexual partners vary on their use of maintenance along two dimensions: passive vs. active and constructive vs. destructive. According to this exit-voice-loyalty-neglect model, exit represents an active but destructive activity that includes threatening to abandon the relationship. Voice is active and constructive and involves attempts to improve the relationship through communication. Loyalty is a passive and constructive approach that involves waiting for relational improvement. Neglect is passive and destructive and involves ignoring the relationship or letting it fall apart (Rusbult, 1987).

The second major commitment framework is the tripartite model of commitment (Johnson, 1991, 1999). According to the tripartite model, commitment is a function of three independent experiences. *Personal commitment* is a desire to remain in a relationship and involves attraction to the partner, attraction to the relationship, and definition of self in terms of the relationship. *Moral commitment* is the feeling that one is obliged or ought to stay in the relationship because of a sense of responsibility or personal values and attitudes. This facet of commitment is made up of values of consistency, values that support stability of relationships, and a personal obligation to stay with a partner. The final component, *structural commitment* (sometimes called constraint commitment), is a feeling that one has to remain in the relationship because there is no better choice or due to feelings of being trapped. Structural commitment emerges from irretrievable investments (e.g., time), social pressure to remain in the relationship, difficulty of ending the relationship, and the availability of alternatives. Both the personal and moral components are internally motivated (i.e., stem from the individual), whereas the structural component is externally motivated (i.e., occurs outside the individual). Although each of these components was theorized to motivate commitment, Johnson (1999) speculated that, in situations of high personal commitment, individuals are likely to maintain their relationships regardless of moral or structural commitments. Moreover, high structural commitment alone should precipitate thoughts of relationship dissolution.

Several studies have shown support for the tripartite model of commitment. One of the first tests of this model showed that the three components were moderately correlated with each other and uniquely predicted a number of important relational characteristics for heterosexual partners (Johnson, Caughlin, & Huston, 1999). Other research has shown that relationship maintenance strategies relate to each of the components of commitment differentially (Ramirez, 2008). Specifically, relationship maintenance had a strong association with personal and moral commitment but little effect on structural commitment.

Centrifugal Forces: Relationship Maintenance Strategies

Another line of relationship maintenance research emerged in the late 1980s that adopted the view that individuals must consciously work to maintain their relationships (Canary & Stafford, 1992; Stafford & Canary, 1991). This research focused on relationship maintenance behaviors, which are specific activities that serve to preserve a relationship. These maintenance behaviors can be classified as either strategic or routine (Dainton & Stafford, 1993). Routine maintenance behaviors generally occur without the intent of relationship maintenance and consist of everyday interactions that serve the implicit function of maintenance. Strategic maintenance behaviors, however, are done with the explicit intent of maintaining a relationship (Dainton & Stafford, 1993). Consistent with the fact that there are many definitions of relationship maintenance, numerous measures of relationship maintenance have been proposed (see Dindia, 2003 for a review of relationship maintenance among heterosexual romantic partners).

The most commonly used typology of relationship maintenance strategies is the relationship maintenance strategy measure (RMSM; Canary & Stafford, 1992; Stafford & Canary, 1991). The RMSM contains five factors (positivity, openness, assurances, social networks, and sharing tasks) that were derived from existing scales and in response to an open-ended survey conducted by the authors (Stafford & Canary, 1991). The "positivity" factor refers to the degree to which one's partner makes interaction cheerful and positive. The "openness" factor measures self-disclosure and conversation within a relationship. The "assurances" factor includes behaviors that focus on commitment, support, love, and faithfulness. The "social networks" factor measures the use of friends and affiliations to maintain a relationship. The "sharing tasks" factor examines the degree of equality in the completion of household tasks that a couple might face (Stafford & Canary, 1991).

Although the majority of research examining relationship maintenance strategies uses the RMSM, there have been several proposed revisions to the measure. One study suggested the addition of five new strategies including joint activities, avoidance, cards-calls-letters, humor, and antisocial acts (Canary, Stafford, Hause, & Wallace, 1993). Using a sample of heterosexual couples, another study retested the factor structure of the original RMSM and found a seven-factor solution in which the positivity factor divided into two distinct factors (positivity and conflict management), as did the openness factor (self-disclosure and advice-giving; Stafford, Dainton, & Haas, 2000). Other work examined the applicability of the RMSM to same-sex couples and found that, with a few exceptions, same-sex couples use the same set of maintenance strategies as different-sex couples (Haas & Stafford, 1998). The three strategies that were unique to same-sex couples were: being out as a couple, experiencing equity in the relationship, and being in gay/lesbian supportive environments (Haas & Stafford, 2002). In a similar vein, Kurdek (2009) developed an inventory to assess how partners monitor the health of their relationships; his work demonstrates a robust relationship between monitoring and commitment for gay, lesbian, and heterosexual couples.

Recently, Stafford (2011) questioned the measurement practices used in the creation of the original RMSM, stating several issues with item construction and conceptual clarity. The result of her criticism was a new measure of relationship maintenance called the relationship maintenance behavior measure (RMBM). The RMBM contains seven factors, including four of the factors from the original RMSM (positivity, assurances, networks, and tasks) in addition to three new factors (understanding, self-disclosure, and relationship talk). In response to this criticism, Canary (2011) argued against discrediting the RMSM and suggested that researchers should determine "which measure better serves the researcher's purpose" (p. 311). Indeed, a recent meta-analysis of this line of research showed that the associations between the maintenance factors and other relational correlates (e.g., satisfaction, commitment) vary significantly depending upon which version of the scale is used (Ogolsky & Bowers, in press).

A considerable amount of research has shown that both one's own enactment of relationship maintenance strategies as well as the perceptions of a partner's strategies are associated with positive relational correlates. In their original work, Stafford and Canary (1991) showed that the perception of maintenance is associated with satisfaction, commitment, liking, and control mutuality (i.e., agreement about the decision-making structure of the relationship). Others have shown that relationship maintenance strategies are positively associated with love (Weigel & Ballard-Reisch, 1999) and trust (Dainton & Aylor, 2001). Despite consistency across most studies of relationship maintenance in heterosexual relationships, two variables, biological sex and relationship duration, have shown less consistent associations with the maintenance factors. For example, one study found that women report using more maintenance strategies (e.g., positivity and openness) than men in married relationships (Dainton & Stafford, 1993). Other researchers argue that there is a weak link between biological sex and relationship maintenance behaviors, yet they have found a strong association between gender roles (e.g., femininity) and maintenance behaviors (Stafford et al., 2000). The results of a recent meta-analysis suggest that, across many studies, women report higher levels of enactment and perception of relationship maintenance, and in most cases women's maintenance is more strongly associated with other relational correlates than men's maintenance (Ogolsky & Bowers, in press). Like biological sex, the association between relationship duration and maintenance is also unclear. One study found a negative association between relationship maintenance and duration (Weigel & Ballard-Reisch, 1999), whereas another found no significant association (Dailey, Hampel, & Roberts, 2010). Across studies, the association between relationship duration and relationship maintenance (namely positivity, openness, and assurances) is quite small in magnitude (Ogolsky & Bowers, in press), suggesting that maintenance strategies are important throughout the duration of the relationship.

Antecedents of Relationship Persistence and Dissolution

Understanding the factors that promote relational persistence is important because romantic relationships are essential to personal well-being. Early studies of heterosexual romantic relationships concentrated on predicting over time which relationships would remain intact, and which relationships would break apart. Burgess and Wallin (1953) conducted one of the first prospective studies of heterosexual relationship breakup. Their classic study of 1,000 engaged couples demonstrated that broken engagements could be predicted by parental disapproval of the engagement, differences in leisure-time preferences, differences in religious faith, lower levels of affectional expression, and less confidence in the happiness of the future marriage. In an early prospective study of heterosexual college couples (Hill, Rubin, & Peplau, 1976) it was found that across the two years of their study, couples who eventually broke apart were characterized by lower levels of love, unequal levels of involvement between the partners, discrepant ages and educational aspirations, differences in intelligence and physical attractiveness, a tendency to date less exclusively, and shorter length of relationship.

Many of Hill and colleagues' and Burgess and Wallin's findings have stood the test of time. In the remainder of this section we discuss the most prominent predictors of relationship persistence versus dissolution. We organize the predictors into three broad categories: individual, dyadic, and external.

Individual Factors

Individual factors, as we define them, are those factors that denote something that is characteristic or dispositional about either partner in a relationship. For example, these factors include variables such as personality characteristics, preferences for activities, attitudes, emotional reactions, and needs. Although classic personality characteristics did not fare well as predictors of relationship phenomena in most early studies (Huston & Levinger, 1978), some studies have begun to examine individual factors that might be more pertinent to understanding relationship stability.

Attachment

Several studies have addressed aspects of adult attachment as predictors of relationship persistence (see Chapter 3 for a discussion of attachment theory). As previously discussed, theorists propose that people's attachment predispositions vary along two dimensions: anxiety and avoidance. *Anxious* individuals worry about the availability of a partner to fulfill their needs and question the extent to which they deserve love. *Avoidant* individuals are prone to distrust their partners and try to remain independent and distant from their partners. *Secure* individuals are those who exhibit low levels of anxiety and avoidance and feel they deserve to be loved, are comfortable with closeness, and believe that relationships are rewarding. According to the theory, attachment should predict relationship persistence because securely attached partners are more likely to use positive communication and manage interpersonal conflict in a constructive way (Shaver & Mikulincer, 2006). A review of attachment in heterosexual romantic relationships reported that secure attachment consistently predicts the stability of romantic relationships (Mikulincer, Florian, Cowan, & Cowan, 2002). For example, one study showed that, in heterosexual relationships, individuals with avoidant attachment were more likely than securely attached individuals to have broken up with their partners over the four-year study duration (Kirkpatrick & Hazan, 1994). Attachment has also been found to be predictive of relationship satisfaction and well-being among same-sex couples (Horne & Bliss, 2009; Keleher, Wei, & Liao, 2010; Mohr, 1999). Still, a recent meta-analysis found that attachment had only a small effect on relationship persistence (Le et al., 2010).

Self-Esteem

Studies of self-esteem in heterosexual relationships suggest that low levels of self-esteem cause individuals to underestimate their partners' feelings toward them (Murray, Holmes, & Griffin, 2000). Such false appraisals set off a series of problematic processes including over-reaction to the partner's behavior, cautiousness, and anger (Murray et al., 2000). Due to the deleterious effects of low self-esteem on relationships, several studies have examined self-esteem as a predictor of relationship persistence. Studies have demonstrated that self-esteem is positively related to heterosexual relationship persistence (Helgeson, 1994; Hendrick, Hendrick, & Adler, 1998), that is, higher self-esteem promotes relationship longevity. These effects, however, are quite small in magnitude (Le et al., 2010).

Personality

Scholars have long been interested in the relationship between personality and relationship stability, particularly in heterosexual marriages. Starting with the work of Terman, Buttenwieser, Ferguson, and Wilson (1938), a succession of studies (both longitudinal and cross-sectional) have assessed the impact of traits such as neuroticism on marital satisfaction and stability (e.g., Bentler & Newcomb, 1978; Burgess & Wallin, 1953; Kelly & Conley, 1987).

Although each of the Big Five personality traits (i.e., extroversion, agreeableness, neuroticism, openness to experience, and conscientiousness) have been explored, the trait of neuroticism has most often been examined as a predictor of relationship dissolution because the other four traits have little effect on relationship outcomes (e.g., Caughlin, Huston, & Houts, 2000; Karney & Bradbury, 1997). Neuroticism refers to the predisposition to experience negative affective states (Caughlin et al., 2000). Neuroticism has consistently been shown to negatively predict satisfaction and persistence in both heterosexual couples (Bentler & Newcomb, 1978; Burgess & Wallin, 1953;

Caughlin et al., 2000; Kelly & Conley, 1987) and gay/lesbian couples (Kurdek, 2008a). Caughlin and colleagues (2000) have explored the mechanisms by which neuroticism exerts its influence on happiness and stability. First, evidence was found for an intrapersonal process (i.e., individuals' levels of neuroticism were negatively related to their satisfaction). Second, neuroticism was positively associated with individuals' and their spouses' negative communication behaviors, which in turn were associated with reduced satisfaction. The findings also suggested that emotional contagion processes (Hatfield, Cacioppo, & Rapson, 1994) might explain the association of neuroticism with reduced satisfaction. The notion that people "catch" the emotions of others was supported by the finding that people's own neuroticism was related to their partners' satisfaction. In other words, the negative emotions of the neurotic individual are "caught" by the partner and manifest as dissatisfaction.

Personal Background

A series of personal background factors have received some attention as predictors of relationship persistence and dissolution, particularly in heterosexual marriages. For example, age at marriage has been consistently shown to be positively related to marital persistence (e.g., Booth, Johnson, White, & Edwards, 1986; Heaton, 2002), particularly in the teens and early twenties (Heaton, 2002). In one study, the rate of dissolution was two-thirds lower among heterosexual women who married after age 25 than among those marrying in their teens (Bumpass, Castro Martin, & Sweet, 1991). In fact, the recent rise in age at marriage is the primary influence on declining divorce in the U.S., offsetting the impact of other factors that promote increasing disruption (Heaton, 2002). It is unlikely that age at marriage has a direct impact on relationship persistence, but likely exerts its influence through other factors associated with age, such as educational attainment (South, 1995). Others have suggested that early marriage coincides with the period in individual development when sexual exploration is at its height, thus leading to sexual infidelity that would cause marital instability (Booth & Edwards, 1985).

Level of Education

Level of education is related to relationship persistence such that the higher the level of education at the time of marriage, the greater the relationship stability (Kurdek, 1991). Some research has suggested that those with higher levels of education are better able than the less educated to cope with stressful life events (Thoits, 2006). This increased ability to cope likely results in lower rates of dissolution.

Family of Origin Factors

The family of origin has a powerful impact on one's romantic relationships, as this is the context within which romantic relationship interaction is modeled and learned. In particular, when the family environment is dysfunctional—that is, disengaged or enmeshed, and chaotic or rigid—emotional regulation and interpersonal competence may be impaired, resulting in higher negativity and less positivity in interpersonal interactions (Larkin, Frazer, & Wheat, 2011). On the other hand, nurturing and involved parenting predicts interpersonally competent (warm and supportive, lacking hostility) romantic relationship interaction among heterosexual youth (Conger, Cui, Bryant, & Elder, 2000; Donnellan, Larsen-Rife, & Conger, 2005).

Bryant and Conger (2002) propose an intergenerational model of romantic relationship development. Their model incorporates four components that affect relationship success: relationship-promoting versus relationship-inhibiting experiences in the family of origin (e.g., effective vs. dysfunctional family problem-solving patterns), social and economic advantage/disadvantage of the young adult (e.g., social support vs. social conflict), individual characteristics of the young adult (e.g., a warm vs. hostile interpersonal style), and attributes of the young couple relationship (e.g., positive vs. negative attributions and cognitions between partners).

Social structural factors may also carry over from family of origin to the developing romantic relationship. Conger, Cui, and Lorenz (2011) present detailed evidence of this carry-over, documenting that the socioeconomic status of the family of origin is a consistent and strong predictor of the economic status of the next generation of romantic partnerships. Additionally, adverse economic circumstances, when coupled with dysfunctional family of origin interaction, increase the likelihood of hostility and conflict in the romantic relationships of emerging adults.

Parental divorce has been studied as well, although largely as a predictor of adult children's own divorces. Considerable research has shown that parental divorce predisposes adult children to experience the dissolution of their own relationships (e.g., Amato, 1996; Bumpass et al., 1991; Martin et al., 1991). There are several explanations for this phenomenon of intergenerational transmission of divorce. First, parental divorce is associated with several socioeconomic and life course factors (e.g., age at marriage, cohabitation, education; Amato, 1996). For example, individuals whose parents have divorced are more likely to marry at earlier ages than those from non-divorced families (Thornton, 1991), and early marriage has been shown to be a robust predictor of relationship dissolution (Heaton, 2002). Second, parental divorce is associated with more liberal attitudes about divorce (Amato, 1996; Amato & Booth, 1991). Pessimistic attitudes about lasting marriages and favorable (vs. unfavorable) attitudes toward divorce have been found to predict relationship dissolution (Booth, Johnson, White, & Edwards, 1985).

Dyadic Factors

Dyadic factors refer to: (1) various "states" (e.g., love, satisfaction) that are assumed to evolve out of the relationship of partners; (2) dyadic interactions of partners (e.g., frequency of interaction, sexual interaction); and (3) dyadic patterns (e.g., attitude similarity, personality complementarity) that derive from the degree of match between individual characteristics of partners in a relationship. In heterosexual couples, there has been consistent documentation of the importance of dyadic factors, including similarity in political and social attitudes (Bleske-Rechek, Remiker, & Baker, 2009), commitment, satisfaction, equality of emotional involvement, and intimacy (Cate et al., 2002; Le & Agnew, 2003; Le et al., 2010; Sprecher, Schmeeckle & Felmlee, 2006), constructive communication, and the absence of aggression (Caughlin & Vangelisti, 2006; Shortt, Capaldi, Kim, & Owen, 2006).

Studies of gay and lesbian couples show a similar pattern of findings. Indeed, one longitudinal study showed that there are many similarities across gay, lesbian, and heterosexual marital relationships; basically, in all three types of relationships, stability is predicted by rewarding relationships and a lack of alternatives (Kurdek, 2001). Beals et al. (2002) found strong support for the investment model (Rusbult, 1983) among lesbian relationships; commitment to the relationship was related to satisfaction, quality of alternatives, and investments, and influenced whether the relationship remained stable over time. Kurdek (2004) documented the role of low levels of positive problem solving and high levels of conflict in predicting relational dissolution among gay and lesbian couples. Gottman and colleagues (2003) found that empathy, reactivity, and expectancy predicted eventual relational dissolution among gay and lesbian couples; in addition, affection was predictive for lesbian couples, and validation was predictive for gay male couples. There are unique factors, however, that affect relational stability among gay and lesbian couples. Gay and lesbian partnerships are characterized by higher levels of autonomy, lower barriers to leaving, and higher rates of dissolution, and, among lesbians, higher levels of equality (as compared to married couples; Kurdek, 1998; Peplau & Spalding, 2002).

Satisfaction

Satisfaction with relationships is one of the most commonly examined variables in the study of close relationships. Consequently, this variable has been used to predict persistence in romantic relationships in several studies. Despite the frequency of scientific inquiry surrounding relationship satisfaction, many researchers have noted the conceptual confusion that plagues this literature (e.g., Fincham & Beach, 2006). For example, in addition to satisfaction, researchers have used terms such as "adjustment," "happiness," "success," and "quality" to study the same underlying phenomenon. Moreover, some have even viewed satisfaction as one indicator of personal commitment (see Johnson, 1982). Fincham and Rogge (2010) outline two overarching approaches that researchers use when studying this construct: the interpersonal/relational approach and the intrapersonal approach. Researchers who use the interpersonal/relational approach examine patterns of behavior under the label of adjustment. Those who use the intrapersonal approach, however, focus on individuals' assessments and beliefs about their partners and their relationships, and tend toward the term "satisfaction" (Fincham & Rogge, 2010).

In addition to conceptual clarity, there is inconsistency in the measurement of satisfaction. Some studies use widely established measures like the Marital Adjustment Test (Locke & Wallace, 1959) or the Dyadic Adjustment Scale (Spanier, 1976) that tap satisfaction by summing people's evaluations of different relationship dimensions (e.g., communication, physical affection, companionship, and others), which blends the intrapersonal and interpersonal approaches. This is problematic because these instruments yield assessments that confound global evaluations of the relationship with relationship behaviors. Consequently, such measures do not allow examination of how relationship behaviors are associated with global evaluations of the relationship. More recent researchers (e.g., Etcheverry & Le, 2005; Lehmiller & Agnew, 2007) have used global assessments of satisfaction, thus avoiding the confounding of relationship behaviors and global satisfaction. Although these approaches are distinct, they have a common underlying premise, which is that satisfaction is a unidimensional phenomenon ranging from satisfied to unsatisfied. An alternative approach to understanding satisfaction posits satisfaction as bidimensional (Fincham & Linfield, 1997). Specifically, this approach assumes that individuals can experience both positive and negative feelings toward their partners concurrently and that these two dimensions are differentially related to other relational characteristics (Fincham & Linfield, 1997).

Although the study of relationship satisfaction is fraught with inconsistencies in conceptualization and measurement, satisfaction has been found to have a robust effect on relationship persistence (Le et al., 2010). Several studies have demonstrated a positive association between satisfaction and heterosexual relationship persistence (e.g., Arriaga, Reed, Goodfriend, & Agnew, 2006; Attridge, Bersheid, & Simpson, 1995). A few studies, however, have found that satisfaction does not uniquely predict relationship stability after controlling for alternatives, investments, and subjective commitment (e.g., Etcheverry & Le, 2005; Rusbult, Coolsen, Kirchner, & Clarke, 2006), whereas a few studies revealed no association between satisfaction and relationship stability (e.g., Drigotas & Rusbult, 1992; Helgeson, 1994). Despite these mixed results, the meta-analysis by Le and colleagues (2010) found a moderate effect of satisfaction on heterosexual relationship stability.

The inability of relationship satisfaction to unambiguously predict relationship stability may be explained by the work of John Gottman and his colleagues (see Gottman, 1993 for a review). In particular, Gottman and Levenson (1992) proposed a cascade model of relationship deterioration that showed that relationship quality predicted considerations of dissolution, which predicted separation and eventual termination. Although this progression seems intuitive, it provided a foundation for a detailed examination of the process by which couples enter the cascade toward dissolution. In fact, results from additional studies showed that the degree of regulation, which was measured by the proportion of positive to negative behaviors, was indicative of relational success versus failure. Specifically, regulated couples maintain a ratio of positive to negative behaviors of approximately 5:1, which was shown to be most predictive of relationship persistence (Gottman & Levenson, 1992). Moreover, Gottman (1993) illustrated four negative behaviors (i.e., "the four horsemen of the apocalypse") that were particularly predictive of relationship dissolution: criticism, contempt, defensiveness, and stonewalling. The work of Gottman and his colleagues clearly illustrates that, although satisfaction is a robust indicator of relationship persistence, it is the interaction patterns of couples that may determine their destiny on the path toward relationship persistence or deterioration.

Finally, satisfaction and relationship quality may interact with unique aspects of being in a gay or lesbian romantic partnership. Same-sex partners high in internalized homophobia report more relationship problems (Frost & Meyer, 2009; Mohr & Daly, 2008). Comparing same-sex couples who were out to non-family members, versus those who were not out, Clausell and Roisman (2009) found that the out couples expressed higher satisfaction with their relationship, and that they displayed more positive and less negative interaction during a problem discussion. Further, gay and lesbian couples display higher levels of satisfaction with their relationships than do heterosexual married couples (Kurdek, 2008b); this is particularly true among same-sex couples who are re-partnered (that is, in a second or subsequent same-sex relationship; Van Eeden-Moorefield, Pasley, Crosbie-Burnett, & King, 2012).

Sexuality

Sexual activity is an integral part of most romantic relationships. Sexual satisfaction and sexual frequency have each been shown to affect relationship persistence. Most couples report that they are satisfied with their sex lives. In fact, approximately 40% of all heterosexual, gay, and lesbian couples report that their sexual relationship is extremely pleasurable (Byers & MacNeil, 2006). High levels of sexual satisfaction have been consistently associated with higher levels of relationship satisfaction in heterosexual dating (Sprecher, 2002) and same-sex couples (Kurdek, 1991). Sprecher (2002) also found that sexual satisfaction positively predicted relationship stability. Although the link between sexual satisfaction and relationship persistence has been clearly documented, sexual frequency also plays a role in the stability of romantic relationships.

Research consistently shows that, in general, sexual frequency declines with age as well as relationship length, although rates of sexual behavior across couples vary considerably (Sprecher, Christopher, & Cate, 2006). Sexual frequency also differs across relationship type. Cohabiting heterosexual and gay male couples tend to report the highest levels of sexual frequency, followed by heterosexual married couples; lesbian couples report the lowest levels of sexual frequency (Blumstein & Schwartz, 1983). Despite variability in the rates of sexual behavior over time, studies still find that sexual frequency is positively related to relationship persistence (Yabiku & Gager, 2009; Yeh, Lorenz, Wickrama, Conger, & Elder, 2006). Some have postulated that sexual frequency may mediate the link between sexual satisfaction and relationship persistence (Sprecher et al., 2006). That is, couples with higher levels of sexual satisfaction may engage in sexual activity more often, which facilitates relationship persistence.

Intimacy

In personal relationships, people can quite easily identify their relationships that are close or intimate. When people describe or talk about their close or intimate relationships, however, it becomes clear that one person's close relationship may bear little resemblance to that of another person. In fact, the terms "intimacy" and "closeness" are often used interchangeably. Here we use the term "intimacy" and discuss research that conceptualizes it as both affective (Aron, Aron, & Smollan, 1992) and behavioral (Kelley et al., 1983). In fact, empirical support exists for the dual nature of intimacy. Research (Aron et al., 1992) shows that intimacy is best characterized along two dimensions, one of "feeling close or intimate" (i.e., affective intimacy) and another of "behaving close or intimate" (i.e., behavioral intimacy).

Behavioral intimacy has been conceptualized in two ways. The Close Relationship Model (Kelley et al., 1983) posits that intimacy exists when relationships have lasted a significant length of time, there are frequent and diverse interactions, and partners have a "strong" impact on each other. In addition, behavioral intimacy has been conceptualized as self-disclosure between partners, which has been seen as the behavioral hallmark of intimacy (Reis & Shaver, 1988).

Studies of behavioral intimacy among heterosexual couples have shown that frequency and diversity of interactions are positively associated with heterosexual relationship stability (e.g., Attridge et al., 1995; Felmlee et al., 1990). The strength of impact of interactions is also positively related to stability (e.g., Aron et al., 1992; Attridge et al., 1995). Several other studies have demonstrated that self-disclosure is related to higher stability in heterosexual romantic relationships (e.g., Fitzpatrick & Sollie, 1999; Surra & Longstreth, 1990). Similarly, psychologically intimate communication among long-term same-sex couples is highly related to satisfaction (Mackey, Diemer, & O'Brien, 2004).

Affective intimacy has also been assessed in various ways. One measure has respondents answer a single Likert-type item that asks how close the person feels to the partner (e.g., Arriaga et al., 2006; Attridge et al., 1995). Others (e.g., Aron et al., 1992; Ickes, Dugosh, Simpson, & Wilson, 2003) have used the Inclusion of Others in Self (IOS; Aron et al., 1992). The IOS asks respondents to pick one of seven Venn-type diagrams that show different degrees of overlap of two circles representing each of the partners; the greater the overlap, the closer the person feels to the other. In general, affective intimacy has been found to be positively related to the persistence of heterosexual romantic relationships (e.g., Aron et al., 1992; Attridge et al., 1995; Ickes et al., 2003; Van Horn et al., 1997). Ironically, high levels of affective intimacy are often negatively described as "fusion" in lesbian relationships; Felicio and Sutherland (2001) argue for an alternative view, emphasizing instead that such intimacy reflects deep communication and emotional support between lesbian partners.

Love

In everyday life, love is seen as the characteristic that defines functional close relationships. Although love is recognized as an important aspect of close relationships, there has been much discussion about what constitutes the phenomenon of love. Love has been viewed as an attitude (Rubin, 1970, 1973), an emotion (Berscheid & Walster, 1974), an attachment (Hazan & Shaver, 1987), and as a combination of some of these (Hatfield & Sprecher, 1986; Sternberg, 1986). Others conceptualize the phenomenon as "styles of loving" (Hendrick & Hendrick, 1986; Lee, 1973; see Hendrick & Hendrick, 1995 for a summary of love in heterosexual relationships).

Several instruments have been developed to measure love in romantic relationships. One commonly used measure is the well known, psychometrically sound measure by Rubin (1970, 1973). This instrument is made up of three components: attachment, caring, and intimacy. Another frequently used instrument is by Braiker and Kelley (1979). This love measure was developed from an analysis of items gleaned from married couples' retrospective reports of the nature of their relationships during dating. The scale taps multiple aspects of love, some of which parallel those in the Rubin scale. The scale taps feelings of attachment, belongingness, closeness, sexual involvement, commitment, and uniqueness of the relationship, but does not include items related to self-disclosure and caring, like the Rubin scale.

Studies have shown that higher levels of love are predictive of heterosexual relationship persistence (e.g., Attridge et al., 1995; Felmlee et al., 1990; Simpson, Ickes, & Grich, 1999). On the other hand, this research has been qualified by findings showing that love does not uniquely predict stability when other relationship factors are considered. For example, in one study, love did not predict persistence when relationship satisfaction was controlled (Van Horn et al., 1997). This suggests that both love and satisfaction may be tapping some common underlying dimension, such as personal commitment (Johnson et al., 1999; see earlier discussion of commitment). Thus, it may be difficult to separate out the unique influence of love and relationship satisfaction on predicting relationship stability. Finally, Peplau and Fingerhut (2007) note that levels of love are similar across gay, lesbian, and heterosexual relationships.

Positive Illusions

How people think about their relationships can be shaped by their motivations and goals, and such motivated reasoning (Kunda, 1990) can lead to *positive illusions* about a relationship that bolster the likelihood of persistence. Illusions can take the form of idealization of partners (i.e., seeing virtues in a partner that the partner does not see in himself/herself; Murray, Holmes, & Griffin, 1996). Positive illusions are also rooted in social comparison processes, such as: (1) perceiving that one's relationship is superior to that of others; (2) having excessive optimism about the current relationship relative to others; and (3) having unrealistic perceptions of control of the relationship compared to others.

Positive illusions have been shown to predict a higher likelihood of persistence in romantic relationships. For example, idealization of the partner has been found to predict heterosexual relationship persistence (e.g., Murray et al., 1996); however, idealization exerted its effect on persistence indirectly through its association with relationship satisfaction. Similarly, positive illusions predict relational satisfaction among gay and lesbian couples (Conley, Roesch, Peplau, & Gold, 2009). Social comparison processes are also predictive of relationship persistence. The perceived superiority of one's relationship in comparison to others is predictive of higher persistence of heterosexual relationships (Rusbult, Van Lange, Wildschut, Yovetich, & Verette, 2000). Similarly, both optimism and control illusions predicted persistence, even after controlling for other relationship variables (Murray & Holmes, 1997). In fact, in Le and colleagues' (2010) meta-analysis, positive illusions was the only relationship variable found to have a large effect on stability.

Similarity

The similarity of partners' individual attributes, attitudes, and preferences has been examined as a predictor of relationship persistence and dissolution. The inclusion of this variable as a predictor arises out of the previously discussed notion that similarity is ostensibly indicative of compatibility in romantic relationships and thus predictive of their persistence (see Chapter 3).

Similarity between heterosexual partners on several background factors (i.e., age, education, race, religion) has been shown to predict relationship persistence (Felmlee et al., 1990; Hill et al., 1976; Lutz-Zois, Bradley, Mihalik, & Moorman-Eavers, 2006). Other studies have examined similarity of attitudes and values as predictors of relationship persistence. Similarity in religious, political, child-rearing, and other attitudes are related to higher relationship persistence in heterosexual dating couples (Bleske-Rechek et al., 2009; Lutz-Zois et al., 2006; Parks & Adelman, 1983). Similarity in the interests and activities of couples is positively related to persistence of relationships (Lutz-Zois et al., 2006; Surra & Longstreth, 1990). Similarity of commitment and involvement are also positively associated with heterosexual romantic relationship continuance (Drigotas et al., 1999; Sprecher, Schmeeckle, & Felmlee, 2006). Persistence may be engendered through the equality of power between partners that results from similarity in commitment and involvement (Drigotas et al., 1999).

External Factors

External factors are those influences that exist outside of the relationship. Little evidence has supported the role of external factors in relationship persistence, with one exception: network factors play a key role in predicting relationship persistence or decline. For heterosexual couples, the positive approval of family and friends lowers the chances of breaking up, whereas disapproval enhances that likelihood (Lehmiller & Agnew, 2007; Sprecher, Felmlee, Schmeeckle & Shu, 2006; Vangelisti, 2006b). Also, friends' negative perceptions of the relationship, particularly friends of the female partner, are predictive of eventual dissolution (Agnew, Loving, & Drigotas, 2001). The friendship networks of gay and lesbian couples may be particularly intertwined, and may actually constitute a barrier to breaking up if partners fear harming their relationships with mutual friends (Elizur & Mintzer, 2003; Weston, 1991). Finally, the larger social context may influence relationship experiences, particularly for same-sex couples, given the experiences of stressors due to being in a minority status, the need to manage a stigmatized lifestyle, and the lack of legal and social protections and barriers afforded by legal marriage (Beals et al., 2002; Peplau & Fingerhut, 2007).

The Process of Relational Deterioration and Dissolution

Given that relationship maintenance and termination can be predicted rather well from the nature and quality of the romantic relationship, the question then becomes: At what point does the future of the relationship become apparent? We think that Surra's (1990) framework of early determination versus gradual differentiation remains a useful tool for analysis here.

Early determinism emphasizes that the demise of romantic relationships can be predicted quite early in the course of the relationship. Ultimately, "future viability" may be apparent very early in a relationship; the ability of partners to communicate comfortably, as well as early attraction and feelings of love, may be the means by which members of the dyad assess their compatibility during the early stages (Loyer-Carlson & Walker, 1990). The gradual differentiation model, on the other hand, argues that relationships progress through periods of growth/deterioration, openness/closedness, and stability/instability throughout their histories (Altman et al., 1981; Baxter & Montgomery, 1996). Consistent with the social ecological perspective espoused in this book, this model proposes that there are multiple pathways to relationship development and dissolution, as well as a variety of causes of changes in relationships (Surra, 1990). Under the gradual differentiation model, future termination would be apparent early on in only a subset of relationships, and unique factors would be hypothesized to affect relationship termination in different types of relationships (smooth vs. turbulent relationships, for example). Thus, due to unique developmental trajectories and interpersonal processes, in some relationships a breakup could be predicted within the first few weeks, whereas in others a breakup could not be predicted until after several years of dating and/or cohabitation.

The gradual differentiation model has, at its core, an emphasis on the process of relationship dissolution (Surra, 1990). Process-oriented research examines the factors that lead to relationship deterioration, the strategies partners use to convey that they wish to terminate the relationship, and the different pathways or trajectories characteristic of the dissolution process.

Relationship Deterioration

Declines in satisfaction, uncertainty about the future of the relationship, and destructive interaction patterns can lead to relationship breakdown (Duck, 1988). What leads to declines in relationship satisfaction? Research on both heterosexual and gay and lesbian romances gives us information on the correlates of dissatisfaction: low levels of rewards, a lack of investment in the relationship, low interdependence, and destructive problem-solving and conflict techniques (Cate et al., 2002; Peplau & Fingerhut, 2007; Rusbult, Johnson, & Morrow, 1986; Rusbult & Van Lange, 2003). Work on interdependence, satisfaction, and communication has fueled an emphasis on processes, that is, the interactions, patterns, and events that fuel cycles of dissatisfaction, disaffection, and detachment. In this section of the chapter, we cover three broad groupings of processes that may lead to relational deterioration: conflict and negativity, turbulence and uncertainty, and relational transgressions.

Conflict and Negativity

It is not surprising that conflict has been examined as a predictor of persistence and deterioration in the romantic relationships of emerging adults. Conflict in romantic relationships is often studied in terms of two dimensions: positive versus negative affect, and engagement versus avoidance (Caughlin & Vangelisti, 2006). Negativity, that is, negative and hostile affect, is predictive of decreasing satisfaction, whereas positive affect predicts satisfaction (although the effect is smaller for positivity). And, although conflict avoidance per se is not associated with dissatisfaction, avoidance that is accompanied by hostility and negative affect does have corrosive effects (Caughlin & Vangelisti, 2006).

In heterosexual romances, men and women may approach conflict from different perspectives. Early on, Lloyd (1987) documented that the key issue contributing to relationship decline for women was difficulty in resolving conflicts, particularly the conflicts that the female partner herself had initiated. For men, on the other hand, the key issue was the stability of the conflict issue (that is, how often the issue has come up in the past); conflict issues that were repeatedly brought up by the partner were particularly distressing. Thus the female partner's "pursuit of resolution" may initiate a cycle of relationship decline if the male partner perceives that the couple is "rehashing the same old issue" (Lloyd, 1987). Subsequent research continued to document gender differences, with women more likely to engage in demands, overt hostility, and criticisms, and men more likely to avoid. In particular, the woman demands/man withdraws pattern occurs more frequently, and predicts dissatisfaction; whereas the man demands/woman withdraws pattern occurs less often (Caughlin & Vangelisti, 2006).

Roloff and Johnson (2002) emphasize the importance of examining "serial arguing" in studying romantic conflict, that is, arguments that occur and reoccur over a given issue. They note that serial arguing emerges as a result of increasing interdependence and conflict over the direction of the relationship. Ongoing arguments that are accompanied by a lack of communication skills and destructive tactics may especially contribute to relational decline and decay (Canary & Messman, 2002). Roberts (2006) presents a particularly complex analysis of the ways in which destructive conflict tactics interface with other relational processes in heterosexual relationships. She notes that non-constructive conflict involves the failure to restrain from expressing negative thoughts, negative reciprocity, and retaliation. Some features of the relationship itself interfere with the de-escalation of destructive conflicts, including low levels of trust, negative attributions, negative relationship expectations, and the perception of low positive regard from one's partner. In addition, negative conflict tactics that involve avoidance, demand/ withdraw, and contempt have been shown to predict relationship dissolution, whereas couples who show a ratio of positive to negative behaviors of approximately 5:1 have more favorable relational outcomes (e.g., Gottman & Levenson, 1992).

Conflict in gay and lesbian relationships has received far less scholarly attention. Scholars have noted that, for lesbian couples in particular, there is some fusion, or high levels of interdependence, that potentially lead to heightened levels of conflict (Causby, Lockhart, White, & Greene, 1995; Felicio & Sutherland, 2001). Sources of conflict for lesbian and gay couples include infidelity, substance abuse, financial problems, and violence (Kurdek, 2001). A further nuance for gay and lesbian couples has been captured by Van Eeden-Moorefield and colleagues (2012); disagreements over whether to be out about one's sexuality are related to a heightened risk of dissolution.

Several researchers (see Kline, Pleasant, Whitton, & Markman, 2006 for a review) have identified a mechanism by which conflict affects relationship persistence, and consequently designed an intervention to minimize these effects. Research by Stanley, Blumberg, and Markman (1999) showed that poor conflict management tactics influence romantic relationships from early on and escalate as these couples navigate more serious and difficult problems. To combat these deleterious effects of poor conflict management, Stanley and his colleagues (1999) designed the Prevention and Relationship Enhancement Program (PREP). In a separate line of research discussed above, Gottman and Levenson (1992) also proposed the cascade model of relationships by which conflict erodes relationships.

Turbulence and Uncertainty

The relational turbulence model accounts for the causes and consequences of the experience of relational turbulence in a romantic relationship (Solomon & Knobloch, 2001, 2004). The model incorporates mechanisms of relational uncertainty (lack of confidence, doubts, and ambiguities about the relationship) that may lead to increased negativity and vigilance during times of relational transitions (see Chapter 3 for a discussion of turbulence; Solomon & Theiss, 2011). These processes are exacerbated by negative cognitions and emotions, difficulty communicating, mistrust, biased information processing, and topic avoidance. Although uncertainty may result in increased intimacy if partners are able to communicate openly about their doubts, it also may be a factor in pushing partners apart, through mechanisms of increasing insecurities, amping up tensions, and contributing to disagreements (Knobloch, 2007; Solomon & Theiss, 2011).

There is evidence that relational uncertainty may contribute to dissolution in heterosexual romances. For example, in relationships where individuals viewed their partners' commitment as fluctuating, the likelihood of a breakup was increased, even after controlling for the individual's commitment and satisfaction (this was true particularly in relationships of less than six months' duration; Arriaga et al., 2006). The trajectory of the relationship did matter; if the relationship was on an upward trend in commitment, uncertainty was predictive of breaking up. If the relationship was on a downward trend, uncertainty did not further increase the chances of dissolution. Similar results were documented for fluctuations in satisfaction, which was predictive of subsequent breakup of the relationship (even after controlling for the absolute level of satisfaction; Arriaga, 2001).

Relational Transgressions

Relational transgressions are defined as "events, actions, and behaviors that violate an implicit or explicit relationship norm or rule" (Metts & Cupach, 2007, p. 245). Metts and Cupach group transgressions into three broad categories: rule violations, hurtful events, and infidelity. *Rule violations* emphasize the rule parameters of the relationship, for example, rules about autonomy, fidelity, shared time, and trust. Studies of romantic heterosexual relationships document nine categories of such rule violations: inappropriate interaction, typically during a conflict; lack of sensitivity, including thoughtless and disrespectful behavior; extra-relational involvement; relational threat confounded by betrayal; disregard for the primary relationship; abrupt termination; broken promises; deception, secrets, privacy; and verbal and physical abuse (Metts & Cupach, 2007).

Hurtful events are related to rule violations, but here, scholars emphasize the ways in which the behaviors cause emotional injury (Metts & Cupach, 2007; Vangelisti, 2007). Such events include betrayal, active dissociation (rejection or active disinterest), passive dissociation (being ignored or excluded), feeling taken for granted, criticism, and deception (Feeney, 2004; Metts & Cupach, 2007). Hurt feelings are intensified when the behavior is perceived as intentional and serious, and when the recipient is not able to respond to or challenge the hurtful behavior (Feeney, 2004; Vangelisti, 2007). When heterosexual dating partners make amends for a betrayal, forgiveness is facilitated (Hannon, Rusbult, Finkel, & Kamashiro, 2010). Moreover, individuals who are dissatisfied with the relationship, and those who are in relationships that contain structural commitments, report greater partner intent in the hurtful event; dissatisfied partners also report more distancing as a result of the hurtful event (Vangelisti, 2007). Vangelisti theorizes that both negative reciprocity (responding to a hurt with a hurt), and demand-withdraw patterns, may set in motion a cycle of relational deterioration over time. The degree of hurt experienced is also related to individual characteristics, with highly anxious attachment, low self-esteem, and high rejection sensitivity being related to higher levels of feeling hurt (Vangelisti, 2006a).

Infidelity encompasses extradyadic interaction that is emotional (sharing love, disclosure, and trust) and/or sexual (sexual attention and access; Tafoya & Spitzberg, 2007). In studies of heterosexual couples, scholars have consistently documented infidelity as a relational transgression or betrayal that typically has more far-reaching consequences on the relationship than other types of transgressions (Metts & Cupach, 2007). The reasons provided for engaging in infidelity include desire for passion/sex, sexual or emotional dissatisfaction in the relationship, revenge/anger, and partner neglect (Barta & Keene, 2005; Hall & Fincham, 2006). Sexual and emotional infidelity in heterosexual dating relationships is also related to lowered investment in the relationship (Tsapelas, Fisher, & Aron, 2010). The impact of infidelity on the romantic relationship is not always negative, and indeed some dating partners report either no effect or a positive effect of infidelity on their relationship (Tafoya & Spitzberg, 2007). Still, infidelity, and the jealousy that accompanies it, are consistently related to relational conflict and breakup (Tafoya & Spitzberg, 2007); in particular, the combination of sexual and emotional infidelity, and lack of partner disclosure of the infidelity, are predictive of dissolution of the romantic relationship (Hall & Fincham, 2006). Additionally, breaking up after infidelity may be mediated by the level of forgiveness (Hall & Fincham, 2006).

In heterosexual relationships, men engage in more sexual infidelity than do women, although the rates for the sexes are converging, especially among younger couples (Tsapelas et al., 2010). Women are more distressed by their partner's emotional infidelity, and men are more distressed by their partner's sexual infidelity (Tafoya & Spitzberg, 2007). In explaining these sex differences, Tafoya and Spitzberg (2007) emphasize evolutionary theory, whereas Hendrick and Hendrick (1995) emphasize gender scripts and constructions.

The patterns of infidelity are somewhat different among gay and lesbian romantic partnerships. Gay men report higher levels of sexual infidelity than do heterosexual men (up to seven times higher), and lesbians also report higher levels of infidelity than heterosexual women (Tsapelas et al., 2010). It should be noted that gay, lesbian, and straight couples do differ in acceptance of non-monogamy. Approximately one-third of gay men not in a civil union, one-half of gay men in civil unions, and three-quarters of heterosexual married men had explicit agreements with their partners that sex outside the relationship was unacceptable. Lesbians and straight married women were more similar, with over 80% reporting such explicit monogamy agreements (Solomon, Rothblum, & Balsam, 2005). Infidelity does affect sexual satisfaction negatively in gay and lesbian relationships, and, although sexual infidelity for gay men may be more acceptable, it does cause pain and jealousy (Blow & Hartnett, 2005).

Strategies for Breaking Off a Romance

What reasons do romantic partners give for breaking off their relationships? And how do people go about breaking the "bad news" to a partner that the relationship is over? The relationship problems that precipitate a heterosexual breakup vary widely and may include low relationship quality, unequal levels of commitment and investments, inequity, alternative opportunities, conflict, or pressure from family (Hill et al., 1976; Rusbult et al., 1986; Sprecher, 2001; Sprecher et al., 2006). Gay and lesbian couples report non-responsiveness of the partner (e.g., lack of communication), partner problems, frequent absence, sexual incompatibility, discrepant incomes and arguments over money, and work intrusion as reasons for breaking apart (Oswald & Clausell, 2006). Many of the problems noted by former romantic partners are constructed as problems of individuals; for example, there is a strong tendency to attribute problems to a trait, disposition, or action of either the partner or the self (Cupach & Metts, 1986).

Baxter presents some of the most detailed research on strategies for breaking off a heterosexual romance. These strategies vary along two dimensions: directness and other-orientation (Baxter, 1985). Directness refers to the extent to which the desire to end the relationship is explicitly stated to the partner; some strategies are quite direct, whereas others involve an attempt to break off the pairing without stating that the breakup is the goal. Direct strategies include *fait accompli* (telling the partner the relationship is over with no hope of repair or compromise), *state of relationship talk* (a statement of the desire to break up in the context of a conversation about relationship problems), *attribution conflict* (an intense argument that becomes the reason for the breakup), and *negotiated farewell* (a clear, bilateral communication that formally ends the relationship). Indirect strategies include *withdrawal* (spending less time with the partner or avoiding contact), *pseudo-de-escalation* (one or both partners state that they want the relationship to be less close or intense), *cost-escalation* (increasing the costs of the relationship in the hopes that the partner will break away), and *fading away* (both partners know that the relationship has ended but do not talk about it). Other-orientation refers to the degree to which the disengager attempts to avoid hurting the partner in the process of breaking up; state of relationship talk, pseudo-de-escalation, fading away, and negotiated farewell are other-oriented, whereas fait accompli, withdrawal, and attribution conflict are self-oriented. The more committed the relationship prior to the breakup, the more likely that direct and other-oriented strategies will be used (Baxter, 1985).

Sprecher, Zimmerman, and Abrahams (2010) extended Baxter's early work to include an examination of the role of compassionate love and compassionate breakup strategies in heterosexual romances. They discovered that strategies that are open and positive in tone are viewed as more compassionate. More compassionate strategies were used when the relationship had been high in compassionate love, and when the reasons for the breakup were located in the dyad or in external factors, whereas strategies low in compassion (such as withdrawal or avoidance) were utilized when the reasons for breaking up involved betrayals, such as infidelity.

Dissolution Processes

Early stage models of heterosexual romantic relationship breakups implied that the process of disentangling follows an orderly set of steps or stages (Rollie & Duck, 2006). Indeed, men and women do identify a "script" for dissolution that follows predictable patterns, including cycles of lack of communication, approach/avoidance, and trying to work things out (Battaglia, Richard, Datteri, & Lord, 1998). As was noted for stage theories of mate selection, however, a stage approach to dissolution has not been well supported across the research; rather, scholars have turned to interpersonal processes as a better lens for understanding romantic relationship breakdown and dissolution.

Vangelisti (2006b) has analyzed the commonalities across both conceptual and empirical studies of the phases of heterosexual relationship dissolution. Dissolution processes may begin with a *recognition of problems* in the relationship; in this phase, partners may focus on each other's behavior, avoid communicating about topics that have caused conflict, highlight their differences, evaluate the state of the relationship, and examine the pros and cons of ending the relationship. Partners typically do *discuss their relationship problems* at some point in the process; this may entail both direct and indirect negotiation, feelings of ambivalence and attempts to repair the relationships. *Social networks* may be consulted in multiple ways; partners may seek advice and support, consult with network members on what to do, and begin to construct the story line of what happened in the dissolving relationship. When a *decision to terminate the relationship* is reached, one or both partners enter a new transitional phase where the breakup is viewed as inevitable and engagement in dissolution behaviors accelerates. The final common feature is *getting over the relationship*, in which interaction with the former partner decreases, each partner reflects on the relationship, the relationship itself is reconceptualized over time, and partners work to heal from the loss. The phases should not be viewed as firm stages; instead, they are "complex, multifaceted, and sometimes even chaotic" (Vangelisti, 2006b, p. 362).

Rollie and Duck (2006) have outlined a model of relationship dissolution that incorporates four processes that involve both fluidity and communication. Rollie and Duck (2006) makes the important point that partners do not always know that they are in the process of breaking up at the time it is occurring, because there are times of uncertainty and difficulty in most relationships. Instead, one or both partners may engage in everyday routines and communication patterns, and may lack a subjective awareness of the importance of events and behaviors until after the fact (Rollie & Duck, 2006). *Intrapsychic processes* encompass the feelings partners go through as their relationships change for the worse; partners may feel resentment and underbenefited, and may withdraw both socially and communicatively, as they focus more on the self. *Dyadic processes* begin when the sense of resentment is expressed to the partner; partners may discover that they both have grievances and resentments to air, and may engage in many "state of the relationship" talks and exchanges. These processes may include attempts to justify one's own behavior, comparison to other people's relationships or to social norms, problem-solving attempts, and reconstructing what happened over the course of the relationship. Additionally, feelings of anger, guilt, and hurt may surface. *Social processes* involve disclosing to the social network that the relationship is in trouble, and may include the construction of the story of one's role in the decline of the relationship, as well as processes of accounting and attribution. The end of the relationship is not the end of the process; both *grave-dressing* (reporting the nature and breakup of the relationship in a socially acceptable manner) and *resurrection processes* (adjustments in views of self, romantic partners, and future relationships) occur after breaking apart (Rollie & Duck, 2006).

Dailey, Rossetto, Pfiester, and Surra (2009) describe "on-again, off-again" romantic relationships. Their work is situated within interdependence theory, and highlights the limitations of viewing romantic relationships as either intact or broken up. Their qualitative analysis provides a rich description of the reasons heterosexual partners reported for breaking up, including conflict, negative characteristics of the partner or oneself, dissatisfaction with time spent together, desire to pursue alternatives, and external factors (such as families, or career opportunities). Reasons for renewals included communicating more effectively, changes in the partner or self, continued attachment to each other, renewed effort, increased time together, increased intimacy, and dissatisfaction with alternative partners. In examining general features of these on-off relationships, Dailey and colleagues note a strong thread of relational uncertainty, which was characterized by ambivalence and indecisiveness.

Van Eeden-Moorefield, Martell, Williams, and Preston (2011) present a thoughtful analysis of the ways in which the negotiation of dissolution for gay and lesbian couples is affected by the heteronormative context. In the current context of heated debates about civil unions and same-sex marriages, there is still a great deal of stigma attached to being a member of a same-sex couple. This context provides different access to resources and places added stressors on couples. Such stress is heightened when one or both partners have internalized the stigma associated with homosexuality, and may lead to lower relationship quality and higher instability.

A recent advancement in the field centers on the study of "post-dissolution" relationships (PDRs); this work goes beyond the notion of a "breakup" as the ultimate end to examine the relationships that develop between former romantic partners (Koenig Kellas, 2008). Lannutti and Cameron (2002) describe the characteristics of post-dissolution relationships for gay, lesbian, and heterosexual former romantic partners. Gay and lesbian former partners reported a high level of satisfaction, moderate interpersonal contact and emotional intimacy, and low sexual intimacy in their PDRs. Straight former partners noted moderate satisfaction and emotional intimacy, and low interpersonal and sexual contact. For same-sex couples, the longer the time since the breakup of the romantic aspect of the relationship, the less interpersonal contact. Both the work of Dailey and colleagues (2009) and Lannutti and Cameron (2002) highlight the importance of examining the post-dissolution phase of relational progressions and processes.

Dissolution Trajectories

Inherent in the gradual differentiation and interpersonal process models is the idea that relationships take different pathways or trajectories as they develop and decline (Surra, 1990). We now present the results of two studies that used the retrospective interview technique to map out different trajectories of relationship development/decline, and post-dissolution relationships.

Cate and Lloyd (1992) reported on a study of the different pathways to heterosexual relationship decline and dissolution. They interviewed 100 partners who had experienced a romantic heterosexual relationship breakup, and identified five relational trajectories. *Accelerated* relationships both developed and deteriorated quite quickly. On average, partners in these relationships reported very high levels of commitment within three months of the first date, with few downturns or negative events as the relationship was developing. When negative turning points did occur, however, these relationships began a process of rapid deceleration and dissolution, ending on average after 10 months of dating. *Low-level* relationships were similarly short (13 months in length); these relationships developed gradually, and evidenced a much lower level of commitment. These relationships were also relatively smooth; when a negative turning point occurred, the relationship broke up soon after.

Moderate relationships were the most symmetrical of the five types, both developing and dissolving at a moderate and even rate. These relationships reached a level of commitment that was between the low-level and accelerated relationships, and evidenced a gradual dissolution phase that might best be characterized as a "fade out" with two to three negative turning points. Moderate relationships lasted 17 months on average. *Prolonged-turbulent* relationships were the most up and down of the types. These were long-term dating relationships, lasting 31 months on average, with a high level of relational commitment. The dissolution phase of these relationships was characterized by an eight-month period of ambivalence and uncertainty, with many downturns, and a pattern of breaking up and getting back together. *Prolonged-smooth* relationships were the longest pattern described, lasting an average of 54 months. These relationships attained the highest level of commitment and were notable in the absence of negative turning points. The dissolution phase of these relationships was quite gradual, with a seven-month period of uncertainty characterized by gradual unbonding.

Koenig Kellas et al. (2008) used a modified retrospective interview technique to examine post-dissolution relationships (PDRs); in this study, they examined romantic heterosexual dating partners' commitment to the post-dissolution relationship. They identified four relational patterns: linear process, relational decline, upward relational progression, and turbulent relational progression. *Linear process* was characterized by a flat trajectory, with a relatively low level of commitment to the PDR. *Relational decline* was characterized by a down-slope, with high levels of commitment soon after the breakup, and a steady drop in commitment thereafter. *Upward relational progression* described relationships where the commitment to the PDR increased over time, although with some drops in commitment along the way. *Turbulent relational progression* relationships were characterized by many drastic ups and downs during the PDR. Koenig Kellas and colleagues (2008) identified 10 types of turning points in these post-dissolution relationship: negative redefinition of the relationship, positive redefinition of a platonic PDR, holding on, letting go, moving on, maintaining contact after the breakup, logistics of uncoupling, ending the PDR, and romantic reconciliation. Finally, partners who reported the linear progression type of PDR reported the least amount of emotional disruption.

The Aftermath of Romantic Relationship Dissolution

Harvey and Hansen (2002) and Orbuch (1992) discuss research and theory on loss and bereavement experienced after the dissolution of a close relationship, with particular emphasis on processes of distress and adaptation. Although the relationship dissolver may experience relief and guilt, both partners (and especially the partner who is broken up with) may experience psychological distress, emotional volatility, and decreased life satisfaction (Cupach & Spitzberg, 2004; Rhoades, Dush, Atkins, Stanley & Markman, 2011; Sbarra & Emery, 2005). Reactions to a romantic relationship loss vary along two dimensions: anger and sadness/withdrawal (Orbuch, 1992). Former romantic partners also note that when a breakup occurs in a heterosexual relationship, members of the social network may downplay the depth of the loss, instead emphasizing the ability to get attached to a new partner and the importance of having avoided marriage.

In heterosexual relationships, emotional distress after a breakup has been studied as a function of a wide variety of factors. Attachment style is related to distress, with those evidencing anxious/ambivalent attachment reporting more difficulties in adjusting to the breakup, and more negative emotions; secure and avoidant individuals report an easier time coping with relational dissolution (Barbara & Dion, 2001; Choo, Levine, & Hatfield, 1996). In terms of coping strategies, former partners who engage in self-blame and catastrophic interpretations report higher levels of post-dissolution emotional problems (Boelen & Reijntjes, 2009). In addition, distress over a breakup is related to the length of time since the breakup occurred, being the non-initiator of the breakup, higher positive ratings of the relationship pre-breakup, and feelings of betrayal (Field, Diego, Pelaez, Deeds & Delgado, 2009).

The post-breakup distress of gay and lesbian partners has been studied less often. The most common emotional reactions were relief from conflict, loneliness, and personal growth (Peplau & Spalding, 2002). Post breakup distress was lower for gay and lesbian partners, who evidenced lower levels of attachment and love, who were better educated, and who lived with the ex-partner a shorter time and did not pool finances (Kurdek, 1991). Anecdotal evidence suggests that there may be pressure from the social network to break off relationships compassionately and tactfully, and to remain friends post-breakup, given the small size and interconnectedness of gay and lesbian communities (Peplau & Spalding, 2002). Both Felicio and Sutherland (2001) and Weinstock (2004) note that lesbians tend to maintain friendship relationships with ex-lovers (more so than do heterosexual couples); Weinstock frames this finding in terms of the strong relational connections that are formed in the face of homophobic oppression, the socialization of female friendships, and the development of positive identities with similar others. In fact, both gay men and lesbians maintain closer relationships to their former partners than do heterosexuals (Harkless & Fowers, 2005).

Finally, not every relationship ends with a clean breaking off of interaction. As noted earlier, the development of the post-dissolution relationship is a complex one, and partners may engage in a pattern of breaking up and getting back together. Additionally, former partners often attempt reconciliation, and may engage in acts of unwanted relational pursuit, continuing to seek out, telephone, and interact with the ex-partner, in the hopes of rekindling the romance (Cupach & Spitzberg, 2004). Continued pursuit is quite common; Langhinrichsen-Rohling, Palarea, Cohen, and Rohling (2000) found that most individuals who were broken up with engaged in some form of pursuit post-breakup, most commonly showing up unexpectedly, telephoning the ex, and asking friends about the ex-partner. Not surprisingly, the relationship dissolvers found these behaviors to be more negative than the partners engaging in the pursuit; dissolvers who experienced high levels of pursuit by the ex-partner described their former partners as displaying insecure and anxious attachment, possessive and dependent love, and jealousy and abusiveness. Indeed, unwanted pursuit may evolve into obsessive relational intrusion and stalking behaviors (Cupach & Spitzberg, 2004), a topic that will be addressed in the next chapter.

Summary

Understanding why some romantic relationships work and others fail is a central question in relationship science because close relationships have a tremendous effect on daily life, health, and life satisfaction. Despite the centrality of this question, there has been much disagreement about how to conceptualize the processes central to relationship success (e.g., stability, satisfaction). We proposed that relationship "stability" is best understood by examining the processes of relationship maintenance and relationship dissolution. The predictors of romantic relationship persistence can be organized into three categories: (1) individual, (2) relational, and (3) external factors. Research clearly shows that relational factors are most predictive of relationship persistence, although several notable individual and external factors also contribute. Scholars examining relationship dissolution have also contributed rich analyses of turbulence, transgressions, deterioration, and trajectories, and have added to our understanding of both the processes and aftermath of disentangling from a romantic pairing. Still, there are areas where more scholarship is sorely needed. In particular, work on the dissolution of gay and lesbian romantic relationships is sparse, and indeed, as noted by Oswald and Clausell (2006), much of what we know has come from the work of only a handful of scholars (Larry Kurdek, in particular), who have catalyzed research in this area. In addition, much of the work on romantic relationships has been conducted on heterogeneous samples of White, mostly middle-class, college students. The need for deeper contextualization of romantic pairings, and for an examination of the intersections of race, class, sexuality, and age, cannot be overstated (Allen et al., 2009; Oswald et al., 2009).

Key Concepts

Affective intimacy/closeness (pp. 100–101)
Anxious attachment (p. 114)
Attachment (p. 114)
Avoidant attachment (p. 114)
Behavioral intimacy/closeness (pp. 100–101)
Breaking up (pp. 109–110, 112–113)
Close Relationship Model (p. 100)
Conflict (pp. 105–106)
Conflict resolution (pp. 105–106)
Deterioration (pp. 104–109)
Dissolution (pp. 110–113)
Distress (pp. 113–115)
Equity (p. 91)
Gay couples (pp. 106, 112, 114)
Hurtful events (pp. 107–108)
Infidelity (pp. 108–109)
Investment model (pp. 88, 89, 97)
Investments (pp. 89, 90, 97, 98, 109)
Lesbian couples (pp. 106, 112, 114)
Loss (pp. 110, 113, 114)
Love (p. 110)
Moral commitment (p. 90)
Negativity (p. 108)
Network support (p. 110)
Personal commitment (pp. 89, 90, 98, 102)
Positive communication (p. 105)
Positive illusions (pp. 102–103)
Post-dissolution relationships (pp. 112, 113)
Relationship maintenance (pp. 87–92, 104)
Rule violations (p. 107)
Secure attachment (pp. 93–94, 114–115)
Self-esteem (pp. 94, 108)
Similarity (pp. 97, 103)
Social network (pp. 110, 114)
Structural commitment (pp. 90, 108)
Subjective commitment (p. 98)
Trajectories (pp. 112–113)
Transgressions (pp. 107–109)
Turbulence (pp. 106–107, 113)
Uncertainty (pp. 106–107, 111, 113)
Underbenefited (p. 111)

Additional Readings

Baxter, L. A. (1985). Accomplishing relationship disengagement. In S. Duck & D. Perlman (Eds.), *Understanding personal relationships* (pp. 243–265). Thousand Oaks, CA: Sage.

Beals, K. P., Impett, E. A., & Peplau, L. A. (2002). Lesbians in love: Why some relationships endure and others end. *Journal of Lesbian Studies, 6*, 53–63.

Canary, D. J., & Stafford, L. (1994). Maintaining relationships through strategic and routine interaction. In D. J. Canary & L. Stafford (Eds.), *Communication and relational maintenance* (pp. 3–22). New York, NY: Academic Press.

Duck, S. (1985). Social and personal relationships. In M. L. Knapp and G. R. Miller (Eds.), *Handbook of interpersonal communication* (pp. 665–686). Beverly Hills, CA: Sage.

Le, B., & Agnew, C. R. (2003). Commitment and its theorized determinants: A meta-analysis of the investment model. *Personal Relationships, 10*(1), 37–57.

Le, B., Dove, N. L., Agnew, C. R., Korn, M. S., & Mutso, A. A. (2010). Predicting nonmarital romantic relationship dissolution: A meta-analytic synthesis. *Personal Relationships, 17*, 377–390.

Oswald, R. F., & Clausell, E. (2006). Same-sex relationships and their dissolution. In M. A. Fine & J. H. Harvey (Eds.), *Handbook of divorce and relationship dissolution* (pp. 499–514). Mahwah NJ: Lawrence Erlbaum.

Roberts, L. J. (2006). From bickering to battering: Destructive conflict processes in intimate relationships. In P. Noller & J. A. Feeney (Eds.), *Close relationships: Functions, forms and processes* (pp. 325–351). New York, NY: Psychology Press.

7

VIOLENCE IN ROMANTIC PARTNERSHIPS

Because intimate pairings are highly romanticized in our culture, the motives and actions of dating, committed, and cohabiting partners are often imbued with both nobility and purity. Although there are a few references to violence and sexual exploitation in early family studies literature (see, for example, Kanin, 1957), scant attention was given to the study of romantic violence until the 1980s. It was not until the work of Makepeace (1981), Cate, Henton, Koval, Christopher, and Lloyd (1982), Laner and Thompson (1982), and Koss and Oros (1982) that issues of physical violence and rape in developing romantic relationships were brought to the forefront.

Work on this dark side of courtship exploded during the 1980s, documenting incidence, correlates, and effects of intimate partner violence (IPV).[1] The result has been an amazing proliferation of work on intimate partner violence, with hundreds of scholarly articles per year by the decade of the 2010s. In this chapter, we review the literature on intimate partner violence that occurs in romantic partnerships. Because of the extensiveness of the literature, we have concentrated here on three types of studies: classic work that catalyzed important trends in the field, research published since 2000, and review articles. Early research on IPV emphasized just two broad types of aggression, physical and sexual, and concentrated almost solely on heterosexual relationships. As the field developed in complexity over time, other forms of partner violence were documented and carefully studied, including stalking, psychological aggression, and intimate partner violence in gay and lesbian partnerships.

---

1 Since the term "intimate partner violence" (IPV) is used in multiple ways in the literature (for example, including married partners and excluding adolescent daters), we want to clarify our use of this term. We use "IPV" to describe physical violence, sexual aggression, stalking, and/or psychological aggression that occurs between teenage and adult romantic partners who are dating or cohabiting.

Physical Violence in Heterosexual Relationships

Definition and Incidence of Physical Violence

Official definitions of IPV are both broad and diverse. For example, the Uniform Crime Report includes as intimate partner violence only those actions that meet the definition of a crime (homicide, aggravated assault, simple assault, and forcible rape), whereas definitions used by the World Health Organization foreground intentionality and harm, and include non-criminal aspects of aggression, such as deprivation and psychological maltreatment (Kilpatrick, 2004).

Definitions used by researchers tend to be more specific and focused. Early researchers defined physical violence as "the use or threat of physical force or restraint carried out with the intent of causing pain or injury to another" (Sugarman & Hotaling, 1989, p. 4). In practice, researchers often operationalize physical violence using the Conflict Tactics Scale—the number of times in the past year (or in one's lifetime) that intimate partners have perpetrated/ experienced pushing, shoving, slapping, kicking, biting, hitting with fists, trying to hit with an object, choking, beatings, and threats/use of a weapon (Straus, 1979; Straus, Hamby, Boney-McCoy, & Sugarman, 1996). Its predominance notwithstanding, the shortcomings of the CTS and the CTS2 have been thoroughly discussed (see DeKeseredy, 2006; Kimmel, 2002).

Fortunately, there are several nationally representative surveys that have assessed the incidence of physical violence in romantic relationships, although it should be noted that these studies typically collapse findings across dating, cohabitation, and marriage. Stets and Henderson (1991) conducted the first nationally representative study of the incidence of physical violence in heterosexual dating relationships and found that 30% reported enacting and 31% reported experiencing physical violence over the previous 12 months. The most comprehensive study, the 2010 *National Intimate Partner and Sexual Violence Survey* (NISVS), found that 32.9% of women and 28.2% of men report having experienced physical violence from an intimate partner (dating, cohabiting, or marital; heterosexual or gay/lesbian); this gender gap widens as the physically violent behavior becomes more severe, with 24.3% of women and 13.8% of men reporting having experienced being hit with a fist, beaten, slammed against something, choked or suffocated, burned, and/or having a weapon threatened or used against them (Black et al., 2011). The *Youth Risk Behavior Surveillance Survey* (YRBSS) documented that among 9th to 12th grade students, 11% of boys and 8.8% of girls reported experiencing physical violence in their heterosexual teen dating relationships (Eaton et al., 2008). And, violence begins early; among women, 22.4% were between 11 and 17 years of age when violence was first experienced, and 47.1% were between 18 and 24 (Black et al., 2011).

Individual Factors in Physical Violence

Individuals with lower incomes and education are more likely to perpetrate and experience physical violence (Barnett, Miller-Perrin, & Perrin, 2005), although effect sizes for these factors are small (Stith, Smith, Penn, Ward, & Tritt, 2004). Whereas younger individuals are more likely to perpetrate intimate partner physical violence in general (Stith et al., 2004), age is not related to physical violence among daters (Lewis & Fremouw, 2001).

Race and gender are also inconsistent risk markers. Although some studies show a heightened risk of experiencing physical violence for minority women, when income is controlled, these differences are largely moderated (Carlson, Worden, van Ryn & Bachman, 2003). Additionally, there has been a three-decade debate over the relative rates of heterosexual physical violence perpetration by women versus men. When the CTS is used, and the definition includes non-injurious violence, gender symmetry is seen consistently (e.g., Straus & Gelles, 1990). On the other hand, the NVAWS, NISVS, and Uniform Crime Reports find gender asymmetry for severe violence, with higher rates of male perpetration and female victimization (see Black et al., 2011; Tjaden & Thoennes, 2000b). Michael Johnson's (2008) typology of IPV has contributed greatly to clarifying the source of this gender debate. His work emphasizes four unique types of IPV: intimate terrorism, situational couple violence, violent resistance, and mutual violent control. Although men and women perpetrate acts of situational couple violence at relatively similar rates, in cases of intimate terrorism men are far more likely to be the perpetrator than are women (Johnson, 2008). And, in dating relationships where violence is perpetrated only by the female partner, the frequency is lower and violence is more likely to desist over time (Testa, Hoffman, & Leonard, 2011). Andersen (2005) and Reed, Raj, Miller, and Silverman (2010) present excellent reviews of the complexity of the intersections of gender and violence; they conclude that, when the full spectrum of violence is taken into account, including sexual violence, stalking, injury, and severity of physical violence, women are at far greater risk of being victimized than are men by their different-sex intimate partners.

Risk factors for physical violence victimization for young women include: the extent to which they exhibit both internalizing and externalizing problems, low academic achievement, substance use, more romantic and sexual partners, and prior victimization in a romantic relationship (Cleveland, Herrera, & Stuewig, 2003; McDonell, Ott, & Mitchell, 2010; Vézina & Hébert, 2007). Young men's risk of violence victimization is related to having been hit as a child by an adult, physical fights with peers, and low self-esteem (Foshee, Benefield, Ennett, Bauman, & Suchindran, 2004).

Characteristics of perpetrators of physical violence have also been carefully examined. Male perpetrators show higher levels of anger, hostility, delinquent behaviors, antisocial behaviors, depression, non-conformity, poor social skills, and impulsivity (Andrews, Foster, Capaldi, & Hops, 2000; Keenan-Miller, Hammen, & Brennen, 2007; Stith et al., 2004; White, McMullin, Swartout, Sechrist, & Gollehon, 2008). They are likely to also engage in forced sex and verbal abuse, have a past history of partner abuse, hold traditional gender role attitudes, and hold attitudes supportive of the use of violence against women (Stith et al., 2004).

The characteristics of female perpetrators of physical violence in dating relationships are less well understood (Edwards, Desai, Gidycz & VanWynsberghe, 2009). There is some evidence that women who perpetrate severe violence are also generally more aggressive (Ehrensaft, Moffitt, & Caspi, 2004), antisocial (Andrews et al., 2000), and have experienced deep trauma in the family of origin (Schaffner, 2007). Women's perpetration of less severe forms of aggression is related to previous victimization experiences, depression, insecure attachment, and to their use of aggression against peers (Carney, Butrell, & Dutton, 2007; Edwards et al., 2009; Foshee, McNaughton, & Ennett, 2010). Edwards and colleagues (2009), using both prospective and retrospective designs, conclude that it is important to understand women's perpetration of intimate aggression within a context of their previous victimization as children/adolescents, the presence of mutual partner aggression, and their previous use of verbal and physical aggression in the relationship.

Alcohol/substance use and abuse are consistent risk markers for physical violence (Foran & O'Leary, 2008; Moore, Stuart, Meehan, Rhatigan, Hellmuth, & Keen, 2008; Stith et al., 2004). Couples report that alcohol and drugs are both a catalyst for violence (due to disinhibition), as well as an excuse for violence (e.g., "I didn't know what I was doing"; Lloyd & Emery, 2000). Physical violence perpetrated by men who abuse alcohol tends to be more frequent and severe, and men who are violent substance abusers display more hostility and suspicion (Christopher & Lloyd, 2000). The alcohol-violence relationship is stronger for men than it is for women (Foran & O'Leary, 2008; Stith et al., 2004).

Finally, prior violent victimization (including community violence, peer harassment, and family of origin violence) is a risk factor for both perpetration and victimization (Crawford & Wright, 2007; Hattery, 2009; Widom et al., 2008). Still, the evidence for a cycle of violence in the family, or the intergenerational transmission of violence, has been both inconsistent and overstated (Lewis & Fremouw, 2001; Widom, Czalja, &Dutton, 2008). Our understanding here has been enhanced by recent prospective and mediated models of transmission; Maas, Fleming, Herrenkohl and Catalano (2010) documented the role of parental bonding and social skills as protective factors for girls, and the mediating role of externalizing behaviors for boys, and Wolf and Foshee (2003) found that adolescents who witness domestic violence "learn anger expression styles that put them at risk of being perpetrators of dating violence" (p. 309). Such models contribute to the development of more complex understanding of the transmission of not only violence, but also trauma and relationship dysfunction (Lloyd, 2012).

Dyadic Factors in Physical Violence

Dyadic factors associated with physical violence in heterosexual relationships encompass a multitude of dynamics, from precipitating events to communication patterns. This section discusses work on precipitating events, motivations and reasons for violent behavior, relationship dynamics, and communication and control.

Precipitating Events, Motivations, and Types of Episodes

What seems to precipitate physical abuse? Emotion-related precipitators include jealousy, perceived threats to the relationship, anger, and frustration. Although aggression may be catalyzed by stressful life events, and alcohol/drug use, it is also clear that "just about anything" can set off an episode of aggression (Lloyd & Emery, 2000).

Another way to understand what triggers violence is by asking romantic partners about the meaning behind their aggression, as well as their motivations. Early on, Henton, Cate, Koval, Lloyd, and Christopher (1983) asked both victims and perpetrators to provide their perceptions of the violent act. Perpetrators were most likely to interpret their aggression as confusion, followed by anger, love, fear and sadness; less than 3% of aggressors interpreted their violence as a sign of hate. Victims interpreted the violence directed at them in similar ways, mentioning anger, confusion, love, and fear. The attribution of love may be indicative of the romantic veneer that surrounds both intimate relationships and dating (Henton et al., 1983; Lloyd & Emery, 2000).

Women's motivations for perpetrating physical violence include playfulness, self-defense, resistance, expression of negative feelings, anger at the partner, ethic enforcement, poor communication, to pay the partner back for past emotional hurts, and to regain control (Caldwell, Swan, Allen, Sullivan, & Snow, 2009; Foshee, Bauman, Linder, Rice, & Wilcher, 2007; Hettrich & O'Leary, 2007; Lloyd, Emery, & Klatt, 2009). Although women attribute their male partners' aggression to jealousy, control, and situational events (Lloyd & Emery, 2000), men's accounts provide a different picture. Men note that their motivations for violence include playfulness and attempts to prevent partner's aggression from escalating (Foshee et al., 2007); they explain their aggression in situational and active terms, suggesting that aggression is seen as an important component of masculinity (Weaver, Vandello, Bosson & Burnaford, 2010). Men also account for their aggression by emphasizing external causes (Mullaney, 2007).

Understanding motivations and precipitators may require digging deeper into types of aggressive episodes. Draucker and colleagues (2010) present an interesting qualitative study of common aggressive events. They identified eight distinct types of aggressive episodes: tumultuous; explosive; scuffling; violating; threatening; controlling; disparaging; and rejecting, ignoring, or disrespecting. Finally, Babcock, Costa, Green, and Eckhardt (2004) theorize that behaviors that potentially precipitate aggression fit into three basic categories: responding to control attempts (either autonomy or control moves), responding out of jealousy, and responding to verbal aggression.

Interpersonal Dynamics

Interpersonal dynamics include initiation of the aggression, how partners react, relational dynamics, and the aftermath of aggression. Studies that have attempted to unravel the question of initiation often simply ask "who initiated the aggression?" and provide a forced choice answer, which may mask the complexity of this dynamic. Olson and Lloyd (2005) conducted a qualitative inquiry and found that, whereas women acknowledged that just over 50% of the time they initiated aggression, probing their answers clarified that initiation meant being angry, being persistent, and bringing up the issue that resulted in conflict. The women rarely described their initiation of aggression in terms of an act of physical aggression such as a slap or a hit.

Finkel (2008) has created the I³ (I-cubed) model as a meta-theoretical framework to account for the interplay of situational and dispositional characteristics in the initiation of aggression. He theorizes that IPV initiation is undergirded by instigation, impellance, and inhibition. *Instigation* is defined as the social dynamics that would normatively trigger aggression, including the partner's verbal aggression, hostility, autonomy/control attempts, and perceived infidelity. *Impellance* is defined as the factors that predispose the individual to feel strong urges to aggress, including dispositional anger, social norms, jealousy, insecurity in the relationship,, and dissatisfaction with one's power in the relationship. *Inhibition* is defined as the factors that lead the individual to override the urge to behave aggressively, including cultural disapproval, alcohol use, and low levels of dispositional self-control, perspective-taking, and relational commitment. The I³ model emphasizes that instigation, impellance, and inhibition all interact with one another to promote or deter IPV perpetration (Finkel & Eckhardt, in press).

How do victims react to the occurrence of physical violence? Female victims speak about feeling angry, hurt, confused, and frightened; the first time aggression is experienced, victims also report a sense of disbelief. Behaviorally, they respond by talking to the partner, fighting back, crying, leaving, and moving out of reach. Most aggressors indicate they felt sorry or hurt after the incident; they responded by apologizing and trying to make up, and talking to the partner (Henton et al., 1983; Lloyd & Emery, 2000). Male aggressors also reacted by acting as if nothing had happened, ignoring their partners, refusing to talk, and blaming the partner (Lloyd & Emery, 2000).

Relational dynamics include commitment levels, satisfaction, and patterns of communication and control. Physical aggression is more likely to occur when the relationship has reached the serious stage or cohabitation, and the risk of aggression increases with the length of the relationship (Lewis & Fremouw, 2001). In short-term prospective studies, physical aggression has been shown to be remarkably stable (Capaldi, Shortt, & Crosby, 2003; O'Leary & Slep, 2003), although Capaldi and colleagues find this to be the case only for mutual aggression, noting that female-only aggression is just as likely to end as it is to continue. Rhoades, Stanley, Kelmer, and Markman (2010) found less dedication to continuing the relationship, yet more barriers to leaving among couples where physical violence was present. Still, the evidence on the stability of physical violence in dating relationships is mixed; proportionately, it is more likely to be infrequent, mild, and unstable, with less than one-fourth of couples reporting stable violence (Spitzberg, 2011).

Surprisingly, the evidence is mixed with regard to relational satisfaction among physically violent couples. Although early research emphasized that partners in physically abusive relationships do not seem to love each other less than those involved in nonviolent relationships, nor are they highly dissatisfied with their relationships (Arias, Samios, & O'Leary, 1987), later research showed that satisfaction and commitment levels are lower (Lewis & Fremouw, 2001; Rhatigan & Street, 2005; Slotter et al., 2012). Lloyd and Emery (2000) explain this dynamic. Because violence may start out with more minor acts, and escalate slowly, it may not initially erode happiness in the relationship. Additionally, female victims actively work to "forgive and forget," by engaging in self-blame for precipitating the violence, and attributing their partners' violence to external stressors or unresolved family of origin traumas. However, violence that continues over time, especially severe violence, does eventually serve to erode the relationship.

Communication and Control

Communication patterns in violent couples have been examined as well. Women describe their aggressive male partners as volatile, unable to talk about feelings without spilling into anger, blaming, and being verbally and psychologically coercive. They also describe patterns of escalating conflicts, wherein aggression is enacted when other communication tactics fail (Lloyd & Emery, 2000). Verbal aggression, jealousy, and controlling behavior may form a latent construct of psychological abuse; these factors predict physical aggression both concurrently and over time (O'Leary & Slep, 2003).

Destructive or inadequate problem-solving skills, relational insecurity, rejection sensitivity, and negative communication patterns—such as harsh start-up, cycles of criticism and defense, flooding, and lower levels of accepting influence and repair attempts—are used more often by aggressive couples (Cornelius, Shorey, & Beebe, 2010; Galliher & Bentley, 2010: Roberts, 2006; Volz & Kerig, 2010). And, physically violent relationships are beset with power imbalances (Giordano, Soto, Manning, & Longmore, 2010).

Dynamics of control are theorized to underlie the relational aspects of men's severe physical aggression. Lloyd and Emery (2000) found multiple patterns of control, including domination of an argument, domination of the woman and the relationship (e.g., controlling her self-confidence, keeping her dependent), physically keeping her in the relationship, and extreme ownership and control of her person (including constant monitoring, ensuring that he controlled all finances, checking the mileage on her car, and even locking her up). Such extreme forms of control are similar to the patterns of intimate terrorism described by Johnson (2008).

Network Factors in Physical Violence

Most physical violence occurs in a private situation; when violence does occur in front of witnesses, intervention is likely to occur less than 50% of the time. Men more than women are likely to report third-party intervention in their violence perpetration (Laner, 1983). Thus, social networks are unlikely to have an influence on a particular occurrence of physical violence.

Networks do play a key role in the norms surrounding violence, as they may either support the legitimacy of such aggression or emphasize the inappropriateness of such behavior (DeKeseredy, 1988). There is consistent evidence that being a member of a friendship network that condones and uses violence is predictive of perpetration of violence for both men and women (Foshee et al., 2010). Similarly, both men's and women's victimization is predicted by knowing other same-sex victims (McDonell et al., 2010).

Adelman and Kil (2007) present a complex analysis of the role of friends in dating conflicts and violence among adolescents. They note five key dynamics of dating conflicts: property or "ownership" rights of daters over their partners, maintenance of a male-centered heterosexual dating culture, distance and competition among girls (with an emphasis on the isolation of the dating couple), difficulty of different-gender friendships due to a framing of them as potentially sexual, and lack of trust and power imbalances between daters and among friends. These norms serve to maintain destructive partner and friend relationships among teens. Adelman and Kil recommend deeper analysis of the ways that dating violence is a means to isolate the partner from the influence of friends, as well as how it is catalyzed by jealousy and norm violation when the partner interacts with both same- and different-sex friends.

The Effects of Physical Violence

Most research on the effects of physical violence examines female survivors, reflecting the typical conceptualization of psychological disorders as causes of men's perpetration, and as consequences of women's victimization (Holtzworth-Munroe, 2005). Over 80% of victimized women report one or more negative effects from IPV (Black et al., 2011). On a short-term basis, women report fear and self-blame (Lloyd & Emery, 2000). Victimized women are more likely to be injured and to require medical attention than are victimized men (Black et al., 2011; Tjaden & Thoennes, 2000b). Consistently documented mental health effects for adolescent girls and women include symptoms of post-traumatic stress disorder (PTSD) and depression (Briere & Jordan, 2004; Holtzworth-Munroe, 2005). Women also evidence heightened levels of somatization, hopelessness, anxiety, suicidal behavior, internalizing disorders, externalizing behaviors, and substance abuse (Barnett et al., 2005; Black et al., 2011; Briere & Jordan, 2004; Vézina & Hébert, 2007), and disruptions in schemas for intimacy, safety, and trust in others (Briere & Jordan, 2004). The experience of coercive behaviors is a stronger predictor of mental health outcomes for victims than is the presence of physical violence, with higher negative effects for women (Prospero, 2009).

The effects of physical violence on women are moderated by several factors, including frequency and severity of violence, comorbid mental disturbance and substance abuse, and a history of prior trauma (Briere & Jordan, 2004). Given the broad range of post-trauma symptoms, and moderating variables, Briere and Jordan conclude that the impact of physical violence on women can best be conceptualized in terms of "response complexity" rather than in a particular syndrome.

There is limited evidence on the effects of physical violence on men (Frieze, 2008). Most studies here examine married partners; this work finds that male victims of minor violence report little distress, and male victims of severe violence report psychological distress at levels that are significantly lower than reported by female victims (Williams & Frieze, 2005). Still, Spitzberg (2011) contends that men are more traumatized by intimate violence victimization than researchers and practitioners assume, and urges further study. Indeed, the recently released NISVS documents that 35% of male victims of IPV (includes physical violence, rape, or stalking) report negative impacts, with fear, safety concerns, and trauma symptoms being the most common (Black et al., 2011).

Sexual Aggression in Heterosexual Relationships

Definition and Incidence of Sexual Aggression

One of the earliest and most comprehensive definitions of sexual aggression in romantic relationships was developed by Koss (1989): sexual interaction, from petting to oral-genital contact to intercourse, which is gained against one's will through use of physical force, threats of force, continual arguments/ pressure, use of alcohol/drugs, and/or position of authority. Subsequent scholars provided refinements; for example, Christopher and Pflieger (2007) break sexual aggression into *sexual coercion*, which includes manipulation, psychological pressure, lying, and incapacitation, and *sexual assault*, which includes threats/use of force. The most widely used assessment is the Sexual Experiences Survey (SES; Koss & Oros, 1982; Koss, Gidycz, & Wisniewski, 1987). Although the revised SES is considered the best assessment of women's sexual victimization (Kolivas & Gross, 2007), it has been carefully critiqued and revised over time (see Cook, Gidycz, Koss, & Murphy, 2011; Koss, Gidycz, et al., 2007).

Incidence rates of sexual aggression vary with the definition used. Restricting the definition to acquaintance rape or date rape (intercourse with a dating partner that occurs in a situation of force or threat of force) yields lifetime incidence rates ranging from 6% to 28% for women (Lloyd & Emery, 2000), with estimates consistently hovering around 15% (Rozee & Koss, 2001). In the NVAWS, Tjaden and Thoennes (2000a) found that 7.7% of women and 0.3% of men report having been raped (either attempted or completed) by an intimate partner (dating, cohabiting, or marital, same- and different-sex relationships). The 2010 NISVS reported that 9.4% of women had experienced intimate partner rape (the corresponding figure for men was not calculated, due to its small size). Lifetime incidence of sexual coercion was 9.8% for women and 4.2% for men; within the category of sexual coercion, 2.2% of men reported being made to penetrate an intimate partner (Black et al., 2011). The overwhelming majority of rape perpetrators are male (Rozee & Koss, 2001); in the NVAWS, men were the perpetrators in 70% of male rapes and 99% of female rapes (Tjaden & Thoennes, 2000a).

Lifetime incidence increases significantly if the definition includes intercourse as a result of verbal pressure or misuse of authority, and attempted intercourse that was accompanied by force or threats of force. Koss (1989), using a national sample of college students, found 39% of college women had experienced an actual rape, attempted rape, or had been coerced into intercourse. Eighty-four percent of the time, the assailant was known to the victim. Studies across the ensuing decades continued to document these figures, with consistent estimates in heterosexual relationships of rape, attempted rape, and coerced intercourse ranging from 22% to 42% of women, and 13% to 22% of men (Peterson, Voller, Polusny, & Murdoch, 2011; Struckman-Johnson, Struckman-Johnson, & Anderson, 2003). Finally, it is important to note that 50% of female victims do not describe their experiences as "rape" or "sexual assault," despite the fact that the assault they experienced meets the legal definition (Littleton, Rhatigan, & Axsom, 2007). Such unacknowledged rapes are more likely to have been perpetrated by a known perpetrator or a romantic partner, and less likely to involve the use of force (Fisher, Daigle, Cullen, & Turner, 2003).

Individual Factors in Sexual Aggression

Research on sexual aggression has also concentrated on the examination of individual risk factors for both victimization and perpetration. As noted above, gender is clearly a very consistent risk factor (for women's victimization and men's perpetration; Struckman-Johnson et al., 2003). Race is related to the incidence of sexual assault, with African American and Native American women being at higher risk than are White women (Bryant-Davis, Chung, & Tillman, 2009). Income and education have not been consistently examined; in part this reflects the wide use of college samples in the study of sexual assault.

Alcohol use has been a consistent risk marker for both perpetration and victimization, with the majority of evidence for alcohol use prior/during sexual aggression, rather than long-term alcohol abuse (Christopher & Lloyd, 2000; Testa, 2004). Although drug-facilitated sexual assault involving surreptitious administration has received a great deal of press, it has been implicated in less than 2% of sexual assaults (Beynon, McVeigh, McVeigh, & Bellis, 2008). Female victims of sexual aggression do not differ substantially from female non-victims on measures of personality and attitudes, such as self-esteem, belief in rape supportive myths, and assertiveness (Lloyd & Emery, 2000). Indeed, the most consistent risk factor for women is prior physical and sexual victimization as children or young adolescents, with those who experienced multiple forms of childhood maltreatment being at the highest risk of subsequent revictimization (Widom et al., 2008). Sexual abuse as a child in particular may be a key risk factor, with heightened risk when the sexual abuse was invasive, intrafamilial, of longer duration, and when sexual assault was experienced during adolescence (Classen, Palesh, & Aggarwal, 2005; Daigneault, Hébert, & McDuff, 2009). Revictimization, both subsequent to childhood sexual abuse, and to adolescent intimate partner sexual assault, is moderated by increased trauma symptoms, risk-taking behaviors (particularly risky sexual behaviors), avoidant coping, and alcohol/substance use (Fargo, 2009; Fortier, DiLillo, Messman-Moore, DeNardi, & Gaffey, 2009; Gidycz, Loh, Lobo, Rich, Lynn & Pashdag, 2007; Messman-Moore, Ward, & Brown, 2009). The dynamics of revictimization include lowered ability to resist, discounting of feelings of danger or inability to defend oneself when childhood traumas are being reenacted, and vulnerability due to negative self-identity and risk-taking behaviors (Fargo, 2009; Messman-Moore et al., 2009).

The factors that place men at risk for heterosexual, dating/romantic partner sexual assault victimization are not well understood. This may be due in part to low occurrence, which even in large representative studies makes accurate estimation difficult (Peterson et al., 2011). What little is known about male sexual assault victims relies on clinical samples (Light & Monk-Turner, 2009). Looking at sexual victimization across the life cycle, it is clear that men's experience of rape evidences a pattern that is quite different from women's (Lloyd, 2012); men are more likely to be raped by an acquaintance than by an intimate partner, by a male perpetrator (85% of cases), and as a child (nearly half of cases occur before the age of 12; Tjaden & Thoennes, 2006).

The research on sexual aggression in close relationships provides a fairly clear profile of male perpetrators (Lloyd, 2012). Men who are sexually coercive in their dating relationships, as compared to non-coercive men, hold more traditional beliefs about women, view their sexual and dating relationships as adversarial, express more anger and hostility toward women, believe in rape-supportive myths, show higher levels of pornography consumption, show lower levels of empathy, and display hypermasculinity (Adams-Curtis & Forbes, 2004; Christopher & Pflieger, 2007; Ryan, 2004; Vega & Malamuth, 2007). Ryan (2004) effectively argues that cognitions play a key role in men's instigation of rape (among both convicted offenders and college students); these include beliefs that men and women are enemies, men are naturally more sexual and sexually aroused, rape can be justified, and that masculinity incorporates the use of sexual force. Finally, sexually aggressive men are not characterized by a lack of sexual outlets; rather they are hypersexual, evidencing more arousal to erotica, more sexual partners and a younger age at first intercourse, more quest for sexual experience, and the use of more exploitative techniques in their pursuit of sex (Christopher & Lloyd, 2000; Christopher & Pflieger, 2007).

Knowledge about women who perpetrate sexual coercion is limited; still, there are a few parallels to the profiles of male perpetrators (Christopher & Lloyd, 2000; Christopher & Pflieger, 2007). Women who engage in sexual coercion hold adversarial beliefs about sexual relationships, display more hostility and anger toward men, and describe their relationships as higher in conflict and lower in satisfaction (Christopher, Madura, & Weaver, 1998).

Dyadic Factors in Sexual Aggression

There are many dyadic factors known to be associated with sexual aggression in heterosexual romantic pairings. Sexual violence perpetrated against a dating partner is likely to begin with trust-gaining tactics as well as romantic overtures (Woods & Porter, 2008). The most common scenario for sexual violence in dating is proximal alcohol use, prior sexual contact, sexual stimulation, and male use of coercion and/or ignoring the woman's "No" (Adams-Curtis & Forbes, 2004). Alcohol use may lower inhibitions, contribute to miscommunication around sexual intent, and serve as an excuse after the fact

(Christopher & Pflieger, 2007). Also, men's estimates of sexual interest are increased in situations where the woman is drinking, dresses in a provocative manner, and initiates the date (Farris, Treat, Viken, & McFall, 2008).

In situations of sexual aggression, men tend to use more forceful, power-assertive, and exploitative tactics than do women, and are more likely to cause serious harm (Struckman-Johnson et al., 2003). Female victims are the most likely to use reasoning in their attempts to resist sexual aggression; when the aggression includes rape or attempted rape, the victim is also highly likely to use physical struggle or force as a resistance technique (Koss, 1989; Lloyd & Emery, 2000).

Miscommunication about sexuality is cited as a dyadic risk factor. Men tend to view women's behaviors as more "sexual," which may result in the interpretation that she desires intercourse, and construction of being led on or mixed signals (Farris et al., 2008; Muehlenhard, 1988). Sexually coercive men, and men who hold traditional ideas about gender roles, are particularly prone to perceive women's behavior as sexual (Farris et al., 2008). This is complicated by a tendency to either ignore or underrate women's resistance (Bouffard & Bouffard, 2011).

Unequal power in the relationship has been documented, with women who are anxiously attached and more highly invested experiencing higher levels of sexual coercion (Christopher & Pflieger, 2007). Indeed, women are more likely to consent to unwanted sex than are men (Impett & Peplau, 2003), and their ability to say no diminishes if the couple has an established sexual relationship (Adams-Curtis & Forbes, 2004). Adolescent girls are at the greatest risk of coercion in a committed relationship; in addition, an age difference between partners results in a dynamic of a younger female being pressured into sex by her older boyfriend (Christopher & Pflieger, 2007).

Sexual coercion and assault are associated with attempts to dominate, change, and impose one's will on a partner (Stets & Pirog-Good, 1990). Lloyd and Emery (2000) described these dynamics of control in their qualitative study of women who experienced sexual aggression in dating relationships. First, some women noted the interplay of physical and sexual force; their partners would use tactics of physical control to force the women to have sex with them and to gain sexual compliance. And, in an unexpected twist, some partners would use sex as a way to make up after physically abusing their partners. Second, some women described a dynamic of possession and ownership; sex became a way to show power over the partner, an expectation that was connected to him paying for their dates, a sign that he now had possession of his woman, and/or a way to show his possessive jealousy. Finally, almost half of the women reported a dynamic of relationship fraud and sexual manipulation: their partners would manipulate them, promising that they loved them and wanted commitment, as a means of gaining sexual access. These women described a dynamic of male manipulation/force and female unwillingness that existed on multiple levels, with the women forced into sex before they were ready and without their consent, and feeling used and manipulated by men who used sex as the price of relationship continuation.

Peterson and Muehlenhard's (2007) analysis of the "missing discourse of ambivalence" is pivotal in contextualizing sexual violence in dating relationships. They note that most research on sexual aggression conceptualizes sex in simplistic terms, as wanted or unwanted. They call instead for more complex examinations of sexual decision making and intimate relationships, and urge further study of unwanted consensual sex, unwanted coerced sex, and non-consensual wanted sex, as well as the ways in which both men's and women's sexual desires and behaviors are intertwined with discourses about masculinity/femininity and intimacy.

Network Factors in Sexual Aggression

Friendship networks play a key role in legitimizing norms of sexual aggression and exploitation, particularly for male perpetrators. Early studies by DeKeseredy (1988) and Gwartney-Gibbs, Stockard, and Bohmer (1987) documented that male peer networks influence the practice of sexual coercion toward women, and that women who have been victimized are more likely to have male friends who are sexually aggressive and female friends who have been victimized. Over the ensuing decades, the influence of male peer networks has continued to be documented. Men who perpetrate sexual coercion in dating relationships have friend networks that are supportive of sexual violence, with the research on this topic being focused largely on men who are members of all-male groups such as fraternities and sports teams (Lloyd, 2012). For example, Murnen and Kohlman (2007) found that fraternity membership and/or athletic participation was associated with hypermasculinity, rape-supportive myths, and perpetration of sexual aggression. Christopher and Pflieger's (2007) review found continued support for the pattern of sexually aggressive men being members of social networks that contain other sexually aggressive men and victimized women.

The Effects of Sexual Aggression

Most of the scholarship on the effects of sexual aggression examines women. Female victims report short-term effects, including fear, emotional distress, lack of trust of men, self-blame, and sexual avoidance (Barnett et al., 2005; Lloyd & Emery, 2000). Consistent long-term effects have been documented, including subsequent alcohol/drug abuse, suicidality, somatic symptoms, chronic illnesses, and gynecological problems (Barnett et al., 2005); these may be heightened for ethnic minority women (Bryant-Davis et al., 2009). Symptoms of trauma and post-traumatic stress disorder have been extensively documented for female victims (Bryant-Davis et al., 2009; Elliott, Mok, & Briere, 2004). Negative effects are magnified when the assault was life-threatening, and when the victim used avoidant coping and self-blame, experienced negative reactions from informal social networks or the judicial system, experienced prior sexual traumas, and had poor pre-assault mental health (Campbell, Dworkin, & Cabral, 2009). Finally, women who were assaulted by their romantic partners report higher levels of trauma and negative mental health effects than those assaulted by a non-partner (Temple, Weston, Rodriguez, & Marshall, 2007).

Very little is known about the effects of sexual assault on men, particularly victimization that occurs inside a heterosexual relationship. Unfortunately, men are highly unlikely to report their victimization or to seek assistance from formal services (Light & Monk-Turner, 2009). Reactions to sexual assault include anger, depression, anxiety, lowered self-esteem, and sexual dysfunction (Christopher & Pflieger, 2007; Tewksbury, 2007). High levels of trauma symptomology are seen as long-term effects of rape for men (Elliott et al., 2004), although most studies of male victims do not examine intimate relationship assaults separately from non-partner assaults, nor do they control for male versus female perpetration. The few studies that do examine female perpetrated rape provide evidence that the psychological consequences are less severe for male victims (as compared to female victims of male rape; Peterson et al., 2011).

Intimate Partner Violence in Gay and Lesbian Partnerships

Definition and Incidence

Over the last three decades, there has been a growing body of research on intimate partner violence that occurs within gay and lesbian partnerships. The extent of physical and sexual aggression in gay and lesbian partnerships is difficult to estimate, for even when representative samples are drawn, the numbers are very small (Christopher & Pflieger, 2007). The most accurate estimates come from the NVAWS; this survey ascertained whether respondents had ever lived with a same-sex partner in a couple relationship, and then looked at experiences of IPV. Looking at physical assault by a same-sex intimate partner, gay men reported a prevalence of 13.8%, and lesbians reported a prevalence of 11.4%. Separate estimates of sexual assault by a same-sex intimate partner were not calculated, because the sample size was too small. Combined estimates of both physical and sexual assault were 11.4% for lesbians and 15.4% for gay men (Tjaden, Thoennes, & Allison, 1999). Both Balsam, Rothblum, and Beauchaine (2005) and Tjaden and colleagues (1999) note that these estimates of IPV are higher among gay-male as compared to heterosexual relationships. The estimates of the incidence of IPV in lesbian relationships is mixed; Tjaden and colleagues (1999) found less physical and sexual violence (as compared to heterosexual relationships), whereas Balsam and colleagues (2005) found higher levels of physical violence. Finally, Messinger (2011) notes that looking across verbal, controlling, physical, and sexual IPV (using NVAWS data), bisexual individuals experience the highest rates, and are the most likely to be victimized by a different-sex partner.

Individual Factors

Because most of the studies of gay and lesbian partnerships utilize convenience samples, clear and consistent individual risk markers have not emerged (Lloyd, 2012). One interesting contextual note in this work is that factors unique to lesbian and gay individuals, such as the lowered self-esteem and self-hatred associated with internalized homophobia, are associated with higher risk of experiencing and perpetrating violence in a same-sex partnership (Balsam & Szymanski, 2005; Murray, Mobley, Buford, & Seaman-DeJohn, 2006).

Perpetrators of same-sex physical violence show higher levels of depression, insecurity, and substance abuse, and lower self-esteem and communication skills (Murray et al., 2006). The link between physical violence experienced in the family of origin and IPV is consistent for gay men, and inconsistent for lesbians (Kulkin, Williams, Borne, de la Betonne, & Laurendine, 2007).

Lesbian/gay/bisexual/transgender (LGBT) individuals are at heightened risk of sexual assault and coercion, as compared to heterosexual individuals, when looking across all types of sexual assault (stranger, acquaintance, intimate partner). This risk is two times higher among lesbians and five times higher among gay men; the perpetrator is most likely to be male for both groups (Balsam et al., 2005; Tjaden et al., 1999). Gay men who grew up in a home characterized by sexual violence and addictive behaviors, and those who were sexually assaulted as a child by a non-family member, are at higher risk of an intimate partner sexual assault (Christopher & Pflieger, 2007; Heidt, Marx, & Gold, 2005).

Relationship Factors

The interpersonal dynamics of physical violence in gay and lesbian partnerships are believed to be similar to those in heterosexual relationships (Murray et al., 2006), although using a heterosexual lens as the basis of such comparisons has been thoroughly critiqued (Ristock, 2003). Early research on same-sex violence emphasized a model of "mutual violence" and made few differentiations between victims and perpetrators; fortunately, more recent work provides finer-tuned analyses (Lloyd, 2012). Both McClennen (2005) and Strike, Myers, Calzavara, and Haubrich (2001) note that perpetrators may use intentional coercive actions against their partners, including use of drugs/alcohol to lower inhibitions, emotional or economic dependency, inducing guilt, and/or threatening to leave the relationship. Physical aggression is often accompanied by psychological aggression (Matte & Lafontaine, 2011). Same-sex intimate partner battering is related to efforts to gain power and control, with power imbalances related to poor conflict resolution skills, attachment fears, jealousy, escalated conflicts, and blaming the victim for provoking violence (Brown, 2008; McClennen, 2005; Murray et al., 2006; Ristock, 2003; Stanley, Bartholomew, Taylor, Oram, & Landolt, 2006). Causby et al. (1995) also found higher levels of intimate partner violence in lesbian relationships to be associated with more control by the partner and more overall fusion in the relationship.

Understanding how relationship dynamics and individual characteristics come together has been advanced by the introduction of mediated models. Balsam and Szymanski (2005) found that the relationship between internalized homophobia and same-sex violence was fully mediated by relational distress. Craft, Serovich, McKenry, and Lim (2008) discovered that the relationship between stress and violence perpetration was mediated by an insecure attachment style.

Contextual Factors

Because of the discrimination and homophobia experienced by LGBT people, there are unique contexts surrounding same-sex partner violence. Perhaps the most important of these is the impact of living in a context of homophobia (Lloyd, 2012). Brown (2008) equates this context to living in a "moral closet" that ignores and denies the IPV experienced by LGBT individuals. Living openly with a same-sex partner may add to the many stressors already associated with being a sexual minority, and increases one's visibility as gay or lesbian (Murray et al., 2006). Alternatively, the threat of being "outed" by the partner may be a unique type of psychological abuse that further isolates the victim (Ristock, 2003). Gay/lesbian partners who are battered may be less likely to reveal their abuse out of fear of exposing the LGBT community to additional prejudice and homophobia (Walters, 2011). Closeted LGBT individuals may experience even more stress, as their ability to seek formal help brings with it the fear of discovery. Homophobia in the legal and intervention systems is routinely noted, and may mitigate against seeking help from these institutions and lead to increased reliance on friendship networks (McClennen, 2005; Murray et al., 2006). Lesbians who are battered may be silenced by the expectations that their relationships are egalitarian and free from the patriarchal strictures of heterosexuality (Barnes, 2011).

Sexual violence in gay/lesbian partnerships adds other dynamics. Lesbian sexual violence does not fit with prevailing cultural norms emphasizing that women do not engage in sex with other women and that women are sexually non-aggressive (Girschick, 2002). Stereotypes about gay men emphasize their hypersexuality, and prevent viewing them as victims (Brown, 2008). Also, men who are HIV positive may be constrained to stay with an abusive partner (Craft & Serovich, 2005).

The Effects of Intimate Partner Violence

There are clear short- and long-term effects related to the experience of both physical and sexual aggression at the hands of a same-sex partner. Victims of same-sex physical violence report emotional distress, self-blame, and conflict avoidance (McClennen, 2005; Murray et al., 2006). Long-term effects include traumatic stress and anxiety disorders (Kulkin et al., 2007). The short-term effects of experiencing lesbian sexual violence include a sense of betrayal, confusion, fear, anger and guilt; long-term effects include PSTD symptomatology, depression, and suicidal ideation (Girschick, 2002; Heidt et al., 2005). The effects of sexual violence for gay men include heightened risk for alcohol abuse, depression, mood disorders, and PTSD symptomatology (Heidt et al., 2005). Depressive and trauma symptoms for both gay and lesbian sexual assault survivors are heightened in contexts of high-internalized homophobia and experiential avoidance (Gold, Dickstein, Marx, & Lexington, 2009; Gold, Marx, & Lexington, 2007). Finally, revictimized gay, lesbian and bi-sexual individuals (that is, those who were sexually victimized both in childhood and adulthood) show the highest levels of psychological distress, PTSD symptoms, and depression (Heidt et al., 2005).

Psychological Aggression in Heterosexual Partnerships

Definition and Incidence of Psychological Aggression

Scholars who research psychological aggression face myriad methodological challenges, beginning with definitional issues. Follingstad (2007) notes that, over time, terms such as "verbal aggression," "psychological maltreatment," and "emotional abuse" have come under the common umbrella term of psychological aggression. She defines psychological aggression as "the *general concepts and range* of behaviors engaged in by intimate adult partners which encompass the range of verbal and mental methods designed to emotionally wound, coerce, control, intimidate, psychologically harm, and express anger" (p. 443). Kelly (2004) describes two dimensions: dominance/control (including hostility, restrictive engulfment, isolation and activity control, and withdrawal) and emotional/verbal (including coercion, denigration, criticism, and ridicule). Spitzberg (2011) emphasizes the need to understand the unique effects of psychological aggression as separately conceptualized from physical or sexual violence.

Nationally representative studies of the prevalence of psychological aggression are rare. The NVAWS documented the prevalence of psychological aggression (with no physical or sexual aggression present) across dating, cohabitation, and marriage; victimization rates for abuse of power/control were 6.9% of women and 6.8% of men, and rates for verbal abuse were 5.2% of women and 10.5% of men (Coker et al., 2002). The 2010 NIVSV documented psychological aggression (with or without sexual or physical aggression present): expressive psychological aggression was experienced by 40.3% of women and 31.9% of men, and coercive control was experienced by 41.1 % of women and 42.5% of men. Community and college sample surveys document a much higher incidence, ranging from 77% to 87% (Dailey, Lee, & Spitzberg, 2007). Follingstad and Edmundson (2010) note that in their national (non-representative) sample, egregious psychological aggression was highly reciprocal across both partners in the relationship.

The vast majority of research examines psychological aggression in relation to physical or sexual aggression; indeed, it is often conceptualized as a precursor to, or covariant with, physical violence (Outlaw, 2009). As a result, the present review will concentrate on the relational dynamics, and the impact of the co-occurrence of these types of aggression.

Dyadic Factors in Psychological Aggression

Psychological aggression occurs in a context of physical aggression at high rates; it is also predictive of the future occurrence and severity of physical aggression (O'Leary & Slep, 2003; Outlaw, 2009). Both men and women commonly report that physical aggression is precipitated by verbal aggression (O'Leary & Slep, 2006). In the context of escalated conflict, verbal aggression is closely linked to control dynamics; indeed, this link is so close that control and psychological aggression may be conceptualizations of the same underlying construct (Winstok & Perkis, 2009).

Anxious attachment is related to both victimization and perpetration of psychological aggression (Miga, Hare, Allen, & Manning, 2010; Riggs & Kaminski, 2010). Weston (2008) documents a mediated relationship, with insecure attachment mediating the link between psychological aggression and relationship quality. How psychological aggression intersects with other relational factors may operate differently for men and women. Lafontaine and Lussier (2005) found that, among men, the relationship of intimacy avoidance and psychological aggression was mediated by anger, whereas among women, abandonment anxiety was related to higher levels of frustration and verbal aggressiveness, which in turn were related to the use of physical violence. Gormley and Lopez (2010) found that the strongest predictor of perpetration of psychological abuse among men was their level of stress; for both men and women, attachment avoidance predicted abuse in a context of high levels of stress.

The Impact of Psychological Aggression

The impact of psychological aggression is difficult to tease out, given the co-occurrence of physical violence, the differing definitions of aggression/abuse, and the failure to control for severity and duration. Follingstad (2009) and Kelly, Warner, Trahan, and Miscavage (2009) find evidence that psychological aggression and depressive symptoms are consistently related. Coker and colleagues (2002) note that individuals experiencing the power/control form of psychological abuse (without physical/sexual violence) show higher levels of depressive symptoms and alcohol/drug use, and poorer health (as compared to individuals experiencing verbal abuse). Also, psychological aggression is associated with women's leaving, or wanting to leave, the relationship (Follingstad, 2009).

There is mixed evidence for the influence of psychological aggression on PTSD (Lloyd, 2012). Babcock, Roseman, Green, and Ross (2008) found that psychological aggression did not predict PTSD symptoms beyond what was predicted by physical assault, whereas Basile, Arias, Desai, and Thompson (2004) found that psychological aggression was related to PTSD symptoms, after controlling for sexual and physical violence, injuries, and stalking. Basile and colleagues (2004) discuss their findings in terms of a dosing effect, with the experience of more types of violence heightening PTSD symptoms. Taft, Schumm, Orazem, Meis, and Pinto (2010) note that the relationship of childhood trauma to psychological aggression is mediated by PTSD symptoms. Follingstad (2007) provides an important caution about the work on psychological aggression, noting that most models do not clearly specify the levels/forms of psychological aggression that produce particular outcomes.

Intimate Partner Stalking

Stalking has been defined as a repeated pattern of threatening or harassing behavior, including actions such as following, property damage, appearing at the victim's home or work, leaving harassing messages or objects, and making harassing phone calls (Tjaden & Thoennes, 1998). Legal definitions of stalking usually include an emphasis on the repetition, intentionality, and the unwanted nature of the behaviors, as well as an emphasis on a pattern of behaviors that would cause fear in a "reasonable person" (Spitzberg & Cupach, 2007). Cupach and Spitzberg (2004) frame intimate partner stalking as a form of obsessive relational intrusion, which involves the unwanted and repeated pursuit of intimacy through the violation of privacy. They note, however, that obsessive relational intrusion does not always result in fear or threat to the victim.

Because of the difficulties of defining and measuring stalking, estimating prevalence has proven difficult (Fox, Nobles, & Fisher, 2011). Prevalence rates vary as a function of definition; Tjaden, Thoennes, and Allison (2002) note prevalence rates using a legal definition of 8.1% of women and 2.2% of men, and rates using a self-identified victim definition of 12.1% of women and 6.2% of men. Within these rates of stalking, 60% of men are pursued by other men, and 6% of women are pursued by other women (Tjaden & Thoennes, 1998).

Women are more likely to be stalked by an intimate partner (59% of cases of stalking) than are men (30% of cases; Tjaden & Thoennes, 1998). Estimates of intimate partner stalking (dating, cohabiting, or marital) from the NISVS document prevalence at 10.7% of women and 2.1% of men (Black et al., 2011). Intimate partner stalking is likely to occur over an extended period of time, lasting from six months to two years (McEwan, Mullen, & Purcell, 2007; Tjaden & Thoennes, 1998). Victims of intimate partner stalking (as compared to non-intimate stalking) are at a higher risk of physical violence, and the closer the relationship, the higher the risk (Logan & Walker, 2009; McEwan et al., 2007). The NVAWS documented that, among women who were stalked by a former or current partner, 81% were physically assaulted and 31% were sexually assaulted (Tjaden & Thoennes, 1998). In cases of male-perpetrated intimate partner homicide/attempted homicide, the man had stalked his partner in the vast majority of cases (McEwan et al., 2007). Indeed, Logan and Walker (2009) argue for the separate study of intimate partner stalking, given its increased risk of violence, greater frequency, wider array of tactics, and greater victim psychological distress.

Individual Factors in Stalking

Gender is a clear risk marker for stalking; in the NVAWS, women were 78% of victims and men were 87% of perpetrators (looking across all types of stalking; Tjaden & Thoennes, 1998). These higher victimization rates for women are evidenced across different samples: on average, women are the victims in 80% of clinical samples, 63% of general population samples, and 69% of college samples (Spitzberg & Cupach, 2007).

Stalking perpetration is predicted by insecure-anxious attachment, harsh parental discipline, and anger issues (Dye & Davis, 2003; Patton, Nobles & Fox, 2010); victimization is predicted by childhood maltreatment (Fox, Gover, & Kaukinen, 2009). Women who exhibit low self-control are at higher risk for stalking victimization, most likely due to the tendency to place themselves in riskier situations and to be in close relationships with controlling men (Fox et al., 2009).

Mullen, Pathé, and Purcell (2009) present a typology of stalkers, based primarily on clinical samples. They describe the rejected stalker as one of the most common forms in which the perpetrator (who is male in 90% of cases) has experienced a unilateral breakup and is seeking either to reconcile with the partner or to exact revenge for the breakup. Rejected intimate stalkers have a history of trouble establishing intimate relationships, as well as overdependence and poor social skills, and have impoverished social networks. Possessiveness and jealousy characterize some of these stalkers as well. Mullen and colleagues' typology includes several types of stalkers who pursue strangers or non-intimates, including intimacy seekers (the only type where women predominated), incompetent suitors, resentful stalkers, predatory stalkers, and erotomaniacs.

Dyadic Factors in Stalking

Intimate partner stalking occurs in a relational context. Although popular notions indicate that women are stalked primarily by ex-partners, the NVAWS found that 21% of victims reported that the stalking occurred during the relationship, 43% reported it occurred after the relationship had ended, and 36% reported stalking both during and after the relationship (Tjaden & Thoennes, 1998). Indeed, Spitzberg and Cupach (2007) conclude that "most stalking represents a distorted version of courtship and romantic relationship failure" (p. 79).

Victims of intimate partner stalking describe a relational context characterized by the perpetrator's jealousy, psychological aggression, hostility, rejection sensitivity, need for control, and obsessive behaviors (Davis, Ace, & Andra, 2000; Dye & Davis, 2003; White, Kowalski, Lyndon, & Valentine, 2002), as well as physical and sexual assault (Logan & Walker, 2009). Verbal and psychological aggression are particularly strong predictors of stalking and the use of physical violence by the stalker (Brewster, 2002; Davis et al., 2000). And, women who are stalked by a physically violent former or current partner also experience higher levels of controlling behaviors, and injuries (Logan & Walker, 2009).

Victims report the primary motivations of the perpetrator of stalking to be instilling fear and control (Tjaden & Thoennes, 1998). Cupach and Spitzberg (2004) note that motivations cut across both power and love, and include reconciliation, desire to be together, intimidation, and revenge. Spitzberg and Cupach (2007) emphasize the "paradoxical ambivalence of stalking" (p. 69). Looking across types of stalking (both intimate partner and non-intimate), their analysis reveals the following motives: 30–40% intimacy (including love, jealousy, abandonment issues, obsession, desire to reconcile, desire for sex), 20–25% aggression (including anger, revenge, control, intimidation, attack), 10% drug/alcohol/mental health, and 10% issue-based.

Logan, Cole, Shannon, and Walker (2006) provide narrative descriptions of intimate partner stalking. Female victims of intimate partner stalking describe patterns of surveillance, including following, showing up unexpectedly, driving by, lying in wait, and monitoring. Their perpetrators engaged in many harassing behaviors, as well as threats, intimidation, and property destruction. For many, these behavior patterns began early in the relationship, and continued on average for over two years. The women reported that stalking intensified during periods of their independence-seeking and/or attempting to leave the relationship, as well as in response to growing jealousy, suspicion, stress, and substance use by the perpetrator.

The Impact of Stalking

Cupach and Spitzberg (2004) synthesize the literature on victims' coping responses to unwanted pursuit into five types. "Moving with" responses include efforts to reason with the pursuer in the hopes of ending or limiting the pursuit. "Moving against" tactics involve deterrence through threats, calling the police, involving third parties, and threatening self-harm. "Moving away" responses include attempts to get away from the pursuer through unlisted phone numbers, moving one's home, and going out in public only in a group. "Moving inward" tactics entail distraction or denial, emphasizing that the stalking is not a big deal, or using alcohol or drugs. "Moving outward" responses include the use of informal and formal interventions, including friend support and advice, counseling, law enforcement, and protective orders. One-fifth of victims moved to a new location to get away from their stalkers, and about half reported it to the police, resulting in prosecution in 12% of cases (Tjaden & Thoennes, 1998).

Women report more psychological consequences of stalking than do men. Women restrict their behavior, go out less often, take time off work, and avoid people/places (McEwan et al., 2007; Mullen et al., 2009). Short-term effects include fear, anxiety, paranoia, feeling besieged, somatic complaints, and injury (Cupach & Spitzberg, 2004; McEwan et al., 2007; Mechanic, 2002; Mullen et al., 2009). Long-term effects include depression, helplessness, deteriorating physical health, suicidal ideation, and PTSD symptomatology (Cupach & Spitzberg, 2004; Logan et al., 2006; Mechanic, 2002), with the mental health consequences being more severe for women than for men (White et al., 2002). The duration of stalking, and self-blame, are related to the severity of trauma symptoms and depression (Kraaij, Arensman, Garnefski, & Kremers, 2007; McEwan et al., 2007).

Summary

Intimate partnerships, although imbued with nobility and romance, clearly have a "dark side." The high rates of aggression and their well-documented deleterious effects on individual physical and mental health underscore the need both to inform romantic partners of the warning signs, and to provide appropriate interventions to stop violence and protect victims.

There are many commonalities across the different forms of intimate partner violence. Common risk factors for perpetration include exposure to violence in the family of origin, anger, hostility, substance use, depression, and anxiety. Common dyadic factors include escalated conflict, relational stress, poor communication skills, and anxious attachment. The effects of the various forms of IPV consistently include trauma symptoms, depression, and physical health issues (Lloyd, 2012). Increasingly, scholars are examining the simultaneous presence of psychological, stalking, physical, and sexual aggression, and using life course perspectives to understand the ways that violence intersects with developmental tasks, life experiences, and past traumas (Sears & Byers, 2010; Williams, 2003). Ultimately, intimate partner violence in romantic pairings is complexly determined, cutting across the many levels of an ecological analysis (Lloyd, 2012).

We must also acknowledge the larger cultural context of intimate partner violence in romantic relationships (Lloyd, 2012). Common cultural values are seen across studies, including attitudes condoning the use of physical and sexual aggression, and hostility toward women. Systemic oppressions such as racism, sexism, and homophobia, as well as norms about family privacy, are also a part of this context; these create critical structural issues that intersect with criminal justice and social service systems, ideas about the origin of violence, and individual responses and constructions of meaning.

Lloyd and Emery (2000) emphasize the importance of contextualizing IPV within the discourses of both romantic relationships and aggression. They use Hare-Mustin's (1994) definition of discourse in their analysis, that is, discourses as systems of practices and structures that share common ideas and meanings, and that build a particular world-view. In this case, discourses work to build a dominant view about how to behave in romantic partnerships. Lloyd and Emery identify three discourses of intimate heterosexual relationships that are important for constructing meaning around the experience of intimate partner violence, and that also serve to underscore its confusing and unexpected nature: the discourse of equality between the sexes, the discourse of romance, and the discourse of gendered sexuality. They further identify dominant discourses around intimate violence that serve to excuse the aggressor, blame the victim, silence the victim's definition of violence, and render intimate aggression invisible.

Ultimately, intimate partner violence is indeed a paradoxical experience because the romantic partner who has promised to love, honor, and care can also be the person who hurts, injures, and creates deep trauma. The analysis presented by Henton and colleagues (1983) three decades ago still stands: romance and violence all too often go hand in hand.

Key Concepts

Aggression, see Intimate partner violence
Intimate partner violence (p. 118)
Physical violence, heterosexual (p. 119)
Physical violence, gay and lesbian (pp. 132–135)
Sexual violence, heterosexual (pp. 126–132)
Sexual violence, gay and lesbian (pp. 132–135)
Stalking (pp. 137–140)

Additional Readings

Adelman, M., & Kil, S. H. (2007). Dating conflicts: Rethinking dating violence and youth conflict. *Violence Against Women, 13*, 1296–1318.

Balsam, K. F., Rothblum, E. D., & Beauchaine, T. P. (2005). Victimization over the life span: A comparison of lesbian, gay, bisexual, and heterosexual siblings. *Journal of Consulting & Clinical Psychology, 73*, 477–487.

Christopher, F. S., & Pflieger, J. C. (2007). Sexual aggression: The dark side of sexuality in relationships. *Annual Review of Sex Research, 18*, 115–142.

Cupach, W. R., & Spitzberg, B. H. (2004). *The dark side of relationship pursuit.* Mahwah, NJ: Lawrence Erlbaum.

Lloyd, S. A. (2012). Family violence. In G. W. Peterson & K. R. Bush (Eds.), *Handbook of marriage and the family* (pp. 449–485). New York, NY: Springer.

Lloyd, S. A., & Emery, B. C. (2000). *The dark side of courtship: Physical and sexual aggression.* Thousand Oaks, CA: Sage.

McClennen, J. C. (2005). Domestic violence between same-gender partners: Recent findings and future research. *Journal of Interpersonal Violence, 20*(2), 149–154.

Outlaw, M. (2009). No one type of intimate partner abuse: Exploring physical and non-physical abuse among intimate partners. *Journal of Family Violence, 24*(4), 263–272.

8

FUTURE DIRECTIONS IN
RELATIONSHIP RESEARCH

It is often said that "courtship" is dead in today's society. Indeed, such rhetoric about the downfall of "the family" and of "traditional marriage" has been heralded for over a century (Bailey, 1988). A recent piece by Leon Kass (1997) is illustrative here:

> Now the vast majority goes to college, but very few—women or men—go with the hope, or even the wish, of finding a marriage partner. . . . Sexually active, in truth—hyperactive—they flop about from one relationship to another; to the bewildered eye of this admittedly much-too-old but still romantic observer, they manage to appear all at once casual and carefree and grim and humorless about getting along with the opposite sex. The young men, nervous predators, act as if any woman is equally good: They are given not to falling in love with one, but to scoring in bed with many. And in this sporting attitude they are now matched by some female trophy hunters. (p. 39)

Such a characterization of how men and women interact today is problematic on a number of fronts, not the least of which is that it is not supported by current research. For example, there is no documented evidence (to our knowledge) that non-married people do not wish or hope to find a life partner, that men consider all women only as potential sexual partners, or that college students engage in hook-up after hook-up.

Still, Kass's lament may reflect the sense that "courtship" has fundamentally changed over time. Indeed, as we proceeded with the rewriting of the original volume, *Courtship*, by Cate and Lloyd, we were struck over and over by the myriad changes in partnering processes that had occurred since that book was published in 1992. As demonstrated by Chapter 2 on the history of romantic partnering, there really was no "golden age" of romantic relationships; instead, there are multiple forces, from economics to urbanization to the advent of reliable birth control to advances in human rights, which have brought about fundamental changes in our ideas about romantic relationships and the ways that we form them. Indeed, it makes no sense to talk about "moral decline" in the absence of a deep understanding of the historical roots of our contemporary romantic relationship practices.

Demographically, the United States witnessed huge changes and great variability across the latter half of the 20th century. The result has been, as Arnett (2000) notes, that the period of emerging adulthood is one of the most diverse developmental stages, demographically speaking. This is the time when young people move out of their parents' homes to form their own households, go to college or trade school, start their lives as economic producers, and most importantly, from the perspective of this book, develop experiences in starting, maintaining, and ending romantic relationships. Indeed, this is a time of identity exploration that "involves trying out various life possibilities and gradually moving toward making enduring decisions" (Arnett, 2000, p. 473). Decisions about love, intimacy, and romantic relationships take on increasing importance as emerging adults mature and develop.

Certainly, decisions about forming legal relationships have been increasingly delayed for heterosexual couples, with the result that the age at first marriage is now at 28 for men and 26 for women (U.S. Centers for Disease Control and Prevention, 2012). For same-sex couples, the right to legally marry is starting to gain momentum, and, in the coming decades, we will hopefully learn more about the decision processes and timing of this external marker of commitment for this group. Emerging adults engage in cohabitation at record levels, and yet cohabitation is not "universal" among this age group as a stage in relationship formation. The variability in romantic relationships for emerging adults is further reflected in the fact that most have multiple relationships, engaging in processes of re-partnering after the breakup of a romantic relationship. Even though there is so much diversity in romantic relationships, they are fundamentally important, as they contribute to well-being and psychological health, and set the stage for romantic relationship functioning in later life (Fincham & Cui, 2011).

This final chapter addresses the implications of these changes for the study of romantic partnerships. We begin with a brief discussion of contemporary partnering practices that are already bringing about changes in the ways we think about finding partners, dating, commitment, and breaking up. We then turn to methodologies that have enriched our ability to study romantic relationships, followed by a discussion of what we see as the major arenas for advancing theory and research.

The Changing Nature of Romantic Partnering

As noted earlier in this book, although the notion that romantic relationships progress to long-term commitment via a discrete series of stages has great heuristic appeal, it simply does not accurately describe the complex nature of romantic relationship development and decline. Instead, there is a wealth of evidence that individual characteristics (such as attachment styles), relationship properties (such as satisfaction, commitment, uncertainty), and couple interaction (e.g., communication, conflict) intersect to form a complex and multifaceted whole that we call a "romantic partnership." The social ecological perspective has influenced a wide range of research on romantic relationships (Cate & Lloyd, 1988), including work on such topics as mate selection (e.g., Arriaga, Goodfriend, & Lohmann, 2004; Chang & Chan, 2007; Niehuis, Huston, & Rosenband, 2006; Ponzetti, 2005; Sassler, 2010; Surra & Longstreth, 1990); sexual decision making (Christopher & Cate, 1985; Lefkowitz, Gillen, & Vasilenko, 2011; O'Sullivan, Cheng, Harris, & Brooks-Gunn, 2007); the formation of gay and lesbian relationships (Kurdek, 2008b; Peplau & Fingerhut, 2007); and romantic relationship dissolution (Kelas, Bean, Cunningham, & Cheng, 2008; Lloyd & Cate, 1985; Oswald & Clausell, 2006).

The social ecological perspective we have highlighted in this volume will continue to undergo refinements and major improvements. Indeed, the changing nature of romantic partnering itself will lead to many interesting avenues for future study, as well as important challenges to current theories and models for understanding romantic relationship formation. Here, we highlight five changes that encompass important arenas for future research: impact of Internet technologies, legalization of same-sex marriage, cohabitation, hooking up versus committed sex, and processes of re-partnering.

Romantic Relationships and Internet Technologies

Twenty years ago, when the first version of this book was published, the idea that Internet matchmaking sites might become a widely used method of meeting new potential romantic partners never even crossed our minds! We have witnessed an amazing transformation in partnering practices due to the availability of social media and Internet technologies; indeed, one prominent matchmaking site claims, "eHarmony is responsible for 5% of marriages in the US" (eHarmony, 2012), and another states, "1 in 5 relationships start online" (Match.com, 2012). A more probable figure comes from Madden and Lenhart (2006), who note that over 10% of Internet users report that they have used Internet dating sites (and it should be noted that it is estimated that over 75% of Americans have access to the Internet; World Bank, n.d.). This large number of users presents many fascinating possibilities and opportunities for research, not the least of which may be the need to fundamentally rethink many of our ideas about the initial stages of dating and getting to know a potential partner. Indeed, the amount of information that may be available about a potential partner, through routine Internet searches and social media sites, may create a very different manner of "initial attraction" (or "detraction," if the information is negative), such that the early stages of face-to-face relationship formation begin with a wealth of background information.

Many other technologies have the potential to affect romantic relationships in fundamental ways. The widespread ownership of cellular telephones, along with texting, is having an impact that is yet to be extensively studied. The potential to transmit both positive and negative messages, to engage in "sexting," and to be instantly in touch with a romantic partner creates possibilities for both positive and negative effects on romantic relationships. Communication is different in both depth and frequency when comparing texts, emails, telephone conversations, and face-to-face interactions, and delving into these differences presents interesting possibilities for relationship researchers.

Sprecher et al. (2008) suggest interesting lines of future research that should increase researchers' knowledge of the initial acquaintance process via Internet dating services and social media sites. First, matchmaking services are likely to increase their proprietary research in order to improve their services and attract additional users. These studies are not likely to be published in academic research journals, but the findings will likely be used in the advertising of these services. Second, if access to members of a dating site is permitted, studies can be done that examine the initiation of relationships and the course of development over time. Third, additional studies could be conducted comparing those relationships formed online with those formed offline. Such comparisons could yield information about the relative advantages of online versus offline romances.

Same-Sex Marriage

One of the most important changes now occurring within the realm of romantic relationships is the legalization of same-sex marriage and civil unions. Although some would portray same-sex marriage as a fundamental challenge to the "institution" of heterosexual marriage, as portrayed in Chapter 2 on the history of romantic relationships, in actuality this change is a continuation of historical trends in romantic partnering. Beginning with the gay and lesbian civil rights movements of the 1970s, activists have worked to change marriage laws state by state, while at the same time opponents have worked to pass defense of (heterosexual) marriage acts (Newton, 2010).

This period of change in the definition of "marriage" brings with it exciting possibilities for scholarship on romantic relationships. For example, Ettlebrick (2007) provides a host of reasons why gays and lesbians would choose not to become legally married. It would be interesting to examine married and unmarried same-sex couples, and to describe the motivations and events that lead members of a couple to decide for or against same-sex marriage.

146

In addition, there is a great need for the development of theories and models of same-sex relationship formation and decline, in particular models that go beyond adapting a theory that was developed on heterosexual couples. These models would need to attend to the particular social context that surrounds gay and lesbian partnerships, as well as the particular strengths and stressors that are concomitant with being a member of a same-sex couple. Finally, scholarship on same-sex relationship development will open new understandings of different-sex relationships—in particular, a deeper understanding of how heterosexual interaction is also gendered interaction (Oswald et al., 2009).

Cohabitation

As discussed in Chapter 5, over one-half of all recently married heterosexual couples cohabited before marriage (Bumpass & Hsien-Hen, 2000), and nearly all highly committed gay and lesbian couples cohabit (Kurdek, 1998). This suggests two things: that cohabitation remains a normative event for gay and lesbian couples, and that cohabitation is approaching the status of a normative event in the progression to heterosexual marriage. Demographers and sociologists have illuminated several important macro-level correlates of cohabitation (e.g., Bumpass & Hsien-Hen, 2000), including education level (Kennedy & Bumpass, 2008), income (Lichter et al., 2010), ethnicity (Rhoades et al., 2007), and nationality (Popenoe, 2008).

Despite the fact that cohabitation occurs with such a high frequency, however, we know relatively little about it from a social ecological perspective, and the study of cohabitation is not prominently featured in the major interdisciplinary personal relationships journals. For example, a search of the *PsycINFO*® database for 2009 and 2010 found only six studies of cohabiting couples in *Personal Relationships* and *Journal of Social and Personal Relationships*. This lack of research is curious at best, because it represents a major gap in our understanding of processes of romantic partnering.

Five types of studies are needed for a more complete understanding of the relationship and individual dynamics of cohabiting relationships. First, studies of the processes that lead same-sex couples to engage in cohabitation are sorely needed, because there is a dearth of scholarship on both early same-sex relationship formation and on the decision to cohabit. Second, prospective studies are needed to identify processes occurring early in relationship formation that may lead to later relationship outcomes (e.g., transition to cohabitation or marriage, breakup of a cohabiting or marital union). Third, the use of daily diary studies of cohabiting and non-cohabiting relationships might allow researchers to uncover daily processes that predict relationship success or failure. Fourth, studies that examine different patterns or types of cohabiting couples are sorely needed, as cohabiters form a quite diverse group, from young heterosexual couples testing their suitability for marriage, to committed gay and lesbian couples in long-term relationships, to elders choosing to cohabit rather than marry for financial reasons. Finally, inclusion of questions about relationship processes in nationally representative studies would provide information about the prevalence of such processes and allow for a better understanding of the generalizability of relationship theory.

Hooking Up versus Sex with Commitment

Several studies have suggested that a significant number of unmarried individuals engage in sexual interactions without an expectation of continuing contact (e.g., Glenn & Marquardt, 2001; Owen, Rhoades, Stanley, & Fincham, 2010). Such casual sexual behavior has been termed "hooking up," and this phenomenon caught widespread interest in the media. The explicit or implicit assumption underlying much of the media coverage is that this type of behavior has been increasing over the past few years. Very little research is cited to substantiate this claim, and some of the research on heterosexual hook-ups is beset with problems, the most important of which is that the conceptualization of hook-ups varies considerably from study to study. Some studies consider behaviors from kissing to intercourse to constitute hooking up (e.g., Paul, McManus, & Hayes, 2000), whereas others (e.g., Fielder & Carey, 2010) included only oral and vaginal sex as "hooking up" behavior. This inconsistent measurement precludes comparison of studies and fails to adequately conceptualize this phenomenon.

The fascination with hook-ups may, in fact, be misplaced, as Armstrong et al. (2010) cite findings from three national surveys that dispute the claim that casual sex is rapidly increasing among youth in the U.S. Moreover, three findings from the Centers for Disease Control and Prevention's Youth Risk Behavior Survey (2010) suggest that sexual behavior among youth has not become more prevalent in recent years. First, the percentage of 9th to 12th graders who have ever had intercourse decreased from 54.1% in 1991 to 46% in 2009. Second, the percentage of youth who have had intercourse with four or more people in their lifetimes decreased from 18.7% in 1991 to 13.8% in 2009. Third, the percentage of youth who have had intercourse with at least one person in the last three months decreased from 37.5% in 1991 to 34.2% in 2009. Additional research by Paula England (cited in Armstrong et al., 2010) on college students suggests that hooking-up experiences are fairly infrequent. This research found that 80% of senior college students averaged less than one hook-up per semester over their college career. This finding argues against the portrayal of college students turning away from traditional forms of relating to more casual sexual encounters. Future researchers could conduct reviews of the literature that might uncover earlier work that measured similar constructs to hooking up and compare to current findings. Earlier research on the incidence of casual sex could be compared to data on hooking up because the contemporary fascination with the latter may simply be a resurrection of the fascination with casual premarital sex seen in earlier works such as Ehrmann (1959) and Reiss (1960). Motivations behind hooking up could be delineated, and questions such as whether some emerging adults use hooking up as a strategy for finding a long-term partner could be addressed. Most importantly, we need more in-depth research on the intertwined processes of sexual interaction and romantic relationship development presented by such authors as Christopher (2001) and Sprecher and Cate (2004). Clearly, young adults continue to value "committed sex," while also valuing the opportunity to engage in sexual interaction without commitment.

Re-partnering

Given relatively high rates of heterosexual divorce and gay/lesbian couple dissolution, many Americans are seeking new partners after many years in a committed relationship (i.e., re-partnering). The re-partnering process is not fully understood and needs considerable research. Fine, Coffelt, and Olson (2008) have suggested several areas for further research on re-partnering. First, they suggest that future research address communication processes in re-partnering. Little is known about how people use communication to show their interest in potential partners and move the relationship forward. Also, work is needed on how divorced people communicate with children, family, and friends about seeking new partners. Second, research needs to address the interrelationship of subsequent relationship partners with each other, for example, how previous relationships affect processes in the present relationship. Third, the use of qualitative methods is encouraged because qualitative methods could explore how former partners develop meaning concerning the initiation of new relationships. Finally, the literature that exists on re-partnering largely focuses on heterosexual relationships for middle- and upper-class couples; future research should engage more diverse groups, addressing re-partnering in same-sex relationships, as well as in those from lower socioeconomic levels.

Methodological and Statistical Developments

Significant advances in the methods used for studying developing relationships have allowed us to explore the dynamics of interpersonal relationships in more detail and with more precision than in the past. Detailed exploration of longitudinal, qualitative, and diary data, as well as non-independent (e.g., data from couples) data, are among some of the methodological innovations that have advanced the study of romantic relationships. In the following sections, we identify some examples of longitudinal, diary, and qualitative studies, and present a detailed discussion of the statistical treatment of non-independent data.

Longitudinal Studies

There has been a virtual explosion of longitudinal studies that address romantic relationships. When we wrote the first edition of this book, only a handful of longitudinal studies had been conducted. Today, at least 137 longitudinal studies of romantic relationships in emerging adulthood have been published (Le et al., 2010). These longitudinal studies allow for a better understanding of the causal factors that operate in romantic relationships, and how relationships develop over time, as well as allowing for the development of comprehensive theories of change processes in romantic partnerships. Examples of outstanding longitudinal work abound. For example, Conger and colleagues have conducted a longitudinal study spanning early adolescence to the late twenties; their work emphasizes the development of interpersonal competence, and examines family of origin factors as well as current relationship functioning (Conger et al., 2000, 2011). In addition, several large, nationally representative data sets allow for investigation of romantic partnering process. For example, the National Longitudinal Study of Adolescent Health (Add Health) data allow for an exploration of partnering from early youth until the mid-twenties. Moreover, the National Survey of Family Growth (NSFG) contains information about sexual partnering and fertility from the teenage years through the mid-forties.

Diary Studies

The development of diary methods for data collection has allowed for a more detailed view of the interactional aspects of romantic partnering. These methods allow research participants to provide information pertinent to their relationships in several forms. Reports can be interval contingent, in which participants respond after a fixed amount of time (e.g., every 24 hours); event contingent, in which they respond after the occurrence of a specific event (e.g., a conflict); or signal contingent, in which participants respond after being signaled by means of an electronic device (e.g., wireless phone or pager). Additionally, information can be obtained using various media, such as daily structured paper-and-pencil measures (e.g., Ridley et al., 2006), telephone interviews (e.g., Ridley, Ogolsky, Payne, Totenhagen, & Cate, 2008), or Internet-based reporting (e.g., Ogolsky, 2009). Obtaining information closer to the occurrence of events than in cross-sectional retrospective reports improves the validity of the information collected and reduces inaccuracy that results from prolonged retrospection. Diary studies frequently take place outside of the laboratory in the participants' natural environments, which increases the ecological validity of the data.

Qualitative Methods

As Surra et al. (1999) note, there is a "baffling disjunction between the way partners act in relationships and the way that others think they should act" (p. 125). Although this observation was made more than a decade ago, it still holds true today. The published literature exploring relationship development has been, and continues to be, heavily focused on outsiders' (e.g., researchers) rather than insiders' (e.g., the relational partners) views.

In 1998, Allen and Walker searched the leading relationship journals in the field to examine the use of qualitative methods, and their search yielded very few studies using these methods. We ran the same search of the three leading publications in the field (*Personal Relationships, Journal of Social and Personal Relationships*, and *Journal of Personality and Social Psychology*) and found that a total of 173 articles using qualitative methods have been published in the past five years (2007–2012), which represents approximately 10% of articles published in those journals. Although this represents a notable increase in the publication of articles using qualitative methods, it still accounts for a small percentage of the knowledge base pertaining to close relationships. Still, there are many examples of qualitative research that have advanced our understanding of relationship processes; see, for example, work on relationship maintenance/support in gay male couples (Haas, 2002; Wrubel, Stumbo, & Johnson, 2010), online dating (Heino, Ellison, & Gibbs, 2010), processes of dissolution and getting back together (Dailey et al., 2009), cohabitation (Manning & Smock, 2005), and the complexities of the initiation of relational aggression (Olson & Lloyd, 2005). Such qualitative work is able to provide rich descriptions about key aspects of romantic partnering, and contributes to an enhanced understanding of relationship processes at large.

Qualitative research allows for a more naturalistic exploration of the lives of couples. Using the personal narratives of partners, qualitative researchers are able to study the dynamic processes by which partners navigate their relationship development. They focus more heavily on understanding process-oriented phenomena such as communication patterns or conflict resolution and do so in more depth than is possible with quantitative methods (Daly, 2007; LaRossa, 2005). Additionally, qualitative research allows the participants to have a voice in the research process, and is a key method for unraveling the complexities of the intersections of culture, gender, race/ethnicity, and social class (Allen et al., 2009). Allowing participants to take part in shaping research provides an outlet for a more contemporary and nuanced understanding of the lived experience of relational partners. Qualitative methods also incorporate researcher reflexivity, allowing critical reflection on their roles in the process, how their theoretical orientations affect the questions they ask, and how their values, motives, and beliefs affect the research process (Allen & Walker, 2000; Daly, 2007). We see these as additional important components of the full variety of research that is needed to fully explicate the complexities of our romantic relationships.

Modeling Non-Independence

Both diary data and dyadic data pose unique complications to researchers because of the presence of non-independence, which occurs when data are collected from one or more related individuals (e.g., romantic partners). In these cases, data from romantic partners are assumed to be interdependent because each partner exerts an influence on the other. Several statistical procedures have emerged to account for this non-independence. Most notably, the emergence of statistical programs like Hierarchical Linear Modeling (HLM) and others that perform Multi-Level Modeling (MLM) has made the challenge of non-independent data much more manageable. Although a complete discussion of HLM and other statistical procedures is beyond the scope of this book (see Campbell & Kashy, 2002, for a complete tutorial), the basic function of MLM is to analyze multiple levels of nested data. Nesting of data occurs when each of the units at a lower level is related at an upper level. For example, data from romantic couples are nested because each of the partners report their own data at the lower level (Level 1) and can report data about the couple at the upper level (Level 2). Diary data also reflect a nested structure, because the repeated daily measurements at Level 1 are nested within the individual at Level 2. By using the MLM procedure, data at the lower levels are not assumed to be independent of each other (e.g., data from romantic partners) but are instead assumed to be independent at Level 2 (e.g., data from different couples). MLM has become a robust tool for the analysis of nested data. When analyzing data from dyads, a model known as the Actor-Partner Interdependence Model (APIM; Kenny, Kashy, & Cook, 2006; see Figure 8.1) has become increasingly useful.

According to the APIM, an individual's behavior is a function of his or her own behaviors (i.e., actor effects) and the partner's behaviors (i.e., partner effects). As shown in Figure 8.1, the actor effects, which are illustrated by the "a" paths, allow researchers to estimate the effects of a wife's depression on her own relationship satisfaction as well as the effects of a husband's depression on his own relationship satisfaction. The partner effects, labeled with a "p," allow researchers to estimate the effects of a wife's depression on her husband's relationship satisfaction, as well as how the husband's depression affects the wife's relationship satisfaction.

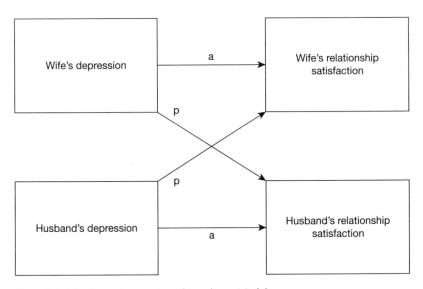

Figure 8.1 The Actor-Partner Interdependence Model

MLM can also be applied to diary methods through the application of a specific technique known as growth curve modeling. Growth curve modeling involves using time as the lower level predictor. By including time as a predictor at Level 1, researchers can estimate change in a dependent variable over time (see Singer & Willett, 2003 for a comprehensive explanation). In addition, by employing a technique known as "lagging," a researcher is able to estimate temporal sequences in data. For example, Ogolsky (2009) collected data on relationship maintenance and commitment over the course of 14 days and by using a lagging procedure estimated the effect of commitment on Day 1 with the experience of relationship maintenance on Day 2. The advantage of using lagged data is that it allows for the closest estimation of causal pathways without an experimental design.

The availability of statistical packages that perform MLM has allowed for tremendous growth in understanding dyadic data. Advancements in the analysis of dyadic data continue to expand at a rapid pace. Several recent studies (Campbell, Simpson, Kashy, & Fletcher, 2001; Ogolsky, 2009) have employed a combination of diary measurement with dyadic data collection in order to explain the course of couple relationships in tremendous detail.

Advancing Future Scholarship on Romantic Relationships

As a deeply interdisciplinary field, the study of romantic relationship processes has benefited from the rich interplay of theoretical and research developments across many social science disciplines, including family studies, psychology, sociology, communication, anthropology, and race, gender and sexuality studies. In this final section we draw from cross-disciplinary developments to discuss the theoretical and methodological challenges that will compel the field to advance and grow in critically important ways. These include life course perspectives, the mind–body connection, understanding heteronormativity, the social construction of gender, incorporating intersections of race, class, and culture, and the interplay of universal properties and unique features.

Life Course Perspectives

One of the conundrums of the body of scholarship on romantic relationships is the fact that much of this research is conducted in relative "silos"; for reasons of theory building and practicality, scholars tend to specialize their work within certain constructs (e.g., deception) and study populations (e.g., heterosexual young adult romantic partners). The unintended consequence of this specialization is a dearth of research on the ebb and flow of romantic relationships across the life span, as well as how relationships are interconnected over time with key developmental experiences and historical events during childhood, adolescence, and adulthood (Bengston & Allen, 1993; Elder, 1985; Williams, 2003).

A life course perspective examines the interconnectedness of the multiple developmental periods and trajectories of people's lives (Elder, 1985). Thus, a life course view of romantic relationship development and decline situates our research and theory within the complexity of human development. We provide three examples of how this perspective integrates with the study of romantic partnering. First, *a life course perspective on partnering processes*, as noted above, would not stop with research on young adults' first major committed relationship, but instead would examine the fascinating histories of partnering and re-partnering across one's lifetime. Indeed, there are many intriguing questions to be asked, including whether/how what we learn/ experience in early romantic relationships carries over into subsequent relationship decisions and dynamics. Second, *a life course view of the dynamics and effects of intimate violence* would acknowledge the impossibility of teasing out the complex web of influences between interpersonal trauma and relationship processes, and instead concentrate on examining how such trauma plays out over a lifetime, as well as the mediating roles of individual resiliency, presence of supportive family and friends, and exposure to multiple forms of violence in both the family and the community (Lloyd, 2012). Third, a life course perspective would encourage us to *attend to the role of context in a deeper way*; examination of period and cohort effects on romantic relationship processes opens up a wealth of future research endeavors that incorporate

154

analyses of historical, political, economic, and global trends as they intersect with our romantic partnerships.

There are several notable applications of such a life course perspective to understanding romantic partnering. First, the application of attachment theory to the study of romantic adult relationships (discussed in detail in Chapter 3) can be viewed as a life course perspective, with its emphasis on how a child's relationships with primary caregivers are later reflected in the romantic partnerships of the early adult. One study (Surra et al., 2006) showed that attachment was the most studied topic on dating and mate selection over the period from 1991 to 2000. The increased interest in attachment theory is due to its ability to illuminate salient processes in romantic relationships across the course of relational development (Shaver & Mikulincer, 2006). Secure attachment facilitates: (1) self-presentation and appropriate self-disclosure early in relationships, (2) trust and commitment as relationships continue to develop, and (3) constructive communication and problem solving required in establishing long-term relationships (Shaver & Mikulincer, 2006).

Second, Bryant and Conger (2002) present an intergenerational model of romantic relationship development that incorporates a life course perspective. They are interested in the interpersonal skills and competencies, developed in the family of origin, that affect the chances of success in adult romantic relationships; that is, the "specific behavioral, cognitive, and emotional characteristics in the family of origin [that] might prime young adults to behave in certain ways with romantic partners" (p. 59). They have tested and supported this model using prospective data (see also Conger et al., 2000, 2011), and they discuss the importance of such a multilayered conceptualization of romantic relationship success.

Contesting Heteronormativity

Oswald et al. (2005) define heteronormativity as:

> the implicit moral system or value framework that surrounds the practice of heterosexuality. Typically, heteronormativity is buttressed by claims (often implicit) that because heterosexuality is "more natural" than other forms of sexuality, it should be standard sexual practice. (p. 144)

Heteronormativity manifests itself through three binaries (Oswald et al., 2005): (1) the gender binary compares "real" men and women with those who do not adhere to accepted gender stereotypes (p. 145); (2) the sexual binary sees heterosexuality as "normal" and pathologizes other types of sexual practice (p. 145); and (3) the family binary treats biological and legal bonds as "genuine," while treating other forms of family structure as "pseudo" (p. 146). The body of literature on personal relationships has, by and large, been conducted within notions of heteronormativity. For example, much of the literature on personal relationships could be very consistently situated within the sexuality binary. An inspection of recent issues of the top two interdisciplinary personal relationships journals, *Personal Relationships* and *Journal of Social and Personal Relationships*, shows that less than 5% of the articles examined gay and lesbian individuals or couples.

Additionally, our very language about romantic relationships is rooted in heterosexuality, a fact that the present authors struggled with in titling and writing this book. The term "courtship" was created and used in an era when the "naturalness" of marriage went unquestioned. Today, the term seems outdated, as scholars have acknowledged the great diversity of intimate relationships, not all of which lead to a legally binding commitment. On the other hand, new terminology, such as "non-marital romantic relationships," can be equally problematic, as it continues to place marriage at the center, implying that all other relationships are on the margin.

Unfortunately, long traditions in scholarship make it unnecessary to name the fact that a study is on heterosexual individuals, while, in contrast, studies of LGBT partners are all too often seen as being mostly about the sexuality of the participants, rather than the variables of interest (such as processes of commitment). Such dynamics within our research traditions contribute to keeping the intimate relationships of gay, lesbian, transgender, and queer individuals in the category of "other" and the intimate relationships of heterosexual individuals in the category of "normal." Certainly, work on queer theory, which challenges the unquestioned centering of heterosexual experience, will continue to push scholars to refine their theorizing and conceptualizations in ways that will resist the tendency toward homogeneity (see, in particular, the chapter titled "Queering the family" by Oswald et al., 2009).

The Social Construction of Gender within Romantic Relationships

One of the exciting prospects for work on romantic relationships is the move toward examination of gender as a process. Early work on gender and courtship concentrated heavily on traditional roles of heterosexual men and women, and current scholarship retains a very strong emphasis on gender differences (Andersen, 2005). As an alternative to these static models of gender, feminist scholars, in particular, have brought to the field an emphasis on gender as a social construction, examining the ways in which individuals enact gender within their everyday social interactions and, in this case, the interlinking of gender processes and relational processes. These lines of research open up examinations of how gender constructions are linked with heteronormativity, how intimate relationship processes may reproduce and/or resist inequitable gender patterns, and how the structural aspects of gender (labor stratification, earnings, assignment of caregiving, power) deeply intersect with partner interactions within romantic relationships (Allen et al., 2009; Johnson, 2005; Lorber, 1994; Oswald et al., 2009).

Intersections of Race, Class, and Culture

Despite repeated pleas for more culturally, economically, and racially diverse samples of study participants, research on romantic relationships still largely examines the lives of young, White, heterosexual, college students. The impact of this continued reliance on relatively homogeneous populations stunts the growth of the field in multiple ways. In particular, despite excellent work on family diversity (see, for example, Demo, Allen, & Fine, 2000), our ability as scholars to examine more deeply the intersections of culture, race/ethnicity, and social class with sexuality and gender has progressed painfully slowly. Although we have come a long way from constructions of deviance and inferiority based on race, class, and sexual orientation, the field still lacks diverse samples, culturally situated analyses, a consistent examination of within-group variation, and culturally sensitive measures (Allen et al., 2009; Kasturirangan, Krishnan, & Riger, 2004). Carefully addressing the need for culturally situated work will do much to advance the development of both theory and research on romantic pairings in emerging adulthood.

Theory and research on close relationships has been influenced in key ways by the work of scholars who study diverse families and scholars who emphasize intersectionality in their work. This work has led to the advancement of theories, such as critical race theory, and multicultural feminisms, which situate understanding of intimate relationships within hierarchies of privilege and power, and structural inequalities (Allen et al., 2009). The concept of intersectionality challenges monolithic views of gender, or race, or sexual orientation, and instead calls for examination of these social locations as overlapping and interlocking (Allen et al., 2009; Andersen, 2005; Collins, 2000). While presenting myriad methodological challenges (McCall, 2005), an emphasis on intersections of race, class, culture, sexuality, and gender holds great promise for understanding the lived experiences of romantic partners in new ways.

The Interplay of Universal Properties and Unique Features

Understanding the intersections of race, class, culture, gender, and sexuality has important implications for assumptions about universal properties. Universal properties are the relational qualities that explain the behavior of individuals across relationship types. In a review of the literature on romantic

157

relationships, Surra and colleagues (2006) found that the majority of studies treated relational variables (e.g., satisfaction, love) as universal, that is, assumed that they operate similarly across relationship types. Moreover, their review highlighted the fact that many of the published studies examining relationships failed to mention the relationship status of the participants at all. Such an omission reflects the underlying assumption that major relationship variables operate the same way across relationships.

This blind acceptance of universal properties, however, can limit the understanding of the unique relationship features that influence the course of romantic relationships. Although many relational variables such as satisfaction and love may behave similarly across relationship types, other variables such as commitment may operate differently. For example, same-sex couples are still unable to marry in the majority of the United States, which eliminates one of the major barriers to dissolution that is present in different-sex relationships. Relationship maintenance can also differ as a function of relationship type. Studies have shown that same-sex couples engage in a number of unique maintenance strategies designed to combat intolerance that are not present among different-sex partners (Haas & Stafford, 1998). We suggest that assuming that relationship processes are universal is problematic. Instead, researchers should examine the diverse characteristics of their participants in order to support or contradict assumptions of universal properties.

Concluding Thoughts

In the introduction to this chapter, we addressed the question of whether the "institution of courtship" is dead. As noted earlier, we disagree with the view that emerging adults no longer search for a close, caring partner, but instead seek sex with as many people as possible. We believe that close interpersonal bonds remain central to most people's lives. Two lines of research support our position. First, research suggests that humans have an innate predisposition to belong; healthy functioning results from fulfillment of this need to seek satisfying relations in enduring and caring relationships (Baumeister & Leary, 1995). Second, satisfying and high-quality relationships have been shown to promote both mental and physical health (Berkman, 1995; Holt-Lunstad et al., 2010).

Still, we must continually expand our understanding of romantic partnership processes. This may well mean that we will have to develop new terminology for our long-term, committed relationships, as well as new theories of their formation, maintenance, and deterioration. The emergence of scholarship on LGBT relationships provides us with a great deal of food for thought here. What happens when we move away from the heteronormative focus on heterosexual marriage as the "end point" of the romantic relationships of emerging adults? Concepts such as "life partnership" (used by Solomon, Rothblum, & Balsam, 2004) would expand our ability to fully incorporate LGBT and heterosexual relationships into the development of universal relationship properties. However, much work remains to be done in developing these concepts—for example, how do people describe their life partnerships? What are the levels of commitment, relationship quality, and time spent together that define these relationships? Although it was much "easier" when legal marriage was a singular end point for the development of romantic relationships, it is truly exciting to be on the cusp of such huge shifts in how we conceptualize our work.

Finally, we challenge Kass's (1997) implication that emerging adults have forsaken time-honored rituals of romantic partnering. This assertion is undoubtedly true, but no truer than past transitions in the romantic partnering process. Are recent changes in partnering processes any more dramatic than the switch from a man "courting" the object of his affection on the front porch of her parents' home to the later practice of "courting" in the back seat of a car (Bailey, 1988)? We think not. For example, many people now choose cohabitation as a step in the partnering process (see Chapter 5) or are relying on Internet dating services to find a partner (see Chapter 2). In other words, people are devising new ways to attract and commit to romantic partners. We are confident that how we form and re-form our relationships, how we work to make them better, and how we grieve when they end, will be a topic for individuals, social science researchers, novelists, poets, and the arts for generations to come.

Summary

The process of romantic partnering has changed drastically over time. The present chapter discussed: (a) current issues in romantic partnering; (b) methodologies used to study partnering processes; and (c) the major needs in theory and research on romantic partnering. The prevailing view of romantic partnering has changed from static stage conceptions to one of interpersonal process. This process perspective assumes that partnering results from the complex interplay of social contexts, individual attributes, relationship attributes, and couple interaction. This complexity calls for further work to better understand partnering processes. Four topics are of particular interest: (a) matchmaking services; (b) cohabitation; (c) hooking up; and (d) re-partnering. Current methodological and statistical advancements also are available to help understand partnering processes. Longitudinal methods assist in teasing out causal processes, whereas daily diary methods help identify micro-level processes of partnering. In addition, qualitative research methods focus on in-depth understanding of the process of partnering. New statistical techniques allow researchers to identify unique effects due to each partner in a relationship. Finally, future research and theorizing on romantic partnering should address: life course perspectives, heteronormativity, the social construction of gender and sexuality, and intersectionality. Ultimately, understanding romantic relationship development and decline requires deep attention to so many levels of analysis, from microprocesses of communication and relational maintenance, to the interplay of gender, sexuality, and race, to the role of changes in societal structures, economies, and technologies.

Key Concepts

Actor-partner interdependence model (pp. 152–153)
Attachment theory (p. 155)
Binaries (pp. 155–156)
Cohabitation (pp. 147–148)
Daily diary methods (pp. 150–151)
Growth curve modeling (p. 153)
Heteronormativity (pp. 155–156)
Hooking up (pp. 148–149)
Internet technologies (pp. 145–146)
Intersectionality (p. 157)
Life course perspectives (pp. 154–155)
Longitudinal studies (p. 150)
Matchmaking services (pp. 145–146)
Nested data (pp. 152–153)
Non-independence (pp. 152–153)
Qualitative research (pp. 151–152)
Re-partnering (p. 149)
Same-sex marriage (pp. 146–147)
Sexuality (pp. 148–149)
Social construction of gender (p. 156)
Universal properties (pp. 157–158)

REFERENCES

Adams-Curtis, L. E., & Forbes, G. B. (2004). College women's experiences of sexual coercion: A review of cultural, perpetrator, victim, and situational variables. *Trauma, Violence, & Abuse, 5*(2), 91–122. doi:10.1177/1524838003262331

Adelman, M., & Kil, S. H. (2007). Dating conflicts: Rethinking dating violence and youth conflict. *Violence Against Women, 13*(12), 1296–1318. doi:10.1177/1077801207310800

Agnew, C. R., Loving, T. J., & Drigotas, S. M. (2001). Substituting the forest for the trees: Social networks and the prediction of romantic relationship state and fate. *Journal of Personality and Social Psychology, 81*(6), 1042–1057. doi:10.1037/0022-3514.81.6.1042

Agnew, C. R., Van Lange, P. A. M., Rusbult, C. E., & Langston, C. A. (1998). Cognitive interdependence: Commitment and the mental representation of close relationships. *Journal of Personality and Social Psychology, 74*(4), 939–954. doi:10.1037/0022-3514.74.4.939

Alexander, E. (2004). The courtship season: Love, race, and elite African American women at the turn of the twentieth century. *OAH Magazine of History, 18*(4), 17.

Allen, K. A., Lloyd, S. A., & Few, A. L. (2009). Reclaiming feminist theory, method and praxis for family studies. In S. A. Lloyd, A. L. Few, & K. A. Allen (Eds.), *Handbook of feminist family studies* (pp. 3–17). Thousand Oaks, CA: Sage.

Allen, K. R., & Walker, A. J. (2000). Constructing gender in families. In R. Milardo & S. Duck (Eds.), *Families as relationships* (pp. 1–17). New York: John Wiley & Sons.

Altman, I., & Taylor, D.A. (1973). *Social penetration: The development of interpersonal relationships.* New York: Holt, Rinehart & Winston.

Altman, I., Vinsel, A., & Brown, B. B. (1981). Dialectical conceptions in social psychology: An application to social penetration and privacy regulation. In L. Berkowitz (Ed.), *Advances in experimental social psychology* (Vol. 14, pp. 107–160). New York: Academic Press.

Amato, P. R. (1996). Explaining the intergenerational transmission of divorce. *Journal of Marriage & the Family, 58*(3), 628–640. doi:10.2307/353723

Amato, P. R., & Booth, A. (1991). The consequences of divorce for attitudes toward divorce and gender roles. *Journal of Family Issues, 12*(3), 306–322. doi:10.1177/019251391012003004

Andersen, M. L. (2005). Thinking about women: A quarter century's view. *Gender & Society, 19*(4), 437–455. doi:10.1177/0891243205276756

Andersen, M. L., & Witham, D. H. (2011). *Thinking about women: Sociological perspectives on sex and gender.* Boston, MA: Allyn & Bacon.

Andrews, J. A., Foster, S. L., Capaldi, D., & Hops, H. (2000). Adolescent and family predictors of physical aggression, communication, and satisfaction in young adult couples: A prospective analysis. *Journal of Consulting and Clinical Psychology, 68*(2), 195–208. doi:10.1037/0022-006X.68.2.195

Antill, J. K. (1983). Sex role complementarity versus similarity in married couples. *Journal of Personality and Social Psychology, 45*(1), 145–155. doi:10.1037/0022-3514.45.1.145

Arias, I., Samios, M., & O'Leary, K. D. (1987). Prevalence and Correlates of physical aggression during courtship. *Journal of Interpersonal Violence, 2*(1), 82–90. doi:10.1177/088626087002001005

Armstrong, E.A., Hamilton, L., & England, P. (2010). Is hooking up bad for young women? *Contexts, 9*(3), http://contexts.org/articles/issues/summer-2010.

Arnett, J. J. (2000). Emerging adulthood: A theory of development from the late teens through the twenties. *American Psychologist, 55*, 469–480.

Aron, A., Aron, E. N., & Smollan, D. (1992). Inclusion of Other in the Self Scale and the structure of interpersonal closeness. *Journal of Personality and Social Psychology, 63*, 596–612.

Arriaga, X. B. (2001). The ups and downs of dating: Fluctuations in satisfaction in newly formed romantic relationships. *Journal of Personality and Social Psychology, 80*(5), 754–765. doi:10.1037/0022-3514.80.5.754

Arriaga, X. B., Goodfriend, W., & Lohmann, A. (2004). *Beyond the individual: Concomitants of closeness in the social and physical environment.* Mahwah, NJ: Lawrence Erlbaum Associates.

Arriaga, X. B., Reed, J. T., Goodfriend, W., & Agnew, C. R. (2006). Relationship perceptions and persistence: Do fluctuations in perceived partner commitment undermine dating relationships? *Journal of Personality and Social Psychology, 91*(6), 1045–1065. doi:10.1037/0022-3514.91.6.1045

Attridge, M., Berscheid, E., & Simpson, J.A. (1995). Predicting relationship stability from both partners versus one. *Journal of Personality and Social Psychology, 69*, 254–268. doi:10.1037/0022-3514.69.2.254

Axinn, W., & Thornton, A. (1992). The relationship between cohabitation and divorce: Selectivity or causal influence. *Demography, 29*(3), 357–374.

Babcock, J. C., Costa, D. M., Green, C. E., & Eckhardt, C. I. (2004). What situations induce intimate partner violence? A reliability and validity study of the proximal antecedents to violent episodes (PAVE) scale. *Journal of Family Psychology, 18*(3), 433–442.

Babcock, J. C., Roseman, A., Green, C. E., & Ross, J. M. (2008). Intimate partner abuse and PTSD symptomatology: Examining mediators and moderators of the abuse-trauma link. *Journal of Family Psychology, 22*(6), 809–818. doi:10.1037/a0013808

Baber, K. M., & Allen, K. R. (1992). *Women & families: Feminist reconstructions.* New York: Guilford Press.

Bailey, B. L. (1988). *From front porch to back seat: Courtship in twentieth-century America.* Baltimore, MD: Johns Hopkins University Press.

Bailey, B. (2004). From front porch to back seat: A history of the date. *OAH Magazine of History, 18*(4), 23.

Baldwin, M., & Fehr, B. (1995). On the instability of attachment style ratings. *Personal Relationships, 2,* 247–261.

Balsam, K. F., Rothblum, E. D., & Beauchaine, T. P. (2005). Victimization over the life span: A comparison of lesbian, gay, bisexual, and heterosexual siblings. *Journal of Consulting and Clinical Psychology, 73*(3), 477–487. doi:10.1037/0022-006X. 73.3.477

Balsam, K. F., & Szymanski, D. M. (2005). Relationship quality and domestic violence in women's same-sex relationships: The role of minority stress. *Psychology of Women Quarterly, 29,* 258–269.

Barbara, A. & Dion, K. (2000). Breaking up is hard to do, especially for strongly "preoccupied" lovers. *Journal of Personal & Interpersonal Loss, 5,* 315–342.

Bargh, J. A., & McKenna, K. Y. A. (2004). The Internet and social life. *Annual Review of Psychology, 55,* 573–590. doi:10.1146/annurev.psych.55.090902.141922

Barnes, R. (2011). "Suffering in a silent vacuum": Woman-to-woman partner abuse as a challenge to the lesbian feminist vision. *Feminism & Psychology, 21*(2), 233–239. doi:10.1177/0959353510370183

Barnett, O. W., Miller-Perrin, C. L., & Perrin, R. D. (2005). *Family violence across the lifespan: An introduction.* Thousand Oaks, CA: Sage.

Barsanti, A. B. (2005). A collage of western women. *OAH Magazine of History, 19*(6), 41.

Bartholomew, K. & Horowitz, L. (1991). Attachment styles among young adults: A test of the four-category model. *Journal of Personality and Social Psychology, 61,* 226–244.

Basile, K. C., Arias, I., Desai, S., & Thompson, M. P. (2004). The differential association of intimate partner physical, sexual, psychological, and stalking violence and posttraumatic stress symptoms in a nationally representative sample of women. *Journal of Traumatic Stress, 17*(5), 413–421. doi:10.1023/B:JOTS. 0000048954.50232.d8

Battaglia, D. M., Richard, F.D., Datteri, D. L., & Lord, C. G. (1998). Breaking up is (relatively) easy to do: A script for the dissolution of close relationships. *Journal of Social and Personal Relationships, 15,* 829–845.

Baumeister, R. F. (1998). The self. In D. Gilbert, S Fiske, & G. Lindzey (Eds.), *The handbook of social psychology* (Vol. 1, 4th ed., pp. 680–740). Oxford: Oxford University Press.

Baumeister, R. F., & Leary, M. R. (1995). The need to belong: Desire for interpersonal attachments as a fundamental human motivation. *Psychological Bulletin, 117*(3), 497–529. doi:10.1037/0033-2909.117.3.497

Baxter, L. A. (1985). Accomplishing relationship disengagement. In S. Duck & D. Perlman (Eds.), *Understanding personal relationships* (pp. 243–265). Thousand Oaks, CA: Sage.

Baxter, L.A. (1990). Dialectical contradictions in relationship development. *Journal of Social and Personal Relationships, 7,* 69–88.

Baxter, L. A. (1993). The social side of personal relationships: A dialectical perspective. In S. Duck (Ed.), *Understanding personal relationship processes* (pp. 139–165). Newbury Park, CA: Sage.

Baxter, L. A. (2004). The dialogues of relating. In R. Anderson, L. A. Baxter, & K. N. Cissna (Eds.), *Dialogue: Theorizing difference in communication studies* (pp. 107–124). Thousand Oaks, CA: Sage.

Baxter, L. A., & Montgomery, B. M. (1996). *Relating: Dialogues and dialectics.* New York: Guilford Press.

Beals, K. P., Impett, E. A., & Peplau, L. A. (2002). Lesbians in love: Why some relationships endure and others end. *Journal of Lesbian Studies, 6,* 53–63.

Bengston, V. L., & Allen, K. R. (1993). The life course perspective applied to families over time. In P. G. Boss, W. J. Doherty, R. LaRossa, W. R. Schumm, & S. K. Steinmetz (Eds.), *Sourcebook of family, theories and methods: A contextual approach* (pp. 469–499). New York: Plenum.

Bentler, P. M., & Newcomb, M. D. (1978). Longitudinal study of marital success and failure. *Journal of Consulting and Clinical Psychology, 46*(5), 1053–1070. doi:10.1037/0022-006X.46.5.1053

Berger, C. R, & Bradac, J. J. (1982). *Language and social knowledge: Uncertainty in interpersonal relationships.* London: Edward Arnold.

Berger, C., & Calabrese, R. (1975). Some explorations in initial interaction and beyond: Toward a developmental theory of interpersonal communication. *Human Communication Research 1,* 99–112.

Berkman, L. F. (1995). The role of social relations in health promotion. *Psychosomatic Medicine, 57*(3), 245–254.

Berscheid, E. (1995). Help wanted: A grand theorist of interpersonal relationships, sociologist or anthropologist preferred. *Journal of Social and Personal Relationships, 12,* 529–533.

Berscheid, E. & Walster, E. (1974). Physical attractiveness. *Advances in Experimental Social Psychology, 7,* 158–216.

Beynon, C. M., McVeigh, C., McVeigh, J., Leavey, C., & Bellis, M. A. (2008). The involvement of drugs and alcohol in drug-facilitated sexual assault: A systematic review of the evidence. *Trauma, Violence, & Abuse, 9*(3), 178–188. doi:10.1177/1524838008320221

Billingsley, A. (1968). *Black families in white America.* Englewood Cliffs, NJ: Prentice-Hall.

Binstock, G., & Thornton, A. (2003). Separations, reconciliations and living apart in cohabiting and marital unions. *Journal of Marriage and Family, 65*(2), 432–443. doi:10.1111/j.1741-3737.2003.00432.

Black, D., Gates, G., Sanders, S., & Taylor, L. (2000). Demographics of the gay and lesbian population in the United States: Evidence from available systematic data sources. *Demography, 37,* 139–154.

Black, M. C., Basile, K. C., Breidling, M. J., Smith, S. G., Walters, M. L., Merrick, M. T., Chen, J., & Stevens, M. R. (2011). *The national intimate partner and sexual violence survey (NISVS): 2010 summary report.* Atlanta, GA: National Center for Injury Prevention and Control, Centers for Disease Control and Prevention.

Bleske-Rechek, A., Remiker, M. W., & Baker, J. P. (2009). Similar from the start: Assortment in young adult dating couples and its link to relationship stability over time. *Individual Differences Research, 7*(3), 142–158.

Blow, A. J., & Hartnett, K. (2005). Infidelity in committed relationships I: A methodological review. *Journal of Marital and Family Therapy, 31*(2), 183–216. doi:10.1111/j.1752-0606.2005.tb01555.x

Blumstein, P. & Schwartz, P. (1983). *American couples: Money, work, sex.* New York: Morrow and Co.

Blumstein, P., & Kollock, P. (1988). Personal relationships. *Annual Review of Sociology, 14,* 467–490.

Boase, J. (2008). Personal networks and the personal communication system: Using multiple communication media to connect with personal networks. *Information, Communication and Society, 11,* 490–508.

Boelen, P. A., & Reijntjes, A. (2009). Negative cognitions in emotional problems following romantic relationship break-ups. *Stress and Health: Journal of the International Society for the Investigation of Stress, 25*(1), 11–19. doi:10.1002/smi.1219

Bogle, K. (2008). *Hooking up: Sex, dating, and relationships on campus.* New York: New York University Press.

Booth, A., & Edwards, J. N. (1985). Age at marriage and marital instability. *Journal of Marriage and the Family, 47,* 67–75.

Booth, A., Johnson. D. R., White, L. K., & Edwards, J. N. (1985). Predicting divorce and permanent separation. *Journal of Family Issues, 6,* 331–346.

Booth, A., Johnson, D. R., White, L. K., & Edwards, J. N. (1986). Divorce and marital instability over the life course. *Journal of Family Issues, 7,* 421–442.

Boss, P., Doherty, W., LaRossa, R., Schumm, W., & Steinmetz, S. (1993). *Sourcebook of family theories and methods: A contextual approach.* New York: Plenum.

Bossard, J. H. S. (1932). Residential propinquity as a factor in marriage selection. *American Journal of Sociology, 38,* 219–224.

Bouffard, L. A., & Bouffard, J. A. (2011). Understanding men's perceptions of risks and rewards in a date rape scenario. *International Journal of Offender Therapy & Comparative Criminology, 55,* 626–645.

Bowlby. J. (1969). *Attachment and loss* (Vol. 1, *Attachment*). New York: Basic Books.

Bradbury, T. N., & Karney, B. R. (2010). *Intimate relationships.* New York: W. W. Norton.

Bradshaw, C., Kahn, A., & Saville, B. (2010). To hook up or date: Which gender benefits? *Sex Roles, 62,* 661–669. doi:10.1007/s11199-010-9765-7

Braiker, H. B., & Kelley, H. H. (1979). Conflict in the development of close relationships. In R. L. Burgess & T. L. Huston (Eds.), *Social exchange in developing relationships* (pp. 135–168). New York: Academic.

Bredow, C. A., Cate, R. M., & Huston, T. L. (2008). Have we met before? A conceptual model of first romantic encounters. In S. Sprecher, A. Wenzel, & J. Harvey (Eds.), *Handbook of relationship initiation* (pp. 3–28). New York: Psychology Press.

Brennan, K. A., Clark, C. L., & Shaver, P. R. (1998). Self-report measurement of adult attachment: An integrative overview. In J. A. Simpson & W. S. Rholes (Eds.), *Attachment theory and close relationships* (pp. 46–76). New York: Guilford Press.

Brewster, M. P. (2002). Stalking by former intimates: Verbal threats and other predictors of physical violence. In K. E. Davis, I. H. Frieze, & R. D. Maiuro (Eds.), *Stalking: Perspectives on victims and perpetrators* (pp. 292–311). New York: Springer Publishing Co.

Briere, J., & Jordan, C. E. (2004). Violence against women: Outcome complexity and implications for assessment and treatment. *Journal of Interpersonal Violence. Special Issue: Toward a National Research Agenda on Violence Against Women—Part 1, 19*(11), 1252–1276. doi:10.1177/0886260504269682

Brines, J., & Joyner, K. (1999). The ties that bind: Principles of cohesion in cohabitation and marriage. *American Sociological Review, 64*(3), 333–355. doi:10.2307/2657490

Brown, C. (2008). Gender-role implications on same-sex intimate partner abuse. *Journal of Family Violence, 23*(6), 457–462. doi:10.1007/s10896-008-9172-9

Brown, S. L. (2000a). The effect of union type on psychological well-being: Depression among cohabitors versus marrieds. *Journal of Health and Social Behavior, 41*(3), 241–255. doi:10.2307/2676319

Brown, S. L. (2000b). Union transitions among cohabitors: The significance of relationship assessments and expectations. *Journal of Marriage & the Family, 62*(3), 833–846. doi:10.1111/j.1741-3737.2000.00833.x

Brown, S. L., Sanchez, L. A., Nock, S. L., & Wright, J. D. (2006). Links between premarital cohabitation and subsequent marital quality, stability, and divorce: A comparison of covenant versus standard marriages. *Social Science Research, 35*(2), 454–470. doi:10.1016/j.ssresearch.2006.03.001

Bryant, C. M., & Conger, R. D. (2002). An intergenerational model of romantic relationship development. In A. Vangelisti, H. Reis, & M. A. Fitzpatrick (Eds.), *Stability and change in relationships* (pp. 57–82). New York: Cambridge University Press. doi:10.1017/CBO9780511499876005

Bryant-Davis, T., Chung, H., & Tillman, S. (2009). From the margins to the center: Ethnic minority women and the mental health effects of sexual assault. *Trauma, Violence, & Abuse, 10*(4), 330–357. doi:10.1177/1524838009339755

Bui, K. T., Peplau, L. A., & Hill, C. T. (1996). Testing the Rusbult model of relationship commitment and stability in a 15-year study of heterosexual couples. *Personality and Social Psychology Bulletin, 22*(12), 1244–1257. doi:10.1177/01461672962212005

Bumpass, L. L., Castro Martin, T., & Sweet, J. A. (1991). The impact of family background and early marital factors on marital disruption. *Journal of Family Issues, 12*(1), 22–42. doi:10.1177/019251391012001003

Bumpass, L., & Hsien-Hen, L. (2000). Trends in cohabitation and implications for children's family contexts in the United States. *Population Studies, 54*, 29–41.

Bureau of Labor Statistics. (2012). *Current population survey.* Retrieved from http://www.bls.gov/cps/.

Burgess, E., & Wallin, P. (1953). *Engagement and marriage.* New York: Lippincott.

Burgess, E. W., Wallin, P., & Schultz, G. D. (1954). *Courtship, engagement and marriage.* Oxford: J. B. Lippincott Co.

Buss, D. (1989). Sex differences in human mate preferences: Evolutionary hypotheses tested in 37 cultures. *Behavioral and Brain Sciences, 12*, 1–49.

Buss, D. M. (1998). Sexual strategies theory: Historical origins and current status. *Journal of Sex Research, 35*(1), 19–31. doi:10.1080/00224499809551914

Buss, D. M., & Schmitt, D. P. (1993). Sexual strategies theory: An evolutionary perspective on human mating. *Psychological Review, 100*(2), 204–232. doi:10.1037/0033-295X.100.2.204

Byers, S. A., & MacNeil, S. (2006). Further validation of the interpersonal exchange model of sexual satisfaction. *Journal of Sex and Marital Therapy, 32*, 53–69. doi:10.1080/00926230500232917

Cadiz Menne, J. M., & Sinnett, E. R. (1971). Proximity and social interaction in residence halls. *Journal of College Student Personnel, 12*(1), 26–31.

Caldwell, J. E., Swan, S. C., Allen, C. T., Sullivan, T. P., & Snow, D. L. (2009). Why I hit him: Women's reasons for intimate partner violence. *Journal of Aggression, Maltreatment & Trauma, 18*, 672–697.

Campbell, L. J. & Kashy, D. A. (2002). Estimating actor, partner, and interaction effects for dyadic data using PROC MIXED and HLM5: A user-friendly guide. *Personal Relationships, 9*, 327–342.

Campbell, L., Simpson, J. A., Kashy, D. A., & Fletcher, G. J. O. (2001). Ideal standards, the self, and flexibility of ideals in close relationships. *Personality and Social Psychology Bulletin, 27*(4), 447–462. doi:10.1177/0146167201274006

Campbell, R., Dworkin, E., & Cabral, G. (2009). An ecological model of the impact of sexual assault on women's mental health. *Trauma, Violence, & Abuse, 10*, 225–246.

Canary, D. J. (2011). On babies, bathwater, and absolute claims: Reply to Stafford. *Journal of Social and Personal Relationships, 28*, 304–311. doi: 10.1177/0265407510397523

Canary, D. J., & Dainton, M. (2006). Maintaining relationships. In A. L. Vangelisti & D. Perlman (Eds.), *The Cambridge handbook of personal relationships* (pp. 727–743). New York: Cambridge University Press.

Canary, D. J., & Messman, S. J. (2002). Relationship conflict. In C. Hendrick & S. S. Hendrick (Eds.), *Close relationships: A sourcebook* (pp. 261–270). Thousand Oaks, CA: Sage.

Canary, D., & Stafford, L. (1992). Relationship maintenance strategies and equity in marriage. *Communication Monographs, 59*, 243–267. doi: 10.1080/03637759209376268

Canary, D. J., & Stafford, L. (1994). Maintaining relationships through strategic and routine interaction. In D. J. Canary & L. Stafford (Eds.), *Communication and relational maintenance* (pp. 3–22). New York: Academic Press.

Canary, D. J., Stafford, L., Hause, K. S., & Wallace, L. A. (1993). An inductive analysis of relational maintenance strategies: Comparisons among lovers, relatives, friends, and others. *Communication Research Reports, 10*, 1993, 5–14. doi: 10.1080/08824099309359913

Capaldi, D. M., Shortt, J. W., & Crosby, L. (2003). Physical and psychological aggression in at-risk young couples: Stability and change in young adulthood. *Merrill-Palmer Quarterly: Journal of Developmental Psychology, 49*(1), 1–27. doi:10.1353/mpq.2003.0001

Caplow, T., Bahr, H., Chadwick, B., Hill, R., & Williamson, M. (1982). *Middletown families: Fifty years of change and continuity.* Minneapolis, MN: University of Minnesota Press.

Carlson, B. E., Worden, A. P., van Ryn, M., & Bachman, R. (2003). *Violence against women: Synthesis of research for practitioners.* Washington, DC: Sage Publications.

Carney, M., Buttell, F., & Dutton, D. (2007). Women who perpetrate intimate partner violence: A review of the literature with recommendations for treatment. *Aggression and Violent Behavior, 12*(1), 108–115. doi:10.1016/j.avb.2006.05.002

Cate, R. M., Henton, J. M., Koval., J. E., Christopher, F. S., & Lloyd, S. A. (1982). Premarital abuse: A social psychological perspective. *Journal of Family Issues, 3*, 79–90.

Cate, R. M., Huston, T. L., & Nesselroade, J. R. (1986). Premarital relationships: Toward the identification of alternative pathways to marriage. *Journal of Social and Clinical Psychology, 4*, 3–22.

Cate, R., Levin, L., & Richmond, L. (2002). Premarital relationship stability: A review of recent research. *Journal of Social and Personal Relationships, 19*, 261–284.

Cate, R. M., & Lloyd, S.A. (1988). Courtship. In S. Duck (Ed.), *Handbook of personal relationships* (pp. 409–428). New York: Wiley.

Cate, R. M., & Lloyd, S. A. (1992). *Courtship*. Newbury Park, CA: Sage.

Cate, R. M., Lloyd, S. A., & Henton, J. M. (1985). The effect of equity, equality, and reward level on the stability of students' premarital relationships. *Journal of Social Psychology, 125*(6), 715–721.

Caughlin, J. P., Huston, T. L., & Houts, R. M. (2000). How does personality matter in marriage? An examination of trait anxiety, interpersonal negativity, and marital satisfaction. *Journal of Personality and Social Psychology, 78*(2), 326–336. doi:10.1037/0022-3514.78.2.326

Caughlin, J. P., & Vangelisti, A. L. (2006). Conflict in dating and romantic relationships. In J. Oetzel & S. Ting-Toomey (Eds.), *The Sage handbook of conflict communication* (pp. 129–157). Thousand Oaks, CA: Sage.

Causby, V., Lockhart, L., White, B., & Greene, K. (1995). Fusion and conflict resolution in lesbian relationships. In C. T. Tully (Ed.), *Lesbian social services: Research issues* (pp. 67–82). New York/England: Harrington Park Press/Haworth Press.

Centers for Disease Control and Prevention. *Morbidity and Mortality Weekly Report.* June 4, 2010, Vol. 59, No. SS-5, www.cdc.gov/mmwr.

Chang, S., & Chan, C. (2007). Perceptions of commitment change during mate selection: The case of Taiwanese newlyweds. *Journal of Social and Personal Relationships, 24*(1), 55–68. doi:10.1177/0265407507072583

Chauncey, G. (1994). *Gay New York: Gender, urban culture, and the making of the gay male world, 1890–1940.* New York: Basic Books.

Cherlin, A. (2009). *The marriage-go-round: The state of marriage and the family in America today.* New York: Alfred Knopf.

Cherlin, A. J. (2010). Demographic trends in the United States: A review of research in the 2000s. *Journal of Marriage and Family, 72*(3), 403–419. doi:10.1111/j.1741-3737.2010.00710.x

Choo, P., Levine, T., & Hatfield, E. (1996). Gender, love schemas, and reactions to romantic break-ups. *Journal of Social Behavior & Personality, 11*, 143–160.

Christopher, F. S. (2001). *To dance the dance: A symbolic interactional exploration of premarital sexuality.* Hillsdale, NJ: Lawrence Erlbaum.

Christopher, F. S., & Cate, R. M. (1985). Premarital sexual pathways and relationship development. *Journal of Social and Personal Relationships, 2*(3), 271–288. doi:10.1177/0265407585023003

Christopher, F. S., & Lloyd, S. A. (2000). Physical and sexual aggression in relationships. In S. Hendrick & C. Hendrick (Eds.), *Close relationships: A sourcebook* (pp. 331–343). Thousand Oaks, CA: Sage.

Christopher, F. S., Madura, M., & Weaver, L. (1998). Premarital sexual aggression: A multivariate analysis of social, relational, and individual correlates. *Journal of Marriage and Family, 60,* 56–69.

Christopher, F. S., & Pflieger, J. C. (2007). Sexual aggression: The dark side of sexuality in relationships. *Annual Review of Sex Research, 18,* 115–142.

Clark, C. L., Shaver, P. R., & Abrahams, M. F. (1999). Strategic behaviors in romantic relationship initiation. *Personality and Social Psychology Bulletin, 25*(6), 707–720. doi:10.1177/0146167299025006006

Clark, R. D., & Hatfield, E. (1989). Gender differences in receptivity to sexual offers. *Journal of Psychology & Human Sexuality, 2,* 39–55. doi:10.1300/J056v02n01_04

Classen, C. C., Palesh, O. G., & Aggarwal, R. (2005). Sexual revictimization: A review of the empirical literature. *Trauma, Violence, & Abuse, 6*(2), 103–129. doi:10.1177/1524838005275087

Clausell, E., & Roisman, G. I. (2009). Outness, big five personality traits, and same-sex relationship quality. *Journal of Social and Personal Relationships, 26,* 211–226.

Cleveland, H. H., Herrera, V. M., & Stuewig, J. (2003). Abusive males and abused females in adolescent relationships: Risk factor similarity and dissimilarity and the role of relationship seriousness. *Journal of Family Violence, 18*(6), 325–339. doi:10.1023/A:1026297515314

Coker, A. L., Davis, K. E., Arias, I., Desai, S., Sanderson, M., Brandt, H. M., & Smith, P. H. (2002). Physical and mental health effects of intimate partner violence for men and women. *American Journal of Preventive Medicine, 23*(4), 260–268. doi:10.1016/S0749-3797(02)00514-7

Collins, P. H. (1990). *Black feminist thought: Knowledge, consciousness, and the politics of empowerment.* Boston: Unwin Hyman.

Conger, R. D., Cui, M., Bryant, C. M., & Elder, G. H. (2000). Competence in early adult romantic relationships: A developmental perspective on family influences. *Journal of Personality and Social Psychology, 79,* 224–237.

Conger, R. D., Cui, M., & Lorenz, F. O. (2011). Intergenerational continuities in economic pressure and couple conflict in romantic relationships. In F. D. Fincham & M. Cui (Eds.), *Romantic relationships in emerging adulthood* (pp. 101–122). New York: Cambridge University Press.

Conley, T. D., Roesch, S. C., Peplau, L. A., & Gold, M. S. (2009). A test of positive illusions versus shared reality models of relationship satisfaction among gay, lesbian, and heterosexual couples. *Journal of Applied Social Psychology, 39,* 1417–1431.

Cook, S. L., Gidycz, C. A., Koss, M. P., & Murphy, M. (2011). Emerging issues in the measurement of rape victimization. *Violence Against Women, 17*(2), 201–218. doi:10.1177/1077801210397741

Coontz, S. (1988). *The origins of private life: A history of American families 1600–1900.* New York: Verso.

Coontz, S. (1992). *The way we never were.* New York: Basic Books.

Coontz, S. (2005). *Marriage, a history: From obedience to intimacy or how love conquered marriage.* New York: Viking.

Coontz, S. (2010). The evolution of American families. In B. Risman (Ed.), *Families as they really are* (pp. 30–47). New York: W. W. Norton.

Cornelius, T. L., Shorey, R. C., & Beebe, S. M. (2010). Self-reported communication variables and dating violence: Using Gottman's marital communication conceptualization. *Journal of Family Violence, 25*(4), 439–448. doi:10.1007/s10896-010-9305-9

Cott, N. F. (2000). *Public vows: A history of marriage and the nation.* Cambridge, MA: Harvard University Press.

Cox, C. L., Wexler, M. O., Rusbult, C. E., & Gaines, S. R. (1997). Prescriptive support and commitment processes in close relationships. *Social Psychology Quarterly, 60*(1), 79–90. doi:10.2307/2787013

Craft, S. M., & Serovich, J. M. (2005). Family-of-origin factors and partner violence in the intimate relationships of gay men who are HIV positive. *Journal of Interpersonal Violence, 20*(7), 777–791. doi:10.1177/0886260505277101

Craft, S. M., Serovich, J. M., McKenry, P. C., & Lim, J. (2008). Stress, attachment style, and partner violence among same-sex couples. *Journal of GLBT Family Studies, 4*, 57–73. doi:10.1080/15504280802084456

Crawford, E., & Wright, M. O. (2007). The impact of childhood psychological maltreatment on interpersonal schemas and subsequent experiences of relationship aggression. *Journal of Emotional Abuse, 7*, 93–116. doi:10.1300/J135v07n02_06

Cunningham, M. R. (1989). Reactions to heterosexual opening gambits: Female selectivity and male responsiveness. *Personality and Social Psychology Bulletin, 15*(1), 27–41. doi:10.1177/0146167289151003

Cunningham, M., & Thornton, A. (2005). The influence of union transitions on white adults' attitudes toward cohabitation. *Journal of Marriage and Family, 67*(3), 710–720. doi:10.1111/j.1741-3737.2005.00164.x

Cupach, W. R., & Metts, S. (1986). Accounts of relational dissolution: A comparison of marital and non-marital relationships. *Communication Monographs, 53*, 311–334.

Cupach, W. R., & Spitzberg, B. H. (2004). *The dark side of relationship pursuit: From attraction to obsession and stalking.* Mahwah, NJ: Lawrence Erlbaum.

Custer, L., Holmberg, D., Blair, K., & Orbuch, T. L. (2008). "So, how did you two meet?" Narratives of relationship initiation. In S. Sprecher, A. Wenzel, & J. Harvey (Eds.), *Handbook of relationship initiation* (pp. 453–470). New York: Psychology Press.

Daigneault, I., Hébert, M., & McDuff, P. (2009). Men's and women's childhood sexual abuse and victimization in adult partner relationships: A study of risk factors. *Child Abuse & Neglect, 33*, 638–647.

Dailey, R. M., Hampel, A. D., & Roberts, J. B. (2010). Relational maintenance in on-again/off-again relationships: An assessment of how relational maintenance, uncertainty, and commitment vary by relationship type and status. *Communication Monographs, 77*, 75–101. doi: 10.1080/03637750903514292

Dailey, R. M., Lee, C. M., & Spitzberg, B. H. (2007). Communicative aggression: Toward a more interactional view of psychological abuse. In B. H. Spitzberg & W. R. Cupach (Eds.), *The dark side of interpersonal communication* (2nd ed., pp. 297–326). Mahwah, NJ: Lawrence Erlbaum Associates.

Dailey, R. M., Rossetto, K. R., Pfiester, A., & Surra, C. A. (2009). A qualitative analysis of on-again/off-again romantic relationships: "It's up and down, all around." *Journal of Social and Personal Relationships, 26*(4), 443–466. doi:10.1177/0265407509351035

Dainton, M., & Aylor, B. (2001). A relational uncertainty analysis of jealousy, trust, and the maintenance of long-distance versus geographically-close relationships. *Communication Quarterly, 49,* 172–188. doi: 10.1080/01463370109385624

Dainton, M., & Stafford, L. (1993). Routine maintenance behaviors: A comparison of relationship type, partner similarity and sex differences. *Journal of Social and Personal Relationships, 10,* 255–271. doi: 10.1177/026540759301000206

Daly, K. J. (2007). *Qualitative methods of family studies and human development.* Thousand Oaks, CA: Sage.

Davis, A. (2006). Reproductive rights. In I. Grewal, & C. Kaplan (Eds.), *An introduction to women's studies* (pp. 103–107). New York: McGraw Hill.

Davis, K. E., Ace, A., & Andra, M. (2000). Stalking perpetrators and psychological maltreatment of partners: Anger-jealousy, attachment insecurity, need for control, and break-up context. *Violence and Victims, 15*(4), 407–425.

Davis. M. S. (1973). *Intimate relations.* New York: Free Press.

DeKeseredy, W. S. (1988). Woman abuse in dating relationships: The relevance of social support theory. *Journal of Family Violence, 3*(1), 1–13. doi:10.1007/BF00994662

DeKeseredy, W. S. (2006). Future directions. *Violence Against Women, 12*(11), 1078–1085. doi:10.1177/1077801206293337

D'Emilio, J. (1999). Capitalism and gay identity. In L. Gross & J. D. Woods (Eds.), *The Columbia reader on lesbians and gay men in media, society, and politics.* New York: Columbia University Press.

D'Emilio, J. (2002). *The world turned: Essays on gay history, politics, and culture.* Durham, NC: Duke University Press.

D'Emilio, J., & Freedman, E. (1988). *Intimate matters: A history of sexuality in America.* New York: Harper & Row.

D'Emilio, J. & Freedman, E. (2002). Family life and the regulation of deviance. In K. M. Phillips & B. Reay (Eds.), *Sexualities in history* (pp. 141–165). New York: Routledge.

Demo, D. H., Allen, K. R., & Fine, M. A. (2000). *Handbook of family diversity.* New York: Oxford University Press.

Demos, J. (1986). *Past, present, and personal: The family and the life course in American history.* New York: Oxford University Press.

Derlega, V. J., Wilson, M., & Chaikin, A. L. (1976). Friendship and disclosure reciprocity. *Journal of Personality and Social Psychology, 34*(4), 578–582. doi:10.1037/0022-3514.34.4.578

Derlega, V. J., Winstead, B. A., & Greene, K. (2008). Self-disclosure and starting a close relationship. In S. Sprecher, A. Wenzel, & J. Harvey (Eds.), *Handbook of relationship initiation* (pp. 153–174). New York: Psychology Press.

Dindia, K. (2003). Definitions and perspectives on relational maintenance communication. In D. Canary & M. Dainton (Eds.), *Maintaining relationships through communication* (pp. 1–28). Mahwah, NJ: Lawrence Erlbaum.

Dindia, K., & Canary, D. J. (1993). Definitions and theoretical perspectives on maintaining relationships. *Journal of Social and Personal Relationships, 10,* 163–173.

Donnellan, M. B., Larsen-Rife, D., & Conger, R. D. (2005). Personality, family history, and competence in early adult romantic relationships. *Journal of Personality and Social Psychology, 88*, 562–576.

Doss, B. D., Rhoades, G. K., Stanley, S. M., & Markman, H. J. (2009). The effect of the transition to parenthood on relationship quality: An 8-year prospective study. *Journal of Personality and Social Psychology, 96*(3), 601–619.

Douglas, W. (1991). Expectations about initial interaction: An examination of the effects of global uncertainty. *Human Communication Research, 17*(3), 355–384. doi:10.1111/j.1468-2958.1991.tb00237.x

Downey, G., & Feldman, S. I. (1996). Implications of rejection sensitivity for intimate relationships. *Journal and Personality and Social Psychology, 70*, 1327–1343.

Downey, G., Freitas, A. L., Michaelis, B., & Khouri, H. (2004). The self-fulfilling prophecy in close relationships: Rejection sensitivity and rejection by romantic partners. In H. T. Reis & C. E. Rusbult (Eds.), *Close relationships: Key readings* (pp. 435–455). Philadelphia, PA: Taylor & Francis.

Draucker, C. B., Martsolf, D., Stephenson, P., Risko, J., Heckman, T., Sheehan, D., & Ferguson, C. (2010). Aggressive events in adolescent dating violence. *Issues in Mental Health Nursing, 31*(9), 599–610. doi:10.3109/01612841003793056

Drigotas, S. M., & Rusbult, C. E. (1992). Should I stay or should I go? A dependence model of breakups. *Journal of Personality and Social Psychology, 62*, 62–87.

Drigotas, S. M., Rusbult, C. E., & Verette, J. (1999). Level of commitment, mutuality of commitment, and couple well-being. *Personal Relationships, 6*, 389–409.

Duck, S. (1985). Social and personal relationships. In M. L. Knapp and G. R. Miller (Eds.), *Handbook of interpersonal communication* (pp. 665–686). Beverly Hills, CA: Sage.

Duck, S. (1988). *Relating to others*. Chicago, IL: Dorsey.

Duck, S., & Sants, H. (1983). On the origin of the specious: Are personal relationships really interpersonal states? *Journal of Social and Clinical Psychology, 1*, 27–41.

Dush, C. M. K., Cohan, C. L., & Amato, P. R. (2003). The relationship between cohabitation and marital quality and stability: Change across cohorts? *Journal of Marriage and Family, 65*(3), 539–549. doi:10.1111/j.1741-3737.2003.00539.x

Dutton, D. G., & Aron, A. P. (1974). Some evidence for heightened sexual attraction under conditions of high anxiety. *Journal of Personality and Social Psychology, 30*(4), 510–517. doi:10.1037/h0037031

Dye, M. L., & Davis, K. E. (2003). Stalking and psychological abuse: Common factors and relationship-specific characteristics. *Violence and Victims, 18*(2), 163–180. doi:10.1891/vivi.2003.18.2.163

Eagly, A. H. (1997). Sex differences in social behavior: Comparing social role theory and evolutionary psychology. *American Psychologist, 52*(12), 1380–1383. doi:10.1037/0003-066X.52.12.1380.b

Eagly, A. H., & Wood, W. (1991). Explaining sex differences in social behavior: A meta-analytic perspective. *Personality and Social Psychology Bulletin Special Issue: Meta-Analysis in Personality and Social Psychology, 17*(3), 306–315. doi:10.1177/0146167291173011

Eaton, D. K., Kann, L., Kinchen, S., Shanklin, S., Ross, J., Hawkins, J., Harris, W. A., et al. (2008). Youth risk behavior surveillance—United States, 2007. *MMWR: Morbidity & Mortality Weekly Report, 57*, 1–130.

Edwards, K. M., Desai, A. D., Gidycz, C. A., & VanWynsberghe, A. (2009). College women's aggression in relationships: The role of childhood and adolescent victimization. *Psychology of Women Quarterly, 33*, 255–265.

eHarmony.com. (2011) *Love is out there, we can help you find it.* Retrieved September 23, 2011, from http://www.eHarmony.com/.

eHarmony.com (2012) From single to soulmate. Retrieved July 15, 2012 from http://www.eharmony.com.

Ehrensaft, M. K., Moffitt, T. E., & Caspi, A. (2004). Clinically abusive relationships in an unselected birth cohort: Men's and women's participation and developmental antecedents. *Journal of Abnormal Psychology, 113*(2), 258–270. doi:10.1037/0021-843X.113.2.258

Ehrmann, W. (1959). *Premarital dating behavior.* Oxford, UK: Henry Holt.

Elder, G. (1985). Perspectives on the life course. In *Life course dynamics* (pp. 23–49). New York: Cornell University Press.

Elizur, Y., & Mintzer, A. (2003). Gay males' intimate relationship quality: The roles of attachment security, gay identity, social support, and income. *Personal Relationships, 10*, 411–435.

Elliott, D. M., Mok, D. S., & Briere, J. (2004). Adult sexual assault: Prevalence, symptomatology, and sex differences in the general population. *Journal of Traumatic Stress, 17*(3), 203–211. doi:10.1023/B:JOTS.0000029263.11104.23

Erbe, B. (1975). Race and socioeconomic segregation. *American Sociological Review, 40*, 801–812.

Etcheverry, P. E., & Agnew, C. R. (2004). Subjective norms and the prediction of romantic relationship state and fate. *Personal Relationships, 11*(4), 409–428. doi:10.1111/j.1475-6811.2004.00090.x

Etcheverry, P. E. & Le, B. (2005). Thinking about commitment: Accessibility of commitment and prediction of relationship persistence, accommodation, and willingness to sacrifice. *Personal Relationships, 12*, 103–124.

Ettlebrick, P. (2007). Since when is marriage a path to liberation? In G. Kirk & M. Okazawa-Rey (Eds.), *Women's lives: Multicultural perspectives* (pp. 305–308). Boston: McGraw-Hill.

Faderman, L. (2000). Romantic friendship. In B. Zimmerman (Ed.), *Lesbian histories and cultures: An encyclopedia* (pp. 648–651). New York: Garland Publishing.

Faludi, S. (1991). *Backlash: The undeclared war against American women.* New York: Crown Publishing Group.

Fargo, J. D. (2009). Pathways to adult sexual revictimization: Direct and indirect behavioral risk factors across the lifespan. *Journal of Interpersonal Violence, 24*(11), 1771–1791. doi:10.1177/0886260508325489

Farris, C., Treat, T. A., Viken, R. J., & McFall, R. M. (2008). Sexual coercion and the misperception of sexual intent. *Clinical Psychology Review, 28*, 48–66.

Feeney, J. A. (2004). Hurt feelings in couple relationships: Towards integrative models of the negative effects of hurtful events. *Journal of Social and Personal Relationships, 21*(4), 487–508. doi:10.1177/0265407504044844

Felicio, D. M., & Sutherland, M. (2001). Beyond the dominant narrative: Intimacy and conflict in lesbian relationships. *Mediation Quarterly, 18*, 363–376. doi:10.1002/crq.3890180405

Felmlee, D. H. (2001). No couple is an island: A social network perspective on dyadic stability. *Social Forces, 79*(4), 1259–1287. doi:10.1353/sof.2001.0039

Felmlee, D., Sprecher, S., & Bassin, E. (1990). The dissolution of intimate relationships: A hazard model. *Social Psychology Quarterly*, 53(1), 13–30. doi:10.2307/ 2786866

Field, T., Diego, M., Pelaez, M., Deeds, O., & Delgado, J. (2009). Breakups distress in university students. *Adolescence*, 44, 705–727.

Fielder, R. L., & Carey, M. P. (2010). Predictors and consequences of sexual "hookups" among college students: A short-term prospective study. *Archives of Sexual Behavior*, 39(5), 1105–1119. doi:10.1007/s10508-008-9448-4

Fields, J., & Casper, L. (2001). America's families and living arrangements. *Current Population Reports*, P-20(537). Washington, DC: U.S. Department of Commerce.

Figley, C. R. (1974). *Tactical self-presentation in a dating decision-making context*. Unpublished doctoral dissertation, Pennsylvania State University, Pennsylvania.

Figley, C. R. (1979). Tactical self-presentation and interpersonal attraction. In M. Cook & G. Wilson (Eds.), *Love and attraction* (pp. 91–99). Oxford: Pergamon Press.

Fincham, F. D., & Beach, S. R. H. (2006). Relationship satisfaction. In D. Perlman & A. Vangelisti (Eds.), *The Cambridge handbook of personal relationships* (pp. 579–594). Cambridge: Cambridge University Press.

Fincham, F. D., & Cui, M. (2011). Emerging adulthood and romantic relationships: An introduction. In F. D. Fincham & M. Cui (Eds.), *Romantic relationships in emerging adulthood* (pp. 3–14). New York: Cambridge University Press.

Fincham, F. D., & Rogge, R. (2010). Understanding relationship quality: Theoretical challenges and new tools for assessment. *Journal of Family Theory and Review*, 2, 227–242.

Fincham, F. D. & Linfield, K. J. (1997). A new look at marital quality: Can spouses feel positive and negative about their marriage? *Journal of Family Psychology*, 11(4), 489–502.

Fine, M. A., Coffelt, T. A., & Olson, L. N. (2008). *Romantic relationship initiation following relationship dissolution*. New York: Psychology Press.

Finkel, E. J. (2008). Intimate partner violence perpetration: Insights from the science of self-regulation. In J. P. Forgas & K. Fitness (Eds.), *Social relationships: Cognitive, affective and motivational processes* (pp. 271–288). New York: Psychology Press.

Finkel, E. J., Eastwick, P. W., Karney, B. R., Reis, H., & Sprecher, S. (2012). Online dating: A critical analysis from the perspective of psychological science. *Psychological Science in the Public Interest*, 13(1), 3–66.

Finkel, E. J., & Eckhardt, C. I. (in press). Intimate partner violence. In J. A. Simpson & L. Campbell (Eds.), *The Oxford handbook of close relationships*. New York: Oxford University Press.

Fisher, B. S., Daigle, L. E., Cullen, F. T., & Turner, M. G. (2003). Acknowledging sexual victimization as rape: Results from a national-level study. *Justice Quarterly*, 20, 535.

Fitzpatrick, J., & Sollie, D. L. (1999). Influence of individual and interpersonal factors on satisfaction and stability in romantic relationships. *Personal Relationships*, 6(3), 337–350. doi:10.1111/j.1475-6811.1999.tb00196.x

Fletcher, G. J. O., Tither, J. M., O'Loughlin, C., Friesen, M., & Overall, N. (2004). Warm and homely or cold and beautiful? Sex differences in trading off traits in mate selection. *Personality and Social Psychology Bulletin*, 30(6), 659–672. doi:10.1177/0146167203262847

Follingstad, D. R. (2007). Rethinking current approaches to psychological abuse: Conceptual and methodological issues. *Aggression and Violent Behavior, 12*(4), 439–458. doi:10.1016/j.avb.2006.07.004

Follingstad, D. R. (2009). The impact of psychological aggression on women's mental health and behavior. *Trauma, Violence, & Abuse, 10,* 271–289.

Follingstad, D., & Edmundson, M. (2010). Is psychological abuse reciprocal in intimate relationships? Data from a national sample of American adults. *Journal of Family Violence, 25,* 495–508.

Foran, H. M., & O'Leary, K. D. (2008). Alcohol and intimate partner violence: A meta-analytic review. *Clinical Psychology Review, 28*(7), 1222–1234. doi:10.1016/j.cpr.2008.05.001

Fortier, M. A., DiLillo, D., Messman-Moore, T. L., Peugh, J., DeNardi, K. A., & Gaffey, K. J. (2009). Severity of child sexual abuse and revictimization: The mediating role of coping and trauma symptoms. *Psychology of Women Quarterly, 33*(3), 308–320. doi:10.1111/j.1471-6402.2009.01503.x

Foshee, V. A., Bauman, K. E., Linder, F., Rice, J., & Wilcher, R. (2007). Typologies of adolescent dating violence: Identifying typologies of adolescent dating violence perpetration. *Journal of Interpersonal Violence, 22*(5), 498–519. doi:10.1177/0886260506298829

Foshee, V. A., Benefield, T. S., Ennett, S. T., Bauman, K. E., & Suchindran, C. (2004). Longitudinal predictors of serious physical and sexual dating violence victimization during adolescence. *Preventive Medicine: An International Journal Devoted to Practice and Theory, 39*(5), 1007–1016. doi:10.1016/j.ypmed.2004.04.014

Foshee, V. A., Reyes, H. L. M., & Ennett, S. T. (2010). Examination of sex and race differences in longitudinal predictors of the initiation of adolescent dating violence perpetration. *Journal of Aggression, Maltreatment & Trauma, 19*(5), 492–516. doi:10.1080/10926771.2010.495032

Fox, K. A., Gover, A. R., & Kaukinen, C. (2009). The effects of low self-control and childhood maltreatment on stalking victimization among men and women. *American Journal of Criminal Justice, 34*(3–4), 181–197. doi:10.1007/s12103-009-9064-4

Fox, K. A., Nobles, M. R., & Fisher, B. S. (2011). Method behind the madness: An examination of stalking measurements. *Aggression and Violent Behavior, 16*(1), 74–84. doi:10.1016/j.avb.2010.12.004

Franklin, D. L. (2010). African Americans and the birth of the modern marriage. In B. Risman (Ed.), *Families as they really are* (pp. 63–74). New York: W. W. Norton.

Frieze, I. H. (2008). Social policy, feminism, and research on violence in close relationships. *Journal of Social Issues, 64*(3), 665–684. doi:10.1111/j.1540-4560.2008.00583.x

Frost, D. M., & Meyer, I. H. (2009). Internalized homophobia and relationship quality among lesbians, gay men, and bisexuals. *Journal of Counseling Psychology, 56,* 97–109.

Furstenberg, F. F., Jr. (1966). Industrialization and the American family: A look backward. *American Sociological Review, 31,* 326–337.

Gadlin, H. (1977). Private lives and public order: A critical view of the history of intimate relations in the United States. In G. Levinger & H. Raush (Eds.), *Close relationships: Perspectives on the meaning of intimacy* (pp. 33–72). Amherst, MA: University of Massachusetts Press.

Gaines, S. O., & Ickes, W. (1997). Perspectives on interracial relationships. In S. Duck (Ed.), *Handbook of personal relationships: Theory, research and interventions* (pp. 197–220). Chichester: Wiley.

Galliher, R. V., & Bentley, C. G. (2010). Links between rejection sensitivity and adolescent romantic relationship functioning: The mediating role of problem-solving behaviors. *Journal of Aggression, Maltreatment & Trauma, 19*(6), 603–623. doi:10.1080/10926771.2010.502066

Gidycz, C. A., Loh, C., Lobo, T., Rich, C., Lynn, S. J., & Pashdag, J. (2007). Reciprocal relationships among alcohol use, risk perception, and sexual victimization: A prospective analysis. *Journal of American College Health, 56*(1), 5–14. doi:10.3200/JACH.56.1.5-14

Giordano, P. C., Soto, D. A., Manning, W. D., & Longmore, M. A. (2010). The characteristics of romantic relationships associated with teen dating violence. *Social Science Research, 39*(6), 863–874. doi:10.1016/j.ssresearch.2010.03.009

Girschick, L. B. (2002). No sugar, no spice: Reflections on research on woman-to-woman sexual violence. *Violence Against Women Special Issue: Women's Use of Violence in Intimate Relationships, Part 2, 8*(12), 1500–1520. doi:10.1177/107780102237967

Glenn, N., & Coleman, M. (1988). *Family relations: A reader.* Belmont, CA: Wadsworth.

Glenn, N., & Marquardt, E. (2001). *Hooking up, hanging out, and hoping for Mr. Right: College women on dating and mating today.* New York: Institute for American Values.

Glick, P. C. (1975). Some recent changes in American families. *Current Population Reports, 52,* 23.

Gold, S. D., Dickstein, B. D., Marx, B. P., & Lexington, J. M. (2009). Psychological outcomes among lesbian sexual assault survivors: An examination of the roles of internalized homophobia and experiential avoidance. *Psychology of Women Quarterly, 33*(1), 54–66. doi:10.1111/j.1471-6402.2008.01474.x

Gold, S. D., Marx, B. P., & Lexington, J. M. (2007). Gay male sexual assault survivors: The relations among internalized homophobia, experiential avoidance, and psychological symptom severity. *Behaviour Research and Therapy, 45*(3), 549–562. doi:10.1016/j.brat.2006.05.006

Goldberg, A. E. & Sayer, A. (2006). Lesbian couples' relationship quality across the transition to parenthood. *Journal of Marriage & the Family, 68*(1), 87–100.

Goode, E. E., & Wagner, B. (1999). Intimate friendships. In L. Gross & J. D. Woods (Eds.), *The Columbia reader on lesbians and gay men in media, society, and politics* (pp. 33–36). New York: Columbia University Press.

Gordon, L. (2002). *The moral property of women: A history of birth control politics in America.* Urbana, IL: University of Illinois Press.

Gordon, R. A. (1996). Impact of ingratiation on judgments and evaluations: A meta-analytic investigation. *Journal of Personality and Social Psychology, 71*(1), 54–70. doi:10.1037/0022-3514.71.1.54

Gormley, B., & Lopez, F. G. (2010). Psychological abuse perpetration in college dating relationships: Contributions of gender, stress, and adult attachment orientations. *Journal of Interpersonal Violence, 25*(2), 204–218. doi:10.1177/0886260509334404

Gottman, J. M. (1993). A theory of marital dissolution and stability. *Journal of Family Psychology, 7*(1), 57–75.

Gottman, J. M., & Levenson, R. W. (1992). Marital processes predictive of later dissolution: Behavior, physiology, and health. *Journal of Personality and Social Psychology, 63*(2), 221–233.

Gottman, J. M., Levenson, R. W., Gross, J., Frederickson, B. L., McCoy, K., Rosenthal, L., Ruef, A., et al. (2003). Correlates of gay and lesbian couples' relationship satisfaction and relationship dissolution. *Journal of Homosexuality, 45,* 23–43.

Greven, P. (1970). *Four generations: Population, land, and family in Colonial Andover, Massachusetts.* Ithaca, NY: Cornell University Press.

Griffen, R. (2005). Courtship contests and the meaning of conflict in the folklore of slaves. *Journal of Southern History, 71,* 769–802.

Gudykunst, W. B. (1985). The influence of cultural similarity, type of relationship, and self-monitoring on uncertainty reduction processes. *Communication Monographs, 52*(3), 203–217. doi:10.1080/03637758509376106

Guerrero, L. K., Andersen, P. A., & Afifi, W. A. (2007). *Close encounters: Communication in relationships,* 2nd ed. Los Angeles, CA: Sage.

Gwartney-Gibbs, P. A., Stockard, J., & Bohmer, S. (1987). Learning courtship aggression: The influence of parents, peers, and personal experiences. *Family Relations: An Interdisciplinary Journal of Applied Family Studies, 36*(3), 276–282. doi:10.2307/583540

Haas, S. M. (2002). Social support as relationship maintenance in gay male couples coping with HIV or AIDS. *Journal of Social and Personal Relationships Special Issue: Personal and Social Relationships of Individuals Living with HIV and/or AIDS, 19*(1), 87–112. doi:10.1177/0265407502191005

Haas, S., & Stafford, L. (1998). An initial examination of maintenance behaviors in gay and lesbian couples. *Journal of Social and Personal Relationships, 14,* 846–855.

Hall, J. H., & Fincham, F. D. (2006). Relationship dissolution following infidelity: The roles of attributions and forgiveness. *Journal of Social and Clinical Psychology, 25*(5), 508–522. doi:10.1521/jscp.2006.25.5.508

Hannon, P., Rusbult, C., Finkel, E., & Kamashiro, M. (2010). In the wake of betrayal: Amends, forgiveness, and the resolution of betrayal. *Personal Relationships, 17,* 253–278.

Hare-Mustin, R. T. (1994). Discourses in the mirrored room: A postmodern analysis of therapy. *Family Process, 33*(1), 19–35. doi:10.1111/j.1545-5300.1994.00019.x

Harkless, L. E., & Fowers, B. J. (2005). Similarities and differences in relational boundaries among heterosexuals, gay men, and lesbians. *Psychology of Women Quarterly, 29,* 167–176.

Harvey, J. H., & Hansen, A. M. (2002). Close relationship loss. In C. Hendrick & S. S. Hendrick (Eds.), *Close relationships: A sourcebook* (pp. 359–370). Thousand Oaks, CA: Sage.

Hatfield, E., Cacioppo, J. T., & Rapson, R. L. (1994). *Emotional contagion.* New York: Cambridge University Press.

Hatfield, E. & Sprecher, S. (1986). Measuring passionate love in intimate relations. *Journal of Adolescence, 9,* 383–410.

Hattery, A. (2009). *Intimate partner violence.* Lanham, MD: Rowman & Littlefield.

Hazan, C., & Shaver, P. (1987). Romantic love conceptualized as an attachment process. *Journal of Personality and Social Psychology, 52*(3), 511–524. doi:10.1037/0022-3514.52.3.511

Heaton, T. B. (2002). Factors contributing to increasing marital stability in the US. *Journal of Family Issues, 23*(3), 392–409. doi:10.1177/0192513X02023003004

Heidt, J. M., Marx, B. P., & Gold, S. D. (2005). Sexual revictimization among sexual minorities: A preliminary study. *Journal of Traumatic Stress, 18*(5), 533–540. doi:10.1002/jts.20061

Heino, R. D., Ellison, N. B., & Gibbs, J. L. (2010). Relationshopping: Investigating the market metaphor in online dating. *Journal of Social and Personal Relationships, 27*(4), 427–447. doi:10.1177/0265407510361614

Helgeson, V. S. (1994). The effects of self-beliefs and relationship beliefs on adjustment to a relationship stressor. *Personal Relationships, 1*(3), 241–258. doi:10.1111/j.1475–6811.1994.tb00064.x

Hendrick, S. S. (1981). Self-disclosure and marital satisfaction. *Journal of Personality and Social Psychology, 40*, 1150–1159.

Hendrick, S. S., & Hendrick, C. (1995). Gender differences and similarities in sex and love. *Personal Relationships, 2*(1), 55–65. doi:10.1111/j.1475-6811.1995.tb00077.x

Hendrick, S. S., Hendrick, C., & Adler, N. L. (1988). Romantic relationships: Love, satisfaction, and staying together. *Journal of Personality and Social Psychology, 54*(6), 980–988. doi:10.1037/0022-3514.54.6.980

Henton, J. M., Cate, R. M., Koval, J. E., Lloyd, S. A. & Christopher, F. S. (1983). Romance and violence in dating relationships. *Journal of Family Issues, 3*, 467–482.

Hettrich, E. L., & O'Leary, K. D. (2007). Females' reasons for their physical aggression in dating relationships. *Journal of Interpersonal Violence, 22*, 1131–1143.

Hill, C. T., Rubin, Z., & Peplau, L. A. (1976). Breakups before marriage: The end of 103 affairs. *Journal of Social Issues, 32*, 147–168.

Hinde, R. (1987). *Individuals, relationships and culture: Links between ethology and the social sciences.* Cambridge, UK: Cambridge University Press.

Hinde, R. (1996). Describing relationships. In A. E. Augagen & M. von Salisch (Eds.), *The diversity of human relationships* (pp. 7–35). Cambridge, UK: Cambridge University Press.

Holt-Lunstad, J., Smith, T. B., & Layton, J. B. (2010). Social relationships and mortality risk: A meta-analytic review. *PLoS Medicine, 7*(7). doi:10.1371/journal.pmed.1000316

Holtzworth-Munroe, A. (2005). Male versus female intimate partner violence: Putting controversial findings into context. *Journal of Marriage and Family, 67*(5), 1120–1125. doi:10.1111/j.1741-3737.2005.00203.x

Homans, G. C. (1961). *Social behavior: Its elementary forms.* New York: Harcourt, Brace & World.

Horne, S. G., & Biss, W. J. (2009). Equality discrepancy between women in same-sex relationships: The mediating role of attachment in relationship satisfaction. *Sex Roles, 60*, 721–730.

Huston, T. L. (2000). The social ecology of marriage and other intimate unions. *Journal of Marriage & the Family, 62*(2), 298–319. doi:10.1111/j.1741-3737.2000.00298.x

Huston, T. L., & Levinger, G. (1978). Interpersonal attraction and relationships. *Annual Review of Psychology, 29,* 115–156. doi:10.1146/annurev.ps.29.020178. 000555

Ickes, W., Dugosh, J. W., Simpson, J. A., & Wilson, C. L. (2003). Suspicious minds: The motive to acquire relationship-threatening information. *Personal Relationships, 10*(2), 131–148. doi:10.1111/1475-6811.00042

Impett, E. A., & Peplau, L. A. (2003). Sexual compliance: Gender, motivational, and relationship perspectives. *Journal of Sex Research Special Issue: Gender and Sexuality, 40*(1), 87–100. doi:10.1080/00224490309552169

Innes, S. A. (2000). Smashes, crushes, spoons. In B. Zimmerman (Ed.), *Lesbian histories and cultures: An encyclopedia* (pp. 707–708). New York: Garland Publishing.

James, S. D. (2011). *Gay Americans make up 4 percent of population.* Retrieved from http://abcnews.go.com/Health/williams-institute-report-reveals-million-gay-bisexual-transgender/story?id=13320565#.UAMaOPV5H1V.

Jensen, J. (1994). Native American women and agriculture: A Seneca case study. In V. L. Ruiz & E. C. DuBois (Eds.), *Unequal sisters: A multicultural reader in U.S. women's history* (pp. 70–84). New York: Routledge.

Johnson, A. (2005). *Unraveling the gender knot.* Thousand Oaks, CA: Pine Forge Press/Sage Publications Co.

Johnson, D. K. (2003). *The lavender scare: The cold war persecution of gays and lesbians in the federal government.* Chicago, IL: University of Chicago Press.

Johnson, M. P. (1982). The social and cognitive features of the dissolution of commitment to relationships. In S. Duck (Ed.), *Personal relationships: Dissolving personal relationships* (pp. 51–73). New York: Academic Press.

Johnson, M. P. (1991). Commitment to personal relationships. In W. H. Jones & D. W. Perlman (Eds.), *Advances in personal relationships* (Vol. 3, pp. 117–143). London: Jessica Kingsley.

Johnson, M. P. (1999). Personal, moral, and structural commitment to relationships: Experiences of choice and constraint. In J. M. Adams & W. H. Jones (Eds.), *Handbook of interpersonal commitment and relationship stability* (pp. 73–87). New York: Plenum Press.

Johnson, M. P. (2008). *A typology of domestic violence: Intimate terrorism, violent resistance, and situational couple violence.* Boston, MA: Northeastern University Press.

Johnson, M. P., Caughlin, J. P., & Huston, T. L. (1999). The tripartite nature of marital commitment: Personal, moral, and structural reasons to stay married. *Journal of Marriage & the Family, 61*(1), 160–177. doi:10.2307/353891

Jose, A., O'Leary, K. D., & Moyer, A. (2010). Does premarital cohabitation predict subsequent marital stability and marital quality? A meta-analysis. *Journal of Marriage and Family, 72*(1), 105–116. doi:10.1111/j.1741-3737.2009.00686.x

Joyner, K. (2009). Justice and the fate of married and cohabiting couples. *Social Psychology Quarterly, 72*(1), 61–76. doi:10.1177/019027250907200106

Kalmijn, M., & Flap, H. (2001). Assortative meeting and mating: Unintended consequences of organized settings for partner choices. *Social Forces, 79*(4), 1289–1312. doi:10.1353/sof.2001.0044

Kanin, E. J. (1957). Male aggression in dating-courtship relations. *American Journal of Sociology, 63,* 197–204. doi:10.1086/222177

Karney, B. R., & Bradbury, T. N. (1997). Neuroticism, marital interaction, and the trajectory of marital satisfaction. *Journal of Personality and Social Psychology, 72*, 1075–1092.

Kass, L. (1997). The end of courtship. *Public Interest, 126*, 39–63.

Kasturirangan, A., Krishnan, S., & Riger, S. (2004). The impact of culture and minority status on women's experience of domestic violence. *Trauma, Violence, & Abuse, 5*(4), 318–332. doi:10.1177/1524838004269487

Keenan-Miller, D., Hammen, C., & Brennan, P. (2007). Adolescent psychosocial risk factors for severe intimate partner violence in young adulthood. *Journal of Consulting and Clinical Psychology, 75*(3), 456–463. doi:10.1037/0022-006X.75.3.456

Keleher, J., Wei, M., & Liao, K. Y. H. (2010). Attachment, positive feelings about being a lesbian, perceived general support, and well-being. *Journal of Social and Clinical Psychology, 29*, 847–873. doi:10.1521/jscp.2010.29.8.847

Kelas, J. K., Bean, D., Cunningham, C., & Cheng, K. Y. (2008). The ex-files: Trajectories, turning points, and adjustment in the development of post-dissolutional relationships. *Journal of Social and Personal Relationships, 25*(1), 23–50. doi:10.1177/0265407507086804

Kelley, H. (1979). *Personal relationships: Their structures and processes*. Hillsdale, NJ: Lawrence Erlbaum.

Kelley, H. H., Berscheid, E., Christensen, A., Harvey, J. H., Huston, T. L., Levinger, G., McClintock, E., Peplau, L. A., & Peterson, D. R. (1983). *Close relationships*. New York: W. H. Freeman.

Kelley, H. H. & Thibaut, J. (1978) *Interpersonal relations: A theory of interdependence*. New York: Wiley.

Kelley, R. K. (1969). *Courtship, marriage and the family*. New York: Harcourt Brace.

Kelly, E. L., & Conley, J. J. (1987). Personality and compatibility: A prospective analysis of marital stability and marital satisfaction. *Journal of Personality and Social Psychology, 52*, 27–40.

Kelly, V. A. (2004). Psychological abuse of women: A review of the literature. *Family Journal, 12*(4), 383–388. doi:10.1177/1066480704267234

Kelly, V., Warner, K., Trahan, C., & Miscavage, K. (2009). The relationship among self-report and measured report of psychological abuse, and depression for a sample of women involved in intimate relationships with male partners. *Family Journal, 17*(1), 51–57. doi:10.1177/1066480708328476

Kennedy, E. L., & Davis, M. D. (1993). *Boots of leather, slippers of gold: The history of a lesbian community*. New York: Routledge.

Kennedy, S., & Bumpass, L. (2008). Cohabitation and children's living arrangements: New estimates from the United States. *Demographic Research, 19*, 1663–1692.

Kenny, D. A., Kashy, D. A., & Cook, W. L. (2006). *Dyadic data analysis*. New York: Guilford Press.

Kerckhoff, A. C. (1974). The social context of interpersonal attraction. In T. L. Huston (Ed.), *Foundations of interpersonal attraction* (pp. 61–78). New York: Academic Press.

Kerckhoff, A. C., & Davis, K. E. (1962). Value consensus and need complementarity in mate selection. *American Sociological Review, 27*, 295–303. doi:10.2307/2089791

Kidd, V. (1975). Happily ever after and other relationship styles: Advice on interpersonal relations in popular magazines. *Quarterly Journal of Speech, 61*, 31–39.

Kiecolt, K. J., & Fossett, M. (1997). The effects of mate availability on marriage among Black Americans: A contextual analysis. In R. Taylor, J. Jackson, & L. Chatters (Eds.), *Family life in Black America* (pp. 63–78). Thousand Oaks, CA: Sage.

Kiernan, K. (2004). Redrawing the boundaries of marriage. *Journal of Marriage and Family, 66*(4), 980–987. doi:10.1111/j.0022-2445.2004.00068.x

Kilpatrick, D. G. (2004). What is violence against women? Defining and measuring the problem. *Journal of Interpersonal Violence Special Issue: Toward a National Research Agenda on Violence Against Women—Part 1, 19*(11), 1209–1234. doi:10.1177/0886260504269679

Kimmel, M. S. (2002). "Gender symmetry" in domestic violence: A substantive and methodological research review. *Violence Against Women, 8,* 1332–1363.

Kirkpatrick, L. A., & Hazan, C. (1994). Attachment styles and close relationships: A four-year prospective study. *Personal Relationships, 1*(2), 123–142. doi:10.1111/j.1475-6811.1994.tb00058.x

Kline, G., Pleasant, N., Whitton, S., & Markman, H. (2006). Understanding couple conflict. In D. Perlman & A. Vangelisti (Eds.), *Handbook of personal relationships* (pp. 445–462). New York: Cambridge University Press.

Kline, G. H., Stanley, S. M., Markman, H. J., Olmos-Gallo, P. A., St. Peters, M., Whitton, S. W., & Prado, L. M. (2004). Timing is everything: Pre-engagement cohabitation and increased risk for poor marital outcomes. *Journal of Family Psychology, 18*(2), 311–318. doi:10.1037/0893-3200.18.2.311

Knapp, Mark. (1984). *Interpersonal communication and human relationships*. Boston: Allyn and Bacon.

Knobloch, L. K. (2007). Perceptions of turmoil within courtship: Associations with intimacy, relational uncertainty, and interference from partners. *Journal of Social and Personal Relationships, 24,* 363–384.

Knobloch, L. K., & Donovan-Kicken, E. (2006). Perceived involvement of network members in courtships: A test of the relational turbulence model. *Personal Relationships, 13,* 281–302.

Knobloch, L., & Miller, L. (2008). Uncertainty and relationship initiation. In S. Sprecher, A. Wenzel, & J. Harvey (Eds.), *Handbook of relationship initiation* (pp. 121–134). New York: Psychology Press.

Knobloch, L. K., & Solomon, D. H. (2002). Information seeking beyond initial interaction: Negotiating relational uncertainty within close relationships. *Human Communication Research, 28,* 243–257.

Knobloch, L., & Solomon, D. H. (2005). Relational uncertainty and relational information processing: Questions without answers? *Communication Research, 32,* 349–388.

Koenig Kellas, J., Bean, D., Cunningham, C., & Cheng, K. Y. (2008). The ex-files: Trajectories, turning points, and the adjustment in the development of post-dissolution relationships. *Journal of Social and Personal Relationships, 25,* 23–50.

Kolivas, E. D., & Gross, A. M. (2007). Assessing sexual aggression: Addressing the gap between rape victimization and perpetration prevalence rates. *Aggression and Violent Behavior, 12*(3), 315–328. doi:10.1016/j.avb.2006.10.002

Koller, M. R. (1951). Some changes in courtship behavior in three generations of Ohio women. *American Sociological Review, 16,* 366–370.

Koss, M.P. (1989). Hidden rape: Sexual aggression and victimization in a national sample of students in higher education. In M. A. Pirog-Good & J. E. Stets (Eds.), *Violence in dating relationships: Emerging social issues* (pp. 145–168). New York: Praeger.

Koss, M. P., Abbey, A., Campbell, R., Cook, S., Norris, J., Testa, M., & White, J. (2007). Revising the SES: A collaborative process to improve assessment of sexual aggression and victimization. *Psychology of Women Quarterly, 31*(4), 357–370. doi:10.1111/j.1471-6402.2007.00385.x

Koss, M. P., Gidycz, C. A., & Wisniewski, N. (1987). The scope of rape: Incidence and prevalence of sexual aggression and victimization in a national sample of higher education students. *Journal of Consulting and Clinical Psychology, 55*(2), 162–170. doi:10.1037/0022-006X.55.2.162

Koss, M. P., & Oros, C. J. (1982). Sexual Experiences Survey: A research instrument investigating sexual aggression and victimization. *Journal of Consulting and Clinical Psychology, 50*(3), 455–457. doi:10.1037/0022-006X.50.3.455

Kraaij, V., Arensman, E., Garnefski, N., & Kremers, I. (2007). The role of cognitive coping in female victims of stalking. *Journal of Interpersonal Violence, 22*(12), 1603–1612. doi:10.1177/0886260507306499

Kreider, R. (2005). Number, timing, and duration of marriages and divorces: 2001, table 3. *Current Population Reports, US Census Bureau*, 70–97.

Kulkin, H. S., Williams, J., Borne, H. F., de la Bretonne, D., & Laurendine, J. (2007). A review of research on violence in same-gender couples: A resource for clinicians. *Journal of Homosexuality, 53*, 71–87.

Kunda, Z. (1990). The case for motivated reasoning. *Psychological Bulletin, 108*(3), 480–498. doi:10.1037/0033-2909.108.3.480

Kurdek, L. A. (1991). Sexuality in homosexual and heterosexual couples. In K. McKinney & S. Sprecher (Eds.), *Sexuality in close relationships* (pp. 177–191). Hillsdale, NJ: Erlbaum.

Kurdek, L. A. (1995). Assessing multiple determinants of relationship commitment in cohabiting gay, cohabiting lesbian, dating heterosexual, and married heterosexual couples. *Family Relations, 44*, 261–266.

Kurdek, L. A. (1998). Relationship outcomes and their predictors: Longitudinal evidence from heterosexual married, gay cohabiting, and lesbian cohabiting couples. *Journal of Marriage and Family, 60*(3), 553–568. doi:10.2307/353528

Kurdek, L. A. (2001). Differences between heterosexual-nonparent couples and gay, lesbian, and heterosexual-parent couples. *Journal of Family Issues, 22*, 727–754.

Kurdek, L. A. (2004). Are gay and lesbian courting couples *really* different from heterosexual married couples? *Journal of Marriage and Family, 66*, 880–900.

Kurdek, L. A. (2008a). A general model of relationship commitment: Evidence from same-sex partners. *Personal Relationships, 15*, 391–405.

Kurdek, L. A. (2008b). Change in relationship quality for partners from lesbian, gay male, and heterosexual couples. *Journal of Family Psychology, 22*, 701–711.

Kurdek, L. A. (2009). Assessing the health of a dyadic relationship in heterosexual and same-sex partners. *Personal Relationships, 16*, 117–127.

Kurdek, L. A., & Schmitt, J. P. (1987). Partner homogamy in married, heterosexual cohabiting, gay, and lesbian couples. *Journal of Sex Research, 23*(2), 212–232.

Lafontaine, M. F., & Lussier, Y. (2005). Does anger towards the partner mediate and moderate the link between romantic attachment and intimate violence? *Journal of Family Violence, 20*, 349–361.

Laner, M. R. (1983). Courtship abuse and aggression: Contextual aspects. *Sociological Spectrum*, 3, 69–83.

Laner, M. R., & Thompson, J. (1982). Abuse and aggression in courting couples. *Deviant Behavior*, 3, 229–244.

Langhinrichsen-Rohling, J., Palarea, R. E., Cohen, J., & Rohling, M. L. (2002). Breaking up is hard to do: Unwanted pursuit behaviors following the dissolution of a romantic relationship. In K. E. Davis, I. H. Frieze, & R. D. Maiuro (Eds.), *Stalking: Perspectives on victims and perpetrator* (pp. 212–236). New York: Springer Publishing Co.

Lannutti, P. J. & Cameron, K. A. (2002). Beyond the break-up: Heterosexual and homosexual post-dissolutional relationships. *Communication Quarterly*, 50, 153–170. doi:10.1080/01463370209385654

Larkin, K. T., Frazer, N. L., & Wheat, A. L. (2011). Responses to interpersonal conflict among young adults: Influence of family of origin. *Personal Relationships*, 18, 657–667.

LaRossa, R. (2005). Grounded theory methods and qualitative family research. *Journal of Marriage and Family Special Issue: Theoretical and Methodological Issues in Studying Families*, 67(4), 837–857. doi:10.1111/j.1741-3737.2005.00179.x

Laumann, E., Gagnon, J. H., Michael, R. T., & Michaels, S. (1994). *The social organization of sexuality: Sexual practices in the United States*. Chicago, IL: University of Chicago Press.

Le, B., & Agnew, C. R. (2003). Commitment and its theorized determinants: A meta-analysis of the investment model. *Personal Relationships*, 10(1), 37–57. doi:10.1111/1475-6811.00035

Le, B., Dove, N. L., Agnew, C. R., Korn, M. S., & Mutso, A. A. (2010). Predicting nonmarital romantic relationship dissolution: A meta-analytic synthesis. *Personal Relationships*, 17, 377–390. doi: 10.1111/j.1475-6811.2010.01285.x

Lee, J. (1973). *The colors of love: An exploration of the ways of loving*. Don Mills, Ontario: New Press.

Lefkowitz, E. S., Gillen, M. M., & Vasilenko, S. A. (2011). Putting the romance back into sex: Sexuality and romantic relationships in emerging adulthood. In F. D. Fincham & M. Cui (Eds.). *Romantic Relationships in Emerging Adulthood* (pp. 213–233). Cambridge, UK: Cambridge University Press.

Lehmiller, J. J., & Agnew, C. R. (2007). Perceived marginalization and the prediction of romantic relationship stability. *Journal of Marriage and Family*, 69(4), 1036–1049. doi:10.1111/j.1741-3737.2007.00429.x

Leonard, K. A. (2011). Containing "perversion": African Americans and same-sex desire in cold war Los Angeles. *Journal of the History of Sexuality*, 20(3), 545–567.

Lewis, R., & Spanier, G. (1979). Theorizing about the quality and stability of marriage. In W. Burr, R. Hill, F. Nye, & I. Reiss (Eds.), *Contemporary theories about the family* (Vol. 2, pp. 268–294). New York: The Free Press.

Lewis, S. F., & Fremouw, W. (2001). Dating violence: A critical review of the literature. *Clinical Psychology Review*, 21(1), 105–127. doi:10.1016/S0272-7358(99)00042-2

Li, N. P., & Kenrick, D. T. (2006). Sex similarities and differences in preferences for short-term mates: What, whether, and why. *Journal of Personality and Social Psychology*, 90(3), 468–489. doi:10.1037/0022-3514.90.3.468

Lichter, D. T., & Qian, Z. (2008). Serial cohabitation and the marital life course. *Journal of Marriage and Family, 70*(4), 861–878.

Lichter, D. T., Qian, Z., & Mellott, M. (2006). Marriage or dissolution? Union transitions among poor cohabiting women. *Demography, 43*, 223–240.

Lichter, D. T., Turner, R. N., & Sassler, S. (2010). National estimates of the rise in serial cohabitation. *Social Science Research, 39*(5), 754–765. doi:10.1016/j. ssresearch.2009.11.002

Light, D., & Monk-Turner, E. (2009). Circumstances surrounding male sexual assault and rape: Findings from the national violence against women survey. *Journal of Interpersonal Violence, 24*(11), 1849–1858. doi:10.1177/0886260508325488

Little, A. C., Penton-Voak, I. S., Burt, M., & Perrett, D. I. (2002). Evolution and individual differences in the perception of attractiveness: How cyclic hormonal changes and self-perceived attractiveness influence female preferences for male faces. In G. Rhodes & L. A. Zebrowitz (Eds.), *Facial attractiveness: Evolutionary, cognitive, and social perspectiveness* (pp. 59–90). Westport, CT: Ablex.

Littleton, H. L., Rhatigan, D. L., & Axsom, D. (2007). Unacknowledged rape: How much do we know about the hidden rape victim? *Journal of Aggression, Maltreatment & Trauma, 14*, 57–74.

Lloyd, S. A. (1987). Conflict in premarital relationships: Differential perceptions of males and females. *Family Relations, 36*, 290–294.

Lloyd, S. A. (2009). Feminist perspectives on relationships. In H. T. Reis & S. Sprecher (Eds.), *Encyclopedia of human relationships* (pp. 579–682). Thousand Oaks, CA: Sage.

Lloyd, S. A. (2012). Family violence. In G. W. Peterson & K. R. Bush (Eds.), *Handbook of marriage and the family* (pp. 449–485). New York: Springer.

Lloyd, S. A., & Cate, R. M. (1985). Attributions associated with significant turning points in premarital relationship development and dissolution. *Journal of Social and Personal Relationships, 2*(4), 419–436. doi:10.1177/0265407585024003

Lloyd, S. A., & Emery, B. C. (2000). *The dark side of courtship: Physical and sexual aggression.* Thousand Oaks, CA: Sage.

Lloyd, S. A., Emery, B. C., & Klatt, S. (2009). Discovering women's agency in response to intimate partner violence. In S. A. Lloyd, A. Few, & K. A. Allen (Eds.), *Handbook of feminist family studies* (pp. 264–278). Thousand Oaks, CA: Sage.

Locke, H. J. & Wallace, K. M. (1959) Short marital adjustment and prediction tests: Their reliability and validity. *Marriage and Family Living, 21*, 251–255.

Logan, T. K., Cole, J., Shannon, L., & Walker, R. (2006). *Partner stalking: How women respond, cope and survive.* New York: Springer.

Logan, T. K., & Walker, R. (2009). Partner stalking: Psychological dominance or "business as usual"? *Trauma, Violence, & Abuse Special Issue: Violence and Women's Mental Health: The Pain Unequalled: A Two-Part Special Issue, 10*(3), 247–270. doi:10.1177/1524838009334461

Lorber, J. (1994). *Paradoxes of gender.* New Haven, CT: Yale University Press.

Loyer-Carlson, V. L. (1990). *Causal attributions and the dissolution of casual-dating relationships* (ProQuest Information & Learning). *Dissertation Abstracts International, 51*, 1547–1548 (electronic and print) 1991-51903-001

Lundberg, F., & Farnham, M. (1947). *Modern woman: The lost sex.* New York: Harper and Bros.

Lutz-Zois, C. J., Bradley, A. C., Mihalik, J. L., & Moorman-Eavers, E. R. (2006). Perceived similarity and relationship success among dating couples: An idiographic approach. *Journal of Social and Personal Relationships*, *23*(6), 865–880. doi:10.1177/0265407506068267

Lynd, R., & Lynd, H. (1937). *Middletown in transition: A study in cultural conflicts*. New York: Harcourt, Brace & Co.

Lystra, K. (1989). *Searching the heart: Men, women and romantic love in nineteenth century America*. New York: Oxford University Press.

Maas, C. D., Fleming, C. B., Herrenkohl, T. I., & Catalano, R. F. (2010). Childhood predictors of teen dating violence victimization. *Violence & Victims*, *25*, 131–149.

Mackey, R. A., Diemer, M. A., & O'Brien, B. A. (2004). Relational factors in understanding satisfaction in the lasting relationships of same-sex and heterosexual couples. *Journal of Homosexuality*, *47*, 111–136. doi:10.1300/J082v47n01_07

Macklin, E. (1972). Heterosexual cohabitation among unmarried students. *Family Coordinator*, *21*, 463–472.

Madden, M., & Lenhart, A. (2006). *Online dating. Washington, DC: Pew internet and American life project*. Retrieved March 5, 2006, from http://www.pewinternet.org/Reports/2006/Online-Dating.aspx.

Makepeace, J. M. (1981). Courtship violence among college students. *Family Relations*, *30*, 97–102.

Manning, W. D., & Smock, P. J. (2002). First comes cohabitation then comes marriage? A research note. *Journal of Family Issues*, *23*(8), 1065–1087. doi:10.1177/019251302237303

Manning, W. D., & Smock, P. J. (2005). Measuring and modeling cohabitation: New perspectives from qualitative data. *Journal of Marriage and Family Special Issue: Theoretical and Methodological Issues in Studying Families*, *67*(4), 989–1002. doi:10.1111/j.1741-3737.2005.00189.x

Margolis, M. (1984). *Mothers and such: Views of American women and why they changed*. Los Angeles, CA: University of California Press.

Martz, J. M., Verette, J., Arriaga, X. B., Slovik, L. F., Cox, C. L., & Rusbult, C. E. (1998). Positive illusion in close relationships. *Personal Relationships*, *5*(2), 159–181. doi:10.1111/j.1475-6811.1998.tb00165.x

Match.com (2012). Site info. Retrieved September 23, 2012, from www.match.com.

Matte, M., & Lafontaine, M. (2011). Validation of a measure of psychological aggression in same-sex couples: Descriptive data on perpetration and victimization and their association with physical violence. *Journal of GLBT Family Studies*, *7*(3), 226–244. doi:10.1080/1550428X.2011.564944

McAdoo, H. P. (1981). *Black families*. Beverly Hills, CA: Sage.

McCall, L. (2005). The complexity of intersectionality. *Signs*, *30*, 1771–1800.

McCary, J. (1973). *Human sexuality: A brief edition*. New York: Van Nostrand.

McClennen, J. C. (2005). Domestic violence between same-gender partners: Recent findings and future research. *Journal of Interpersonal Violence*, *20*(2), 149–154. doi:10.1177/0886260504268762

McDonell, J., Ott, J., & Mitchell, M. (2010). Predicting dating violence victimization and perpetration among middle and high school students in a rural southern community. *Children and Youth Services Review*, *32*(10), 1458–1463. doi:10.1016/j.childyouth.2010.07.001

McEwan, T., Mullen, P. E., & Purcell, R. (2007). Identifying risk factors in stalking: A review of current research. *International Journal of Law and Psychiatry, 30*(1), 1–9. doi:10.1016/j.ijlp.2006.03.005

McNamara, R. P., Tempenis, M., & Walton, B. (1999). *Crossing the line: Interracial couples in the south*. Westport, CT: Greenwood.

McWhirter, D. P., & Mattison, A. M. (1984). *The male couple: How relationships develop*. Englewood Cliffs, NJ: Prentice-Hall.

Mechanic, M. (2002). Stalking victimization: Clinical implications for assessment and intervention. In I. H. Frieze, K. E. Davis., & R. D. Maiuro (Eds.), *Stalking and obsessive behavior: Perspectives on victims and perpetrators* (pp. 31–61). New York: Springer.

Messinger, A. M. (2011). Invisible victims: Same-sex IPV in the national violence against women survey. *Journal of Interpersonal Violence, 26*, 2228–2243.

Messman-Moore, T. L., Ward, R. M., & Brown, A. L. (2009). Substance use and PTSD symptoms impact the likelihood of rape and revictimization in college women. *Journal of Interpersonal Violence Special Section: Research Methodology, 24*(3), 499–521. doi:10.1177/0886260508317199

Metts, S., & Cupach, W. R. (2007). Responses to relational transgressions: Hurt, anger and sometimes forgiveness. *The dark side of interpersonal communication*, 2nd ed., pp. 243–274.

Miga, E. M., Hare, A., Allen, J. P., & Manning, N. (2010). The relation of insecure attachment states of mind and romantic attachment styles to adolescent aggression in romantic relationships. *Attachment & Human Development, 12*, 463–481.

Mikulincer, M., Florian, V., Cowan, P. A., & Cowan, C. P. (2002). Attachment security in couple relationships: A systemic model and its implications for family dynamics. *Family Process, 41*(3), 405–434.

Mintz, S., & Kellogg, S. (1988). *Domestic revolutions: A social history of American family life*. New York: Free Press.

Modell, J. (1983). Dating becomes a way of American youth. In D. Levine, L. Moch, J. Tilly, J. Modell, & E. Pleck (Eds.), *Essays on the family and historical change* (pp. 169–175). College Station, TX: Texas A & M University Press.

Modell, J. (1989). *Into one's own: From youth to adulthood in the United States: 1920–1975*. Berkeley, CA: University of California Press.

Mohr, J. J. (1999). Same-sex romantic attachment. In J. Cassidy & P. R. Shaver (Eds.), *Handbook of attachment: Theory, research, and clinical applications* (pp. 378–394). New York: Guilford.

Mohr, J. J., & Daly, C. A. (2008). Sexual minority stress and changes in relationship quality in same-sex couples. *Journal of Social and Personal Relationships, 25*, 989–1007. doi:10.1177/0265407508100311

Moore, T. M., Stuart, G. L., Meehan, J. C., Rhatigan, D., Hellmuth, J. C., & Keen, S. M. (2008). Drug abuse and aggression between intimate partners: A meta-analytic review. *Clinical Psychology Review, 28*(2), 247–274. doi:10.1016/j.cpr.2007.05.003

Mosher, W. D., Chandra, A., & Jones, J. (2005). Sexual behavior and selected health measures: Men and women 15–44 years of age, United States, 2005. *Advance data from vital and health statistics, no. 362*. Hyattsville, MD: National Center for Health Statistics.

Muehlenhard, C. L. (1988). Misinterpreted dating behaviors and the risk of date rape. *Journal of Social and Clinical Psychology*, 6(1), 20–37.

Mullaney, J. L. (2007). Telling it like a man: Masculinities and battering men's accounts of their violence. *Men and Masculinities*, 10(2), 222–247. doi:10.1177/1097184X06287758

Mullen, P. E., Pathé, M., & Purcell, R. (2009). *Stalkers and their victims*, 2nd ed. New York: Cambridge University Press.

Murnen, S. K., & Kohlman, M. H. (2007). Athletic participation, fraternity membership, and sexual aggression among college men: A meta-analytic review. *Sex Roles*, 57(1–2), 145–157. doi:10.1007/s11199-007-9225-1

Murray, S. L., & Holmes, J. G. (1997). A leap of faith? Positive illusions in romantic relationships. *Personality and Social Psychology Bulletin*, 23(6), 586–604. doi:10.1177/0146167297236003

Murray, S. L., Holmes, J. G., & Griffin, D. W. (1996). The self-fulfilling nature of positive illusions in romantic relationships: Love is not blind, but prescient. *Journal of Personality and Social Psychology*, 71(6), 1155–1180. doi:10.1037/0022-3514.71.6.1155

Murray, S. L., Holmes, J. G., & Griffin, D. W. (2000). Self-esteem and the quest for felt security: How perceived regard regulates attachment processes. *Journal of Personality and Social Psychology*, 78(3), 478–498.

Murray, C. E., Mobley, K. A., Buford, A. P., & Seaman-DeJohn, M. M. (2006). Same-sex intimate partner violence: Dynamics, social context, and counseling implications. *Journal of LGBT Issues in Counseling*, 1, 7–30.

Murstein, B. I. (1970). Stimulus value role: A theory of marital choice. *Journal of Marriage and Family*, 32(3), 465–481. doi:10.2307/350113

Murstein, B. I. (1974). *Love, sex and marriage through the ages*. New York: Springer.

Murstein, B. I. (1976). *Who will marry whom? Theories and research in marital choice*. New York: Springer.

Newton, D. E. (2010). *Same-sex marriage: A reference handbook*. Santa Barbara, CA: ABC-CLIO.

Niehuis, S., Huston, T. L., & Rosenband, R. (2006). From courtship into marriage: A new developmental model and methodological critique. *Journal of Family Communication*, 6, 23–47. doi:10.1207/s15327698jfc0601_3

Ogolsky, B. G. (2009). Deconstructing the association between relationship maintenance and commitment: Testing two competing models. *Personal Relationships*, 16(1), 99–115. doi:10.1111/j.1475-6811.2009.01212.x

Ogolsky, B., & Bowers, J. (in press). A meta-analytic review of relationship maintenance and its correlates. *Journal of Social and Personal Relationships*.

Ogolsky, B., Niehuis, S., & Ridley, C. (2009). Using online methods and designs to conduct research on personal relationships. *Marriage and Family Review*, 45, 610–628.

O'Leary, K. D., & Slep, A. M. (2003). A dyadic longitudinal model of adolescent dating aggression. *Journal of Clinical Child & Adolescent Psychology*, 32, 314–327.

O'Leary, S. G., & Slep, A. M. S. (2006). Precipitants of partner aggression. *Journal of Family Psychology*, 20, 344–347.

O'Sullivan, L. F., Cheng, M. M., Harris, K. M., & Brooks-Gunn, J. (2007). I wanna hold your hand: The progression of social, romantic and sexual events in adolescent relationships. *Perspectives on Sexual and Reproductive Health*, 39, 100–107.

Olson, L. N., & Lloyd, S. A. (2005). "It depends on what you mean by starting": An exploration of how women define initiation of aggression and their motives for behaving aggressively. *Sex Roles, 53*(7–8), 603–617. doi:10.1007/s11199-005-7145-5

Olson, L., Fine, M., & Lloyd, S. A. (2005). A dialectical approach to theorizing about violence between intimates. In V. Bengston, A. Acock, K. Allen, P. Dilworth-Anderson, & D. Klein (Eds.), *Sourcebook of family theory and research* (pp. 315–331). Thousand Oaks, CA: Sage.

Opie, F. D. (2008). Eating, dancing, and courting in New York Black and Latino relations, 1930–1970. *Journal of Social History, 42*(1), 79.

Orbuch, T. L. (1992). A symbolic interactionist approach to the study of relationship loss. In *Close Relationship Loss: Theoretical Approaches* (pp. 192–206). New York: Springer.

Orth-Gomér, K., Wamala, S. P., Horsten, M., Schenck-Gustafsson, K., Schneiderman, N., & Mittleman, M. A. (2000). Marital stress worsens prognosis in women with coronary heart disease: The Stockholm female coronary risk study. *JAMA: Journal of the American Medical Association, 284*(23), 3008–3014. doi:10.1001/jama.284.23.3008

Osborne, C., Manning, W. D., & Smock, P. J. (2007). Married and cohabiting parents' relationship stability: A focus on race and ethnicity. *Journal of Marriage and Family, 69*(5), 1345–1366.

Oswald, R. F., Blume, L. B., & Marks, S. R. (2005). Decentering heteronormativity: A model for family studies. In V. Bengston, A. Acock, K. Allen, P. Dilworth-Anderson, & D. Klein (Eds.), *Sourcebook of family theory and research* (pp. 143–165). Thousand Oaks, CA: Sage.

Oswald, R., & Clausell, E. (2006). Same-sex relationships and their dissolution. In M. Fine & J. Harvey (Eds.), *Handbook of divorce and relationship dissolution* (pp. 499–513). Mahwah, NJ: Lawrence Erlbaum Associates.

Oswald, R., Blume, L., Berkowitz, D., & Kuvalanka, K. (2009). Queering "the family". In S. A. Lloyd, A. L. Few, & K. R. Allen (Eds.), *Handbook of feminist family studies* (pp. 43–55). Thousand Oaks, CA: Sage.

Outlaw, M. (2009). No one type of intimate partner abuse: Exploring physical and non-physical abuse among intimate partners. *Journal of Family Violence, 24*(4), 263–272. doi:10.1007/s10896-009-9228-5

Owen, J. J., Rhoades, G. K., Stanley, S. M., & Fincham, F. D. (2010). "Hooking up" among college students: Demographic and psychosocial correlates. *Archives of Sexual Behavior, 39*(3), 653–663. doi:10.1007/s10508-008-9414-1

Parent, A. S., & Wallace, S. B. (1993). Childhood and sexual identity under slavery. In J. C. Fout & M. S. Tantillo (Eds.), *American sexual politics: Sex, gender, and race since the Civil War* (pp. 19–57). Chicago, IL: University of Chicago Press.

Parks, M. R., & Adelman, M. B. (1983). Communication networks and the development of romantic relationships: An expansion of uncertainty reduction theory. *Human Communication Research, 10*, 55–79. doi:10.1111/j.1468-2958.1983.tb00004.x

Patton, C. L., Nobles, M. R., & Fox, K. A. (2010). Look who's stalking: Obsessive pursuit and attachment theory. *Journal of Criminal Justice, 38*(3), 282–290. doi:10.1016/j.jcrimjus.2010.02.013

Paul, E. L., McManus, B., & Hayes, A. (2000). "Hookups": Characteristics and correlates of college students' spontaneous and anonymous sexual experiences. *Journal of Sex Research, 37*(1), 76–88. doi:10.1080/00224490009552023

Pederson, F. A. (1991). Secular trends in human sex ratios: Their influence on individual and family behavior. *Human Nature, 2*(3), 271–291. doi:10.1007/BF02692189

Peiss, K., Jeannette P. (2004). Charity girls and city pleasures. *OAH Magazine of History, 18*(4), 14.

Peplau, L. A. (1982). Research on homosexual couples: An overview. *Journal of Homosexuality, 8*(2), 3–8.

Peplau, L. A., & Fingerhut, A. W. (2007). The close relationships of lesbians and gay men. *Annual Review of Psychology, 58*, 405–424.

Peplau, L. A., & Spalding, L. R. (2002). The close relationships of lesbians, gay men and bisexuals. In C. Hendrick & S. S. Hendrick (Eds.), *Close relationships: A sourcebook* (pp. 111–123). Thousand Oaks, CA: Sage.

Perdue, T. (1994). Cherokee women and the trail of tears. In V. L. Ruiz & E. C. DuBois (Eds.), *Unequal sisters: A multicultural reader in U.S. women's history* (pp. 32–43). New York: Routledge.

Peterson, Z. D., & Muehlenhard, C. L. (2007). Conceptualizing the "wantedness" of women's consensual and nonconsensual sexual experiences: Implications for how women label their experiences with rape. *Journal of Sex Research, 44*(1), 72–88. doi:10.1207/s15598519jsr4401_8

Peterson, Z. D., Voller, E. K., Polusny, M. A., & Murdoch, M. (2011). Prevalence and consequences of adult sexual assault of men: Review of empirical findings and state of the literature. *Clinical Psychology Review, 31*(1), 1–24. doi:10.1016/j.cpr. 2010.08.006

Ponzetti, J. J. (2005). Family beginnings: A comparison of spouses' recollections of courtship. *Family Journal, 13*(2), 132–138. doi:10.1177/1066480704271249

Popenoe, D. (2008). *Cohabitation, marriage, and child wellbeing.* Piscataway, NJ: Rutgers University/The National Marriage Project. Retrieved from http://www.virginia.edu/marriageproject/pdfs/NMP2008CohabitationReport.pdf.

Price, R. A. & Vandenberg, S. G. (1979). Matching for physical attractiveness in married couples. *Personality and Social Psychology Bulletin, 5*, 398–400.

Prospero, M. (2009). Sex-symmetric effects of coercive behaviors on mental health? Not exactly. *Journal of Interpersonal Violence, 24*(1), 128–146. doi:10.1177/0886260508315778

Qu, L., Weston, R., & de Vaus, D. (2009). Cohabitation and beyond: The contribution of each partner's relationship satisfaction and fertility aspirations to pathways of cohabiting couples. *Journal of Comparative Family Studies, 40*, 585–601.

Ramírez, A. (2008). An examination of the tripartite approach to commitment: An actor-partner interdependence model analysis of the effect of relationship maintenance behavior. *Journal of Social and Personal Relationships, 25*, 943–965. doi:10.1177/0265407508100309

Ramírez, H. N. R. (2003). "That's my place!": Negotiating racial, sexual, and gender politics in San Francisco's gay Latino alliance, 1975–1983. *Journal of the History of Sexuality, 12*(2), 224–258.

Reed, E., Raj, A., Miller, E., & Silverman, J. G. (2010). Losing the "gender" in gender-based violence: The missteps of research on dating and intimate partner violence. *Violence Against Women, 16*(3), 348–354. doi:10.1177/1077801209361127

Reis, H. T., Caprariello, P. A., & Velickovic, M. (2011). The relationship superiority effect is moderated by the relationship context. *Journal of Experimental Social Psychology, 47*(2), 481–484. doi:10.1016/j.jesp.2010.10.008

Reis, H. T., & Patrick, B. C. (1996). *Attachment and intimacy: Component processes.* New York: Guilford Press.

Reis, H. T., & Shaver, P. (1988). Intimacy as an interpersonal process. In S. Duck (Ed.), *Handbook of personal relationships: Theory, research, and interventions* (pp. 367–389). Chichester, UK: Wiley.

Reiss, I. (1960). *Premarital sexual standards.* New York: Sex Information and Education Council of the United States.

Rhatigan, D. L., & Street, A. E. (2005). The impact of intimate partner violence on decisions to leave dating relationships: A test of the investment model. *Journal of Interpersonal Violence, 20*(12), 1580–1597. doi:10.1177/0886260505280344

Rhoades, G. K., Kamp Dush, C. M., Atkins, D., Stanley, S., & Markman, H. (2011) Breaking up is hard to do: The impact of unmarried relationship dissolution on mental health and life satisfaction. *Journal of Family Psychology, 25,* 366–374.

Rhoades, G. K., Petrella, J. N., Stanley, S. M., & Markman, H. J. (2007). Premarital cohabitation, husbands' commitment, and wives' satisfaction with the division of household contributions. *Marriage & Family Review, 40,* 5–22. doi:10.1300/J002v40n04_02

Rhoades, G. K., Stanley, S. M., Kelmer, G., & Markman, H. J. (2010). Physical aggression in unmarried relationships: The roles of commitment and constraints. *Journal of Family Psychology, 24*(6), 678–687. doi:10.1037/a0021475

Rhoades, G. K., Stanley, S. M., & Markman, H. J. (2006). Pre-engagement cohabitation and gender asymmetry in marital commitment. *Journal of Family Psychology, 20*(4), 553–560. doi:10.1037/0893-3200.20.4.553

Rhoades, G. K., Stanley, S. M., & Markman, H. J. (2009a). Couples' reasons for cohabitation: Associations with individual well-being and relationship quality. *Journal of Family Issues, 30*(2), 233–258. doi:10.1177/0192513X08324388

Rhoades, G. K., Stanley, S. M., & Markman, H. J. (2009b). The pre-engagement cohabitation effect: A replication and extension of previous findings. *Journal of Family Psychology, 23*(1), 107–111. doi:10.1037/a0014358

Rice, F. (1990). *Intimate relationships, marriages, and families.* Mountain View, CA: Mayfield.

Rich, A. (1980). Compulsory heterosexuality and lesbian experience. *Signs: Journal of Women in Culture & Society, 5,* 631–660.

Ridley, C. A., Cate, R. M., Collins, D. M., Reesing, A. L., Lucero, A. A., Gilson, M. S., & Almeida, D. M. (2006). The ebb and flow of marital lust: A relational approach. *Journal of Sex Research, 43*(2), 144–153.

Ridley, C., Ogolsky, B., Payne, P., Totenhagen, C., & Cate, R. (2008). Sexual expression: Its emotional context in heterosexual, gay, and lesbian couples. *Journal of Sex Research, 45*(3), 305–314.

Riggs, S. A., & Kaminski, P. (2010). Childhood emotional abuse, adult attachment, and depression as predictors of relational adjustment and psychological aggression.

Journal of Aggression, Maltreatment & Trauma, 19(1), 75–104. doi:10.1080/10926770903475976

Riley, G. (1996). *Building and breaking families in the American west*. Albuquerque, NM: University of New Mexico Press.

Ristock, J. L. (2003). Exploring dynamics of abusive lesbian relationships: Preliminary analysis of a multisite, qualitative study. *American Journal of Community Psychology, 31*(3–4), 329–341. doi:10.1023/A:1023971006882

Roberts, L. J. (2006). From bickering to battering: Destructive conflict processes in intimate relationships. In P. Noller & J. A. Feeney (Eds.), *Close relationships: Functions, forms and processes* (pp. 325–351). New York: Psychology Press.

Robinson, I., & Jedlicka, D. (1982). Changes in sexual attitudes and behaviors of college students. *Journal of Marriage & Family, 43*, 77–83.

Robinson, L. C., & Blanton, P. W. (1993). Marital strengths in enduring marriages. *Family Relations: An Interdisciplinary Journal of Applied Family Studies, 42*(1), 38–45. doi:10.2307/584919

Rollie, S. S., & Duck, S. (2006). *Divorce and dissolution of romantic relationships: Stage models and their limitations*. Mahwah, NJ: Lawrence Erlbaum Associates.

Roloff, M. E., & Johnson, K. L. (2002). Serial arguing over the relational life course: Antecedents and consequences. In A. L. Vangelisti & H. T. Reis (Eds.), *Stability and change in relationships* (pp. 107–128). New York: Cambridge University Press. doi:10.1017/CBO9780511499876.008

Rothman, E. K. (1984). *Hands and hearts: A history of courtship in America*. New York: Basic Books.

Rozee, P. D., & Koss, M. P. (2001). Rape: A century of resistance. *Psychology of Women Quarterly Special Issue: Women's Lives, Feminist Research, and the Decade of Behavior, 25*(4), 295–311. doi:10.1111/1471-6402.00030

Rubin, L. B. (1976). *Worlds of pain: Life in the working-class family*. New York: Basic Books.

Rubin, Z. (1970). Measurement of romantic love. *Journal of Personality and Social Psychology, 16*, 265–273.

Rubin, Z. (1973). *Liking and loving: An invitation to social psychology*. New York: Holt, Rinehart, & Winston.

Rubin, Z., & Levinger, G. (1974). Theory and data badly mated: A critique of Murstein's SVR and Lewis's PDF models of mate selection. *Journal of Marriage and Family, 36*, 226–231.

Rupp, L. J. (1989). "Imagine my surprise": Women's relationships in mid-twentieth century America. In M. Duberman, M. Vincus, & G. Chauncey Jr., (Eds.), *Hidden from history: Reclaiming the gay and lesbian past* (pp. 395–410). New York: NAL Books.

Rupp, L. J. (2001). Toward a global history of same-sex sexuality. *Journal of the History of Sexuality, 10*(2), 287–302.

Rusbult, C. E. (1980). Commitment and satisfaction in romantic associations: A test of the investment model. *Journal of Experimental Social Psychology, 16*, 172–186. doi:10.1016/0022-1031(80)90007-4

Rusbult, C. E. (1983). A longitudinal test of the investment model: The development (and deterioration) of satisfaction and commitment in heterosexual involvements. *Journal of Personality and Social Psychology, 45*(1), 101–117. doi:10.1037/0022-3514.45.1.101

Rusbult, C. E. (1987). Responses to dissatisfaction in close relationships: The exit-voice-loyalty-neglect model. In D. Perlman & S. Duck (Eds.), *Intimate relationships: Development, dynamics, and deterioration* (pp. 209–237). Newbury Park, CA: Sage.

Rusbult, C. E., Coolsen, M. K., Kirchner, J. L., & Clarke, J. A. (2006). *Commitment.* New York: Cambridge University Press.

Rusbult, C. E., Drigotas, S. M., & Verette, J. (1994). The investment model: An interdependence analysis of commitment processes and relationship maintenance phenomena. In D. Canary & L. Stafford (Eds.), *Communication and relational maintenance* (pp. 115–139). New York: Academic Press.

Rusbult, C. E., Johnson, D. J., & Morrow, G. D. (1986). Predicting satisfaction and commitment in adult romantic involvements: An assessment of the generalizability of the investment model. *Social Psychology Quarterly, 49*(1), 81–89. doi:10.2307/2786859

Rusbult, C. E., Martz, J. M., & Agnew, C. R. (1998). The investment model scale: Measuring commitment level, satisfaction level, quality of alternatives, and investment size. *Personal Relationships, 5,* 357–391.

Rusbult, C. E., & Van Lange, P. A. M. (2003). Interdependence, interaction and relationships. *Annual Review of Psychology, 54,* 351–375. doi:10.1146/annurev.psych.54.101601.145059

Rusbult, C. E., Van Lange, P. A. M., Wildschut, T., Yovetich, N. A., & Verette, J. (2000). Perceived superiority in close relationships: Why it exists and persists. *Journal of Personality and Social Psychology, 79*(4), 521–545. doi:10.1037/0022-3514.79.4.521

Rusbult, C. E., Wieselquist, J., Foster, C. A., & Witcher, B. S. (1999). Commitment and trust in close relationships: An interdependence analysis. In J. M. Adams & W. H. Jones (Eds.), *Handbook on interpersonal commitment and relationship stability* (pp. 427–449). New York: Kluwer Academic/Plenum.

Ryan, K. M. (2004). Further evidence for a cognitive component of rape. *Aggression and Violent Behavior, 9*(6), 579–604. doi:10.1016/j.avb.2003.05.001

Salholz, E., Michael, R., Starr, M., Doherty, S., Abramson, P., & Wingert, P. (1986). Too late for prince charming? *Newsweek, 107*(2), 54–61.

Sassler, S. (2010). Partnering across the life course: Sex, relationships, and mate selection. *Journal of Marriage and Family, 72*(3), 557–575. doi:10.1111/j.1741-3737.2010.00718.x

Sassler, S., & McNally, J. (2003). Cohabiting couples' economic circumstances and union transitions: A re-examination using multiple imputation techniques. *Social Science Research, 32*(4), 553–578. doi:10.1016/S0049-089X(03)00016-4

Sbarra, D. A., & Emery, R. E. (2005). The emotional sequelae of nonmarital relationship dissolution: Analysis of change and intraindividual variability over time. *Personal Relationships, 12*(2), 213–232. doi:10.1111/j.1350-4126.2005.00112.x

Schaffner, L. (2007). Violence against girls provokes girls' violence: From private injury to public harm. *Violence Against Women, 13*(12), 1229–1248. doi:10.1177/1077801207309881

Schellenberg, J. A. (1960). Homogamy in personal values and the "field of eligibles." *Social Forces, 39,* 157–162.

Scheurs, K. M. G., & Buunk, B. P. (1996). Closeness, autonomy, equity, and relationship satisfaction in lesbian couples. *Psychology of Women Quarterly, 20*, 577.

Sears, H. A., & Byers, E. S. (2010). Adolescent girls' and boys' experiences of psychologically, physically, and sexually aggressive behaviors in their dating relationships: Co-occurrence and emotional reaction. *Journal of Aggression, Maltreatment & Trauma, 19*(5), 517–539. doi:10.1080/10926771.2010.495035

Seltzer, J. A. (2000). Families formed outside of marriage. *Journal of Marriage and Family, 62*(4), 1247–1268. doi:10.1111/j.1741-3737.2000.01247.x

Seyfried, B. A. (1977). Complementarity in interpersonal attraction. In S. Duck (Ed.), *Theory and Practice in Interpersonal Attraction* (pp. 165–184). London: Academic Press.

Shanteau, J., & Nagy, G. F. (1979). Probability of acceptance in dating choice. *Journal of Personality and Social Psychology, 37*(4), 522–533. doi:10.1037/0022-3514.37.4.522

Shaver, P. R., & Mikulincer, M. (2006). Attachment theory, individual psychodynamics, and relationship functioning. In D. Perlman & A. Vangelisti (Eds.), *Handbook of personal relationships* (pp. 251–272). New York: Cambridge University Press.

Shortt, J. W., Capaldi, D. M., Kim, H. K., & Owen, L. D. (2006). Relationship separation for young, at-risk couples: Prediction from dyadic aggression. *Journal of Family Psychology, 20*(4), 624–631. doi:10.1037/0893-3200.20.4.624

Simpson, J. A., Ickes, W., & Grich, J. (1999). When accuracy hurts: Reactions of anxious-ambivalent dating partners to a relationship-threatening situation. *Journal of Personality and Social Psychology, 76*(5), 754–769. doi:10.1037/0022-3514.76.5.754

Singer, J. D., & Willett, J. B. (2003). *Applied longitudinal data analysis: Modeling change and event occurrence.* New York: Oxford University Press.

Slotter, E. B., Finkel, E. J., Dewall, C. N., Pond, R. S., Lambert, N. M., Bodenhausen, G. V., & Fincham, F. D. (2012). Putting the brakes on aggression toward a romantic partner: The inhibitory influence of relationship commitment. *Journal of Personality and Social Psychology, 102*(2), 291–305.

Smith-Rosenberg, C. (1985). *Disorderly conduct: Visions of gender in Victorian America.* New York: Oxford University Press.

Smock, P. J. (2000). Cohabitation in the United States: An appraisal of research themes, findings, and implications. *Annual Review of Sociology, 26*, 1–20. doi:10.1146/annurev.soc.26.1.1

Snyder, M., Tanke, E. D., & Berscheid, E. (1977). Social perception and interpersonal behavior: On the self-fulfilling nature of social stereotypes. *Journal of Personality and Social Psychology, 35*(9), 656–666. doi:10.1037/0022-3514.35.9.656

Solomon, D. H., & Knobloch, L. K. (2001). Relationship uncertainty, partner interference, and intimacy within dating relationships. *Journal of Social and Personal Relationships, 18*(6), 804–820. doi:10.1177/0265407501186004

Solomon, D. H., & Knobloch, L. K. (2004). A model of relational turbulence: The role of intimacy, relational uncertainty, and interference from partners in appraisals of irritations. *Journal of Social and Personal Relationships, 21*(6), 795–816. doi:10.1177/0265407504047838

Solomon, D. H., & Theiss, J. A. (2011). Relational turbulence: What doesn't kill us makes us stronger. In W. R. Cupach and B. H. Spitzberg (Eds.) *The dark side of close relationships* (pp. 197–216). New York: Routledge/Taylor & Francis.

Solomon, S. E., Rothblum, E. D., & Balsam, K. F. (2004). Pioneers in partnership: Lesbian and gay male couples in civil unions as compared with those not in civil unions and married heterosexual siblings. *Journal of Family Psychology, 18*, 275–286.

Solomon, S. E., Rothblum, E. D., & Balsam, K. F. (2005). Money, housework, sex and conflict: Same-sex couples in civil unions, those not in civil unions, and heterosexual married siblings. *Sex Roles, 52*, 561–575.

South, S. J. (1995). Do you need to shop around? Age at marriage, spousal alternatives, and marital dissolution. *Journal of Family Issues, 16*, 432–449.

South, S. J., & Lloyd, K. M. (1992). Marriage opportunities and family formation: Further implications of imbalanced sex ratios. *Journal of Marriage and Family, 54*(2), 440–451. doi:10.2307/353075

Spanier, G. (1976). Measuring dyadic adjustment: New scales for assessing the quality of marriage and similar dyads. *Journal of Marriage and Family, 38*, 15–28.

Spitzberg, B. H. (2011). Intimate partner violence and aggression: Seeing the light in a dark place. In W. R. Cupach & B. H. Spitzberg (Eds.), *The dark side of close relationships* (pp. 327–380). New York: Taylor & Francis.

Spitzberg, B. H., & Cupach, W. R. (2007). The state of the art of stalking: Taking stock of the emerging literature. *Aggression and Violent Behavior, 12*(1), 64–86. doi:10.1016/j.avb.2006.05.001

Sprecher, S. (1989). The importance to males and females of physical attractiveness, earning potential, and expressiveness in initial attraction. *Sex Roles, 21*(9–10), 591–607. doi:10.1007/BF00289173

Sprecher, S. (2001). Equity and social exchange in dating couples: Associations with satisfaction, commitment, and stability. *Journal of Marriage and Family, 63*(3), 599–613. doi:10.1111/j.1741-3737.2001.00599.x

Sprecher, S. (2002). Sexual satisfaction in premarital relationships: Associations with satisfaction, love, commitment, and stability. *Journal of Sex Research, 39*(3), 190–196. doi:10.1080/00224490209552141

Sprecher, S., & Cate, R. M. (2004). *Sexual satisfaction and sexual expression as predictors of relationship satisfaction and stability*. Mahwah, NJ: Lawrence Erlbaum Associates.

Sprecher, S., Christopher, F. S., & Cate, R. (2006). Sexuality in close relationships. In D. Perlman, & A. Vangelisti (Eds.), *Handbook of personal relationships* (pp. 463–482). New York: Cambridge University Press.

Sprecher, S., & Felmlee, D. (1992). The influence of parents and friends on the quality and stability of romantic relationships: A three-wave longitudinal investigation. *Journal of Marriage and Family, 54*(4), 888–900. doi:10.2307/353170

Sprecher, S., Felmlee, D., Schmeeckle, M., & Shu, X. (2006). *No breakup occurs on an island: Social networks and relationship dissolution*. Mahwah, NJ: Lawrence Erlbaum Associates.

Sprecher, S., Schmeeckle, M., & Felmlee, D. (2006). The principle of least interest: Inequality in emotional involvement in romantic relationships. *Journal of Family Issues, 27*(9), 1255–1280. doi:10.1177/0192513X06289215

Sprecher, S., & Schwartz, P. (1996). Equity and balance in the exchange of contributions in close relationships. In M. J. Lerner & G. Mikula (Eds.), *Entitlement and the affectional bond: Justice in close relationships* (pp. 11–41). New York: Plenum.

Sprecher, S., Schwartz, P., Harvey, J., & Hatfield, E. (2008). Thebusinessoflove.com: Relationship initiation at Internet matchmaking services. In S. Sprecher, A. Wenzel, & J. Harvey (Eds.), *Handbook of relationship initiation* (pp. 249–265). New York: Psychology Press.

Sprecher, S., Wenzel, A., & Harvey, J. (Eds.) (2010). *Handbook of relationship initiation*. New York: Psychology Press.

Sprecher, S., Zimmerman, C., & Abrahams, E. M. (2008). Choosing compassionate strategies to end a relationship: Effects of compassionate love for partner and the reason for the breakup. *Social Psychology, 41*(2), 66–75. doi:10.1027/1864-9335/a000010

Stafford, L. (1994). Tracing the threads of spider webs. In D. J. Canary & L. Stafford (Eds.), *Communication and relational maintenance* (pp. 297–306). San Diego, CA: Academic Press.

Stafford, L. (2011). Measuring relationship maintenance behaviors: Critique and development of the revised relationship maintenance behaviors scale. *Journal of Social and Personal Relationships, 28,* 278–303. doi: 10.1177/0265407510378125

Stafford, L., & Canary, D. J. (1991). Maintenance strategies and romantic relationship type, gender and relational characteristics. *Journal of Social and Personal Relationships, 8,* 217–242. doi: 10.1177/0265407591082004

Stafford, L., Dainton, M., & Haas, S. (2000). Measuring routine and strategic relational maintenance: Scale revision, sex versus gender roles, and the prediction of relational characteristics. *Communication Monographs, 67,* 306–323. doi: 10.1080/03637750009376512

Stanley, J. L., Bartholomew, K., Taylor, T., Oram, D., & Landolt, M. (2006). Intimate violence in male same-sex relationships. *Journal of Family Violence, 21*(1), 31–41. doi:10.1007/s10896-005-9008-9

Stanley, S. (2010). Sliding vs. deciding. Web log. Retrieved from *http://www.slidingvsdeciding.blogspot.com/*.

Stanley, S. M., Amato, P. R., Johnson, C. A., & Markman, H. J. (2006). Premarital education, marital quality, and marital stability: Findings from a large, random household survey. *Journal of Family Psychology, 20*(1), 117–126. doi:10.1037/0893-3200.20.1.117

Stanley, S., Blumberg, S., & Markman, H. (1999). Helping couples fight for their marriages: The PREP approach. In R. Berger & M. Hannah (Eds.), *Preventative approaches in couples therapy* (pp. 279–303). Philadelphia, PA: Brunner-Mazel.

Stanley, S. M., & Markman, H. J. (1992). Assessing commitment in personal relationships. *Journal of Marriage and Family, 54,* 595–608. doi:10.2307/353245

Stanley, S. M., Whitton, S. W., & Markman, H. J. (2004). Maybe I do: Interpersonal commitment and premarital or nonmarital cohabitation. *Journal of Family Issues, 25*(4), 496–519. doi:10.1177/0192513X03257797

Stein, P. (1976). *Singleness*. Englewood Cliffs, NJ: Prentice-Hall.

Stephen, T. D. (1985). Fixed-sequence and circular-casual models of relationship development: Divergent views on the role of communication in intimacy. *Journal of Marriage and Family, 47,* 955–963.

Sternberg, R. J. (1986). A triangular theory of love. *Psychological Review, 93*(2), 119–135.

Stets, J. E., & Henderson, D. A. (1991). Contextual factors surrounding conflict resolution while dating: Results from a national study. *Family Relations: An Interdisciplinary Journal of Applied Family Studies, 40*(1), 29–36. doi:10.2307/585655

Stets, J. E., & Pirog-Good, M. A. (1990). Interpersonal control and courtship aggression. *Journal of Social and Personal Relationships, 7*(3), 371–394. doi:10.1177/0265407590073005

Stith, S. M., Smith, D. B., Penn, C. E., Ward, D. B., & Tritt, D. (2004). Intimate partner physical abuse perpetration and victimization risk factors: A meta-analytic review. *Aggression and Violent Behavior, 10*(1), 65–98. doi:10.1016/j.avb.2003.09.001

Stone, E. A., Shackelford, T. K., & Buss, D. M. (2007). Sex ratio and mate preferences: A cross-cultural investigation. *European Journal of Social Psychology, 37*(2), 288–296. doi:10.1002/ejsp.357

Straus, M. A. (1979). Measuring intrafamily conflict and violence: The conflict tactics (CT) scales. *Journal of Marriage and Family, 41*(1), 75–88. doi:10.2307/351733

Straus, M. A., Hamby, S. L., Boney-McCoy, S., & Sugarman, D. B. (1996). The revised conflict tactics scales (CTS2): Development and preliminary psychometric data. *Journal of Family Issues, 17*(3), 283–316. doi:10.1177/019251396017003001

Straus, M. A., & Gelles, R. J. (1990). *Physical violence in American families.* New Brunswick, NJ: Transaction Press.

Strike, C., Myers, T., Calzavara, L., & Haubrich, D. (2001). Sexual coercion among young street-involved adults: Perpetrators' and victims' perspectives. *Violence and Victims, 16*(5), 537–551.

Struckman-Johnson, C., Struckman-Johnson, D., & Anderson, P. B. (2003). Tactics of sexual coercion: When men and women won't take no for an answer. *Journal of Sex Research Special Issue: Gender and Sexuality, 40*(1), 76–86. doi:10.1080/00224490309552168

Sugarman, D. B., & Hotaling, G. T. (1989). Dating violence: Prevalence, context, and risk markers. In M. A. Pirog-Good & J. E. Stets (Eds.), *Violence in dating relationships: Emerging social issues* (pp. 3–32). New York: Praeger.

Surra, C. A. (1990). Research and theory on mate selection and premarital relationships in the 1980s. *Journal of Marriage and Family, 52*, 844–865.

Surra, C. A., Gray, C. R., Boettcher, T. M. J., Cottle, N. R., & West, A. R. (2006). *From courtship to universal properties: Research on dating and mate selection, 1950 to 2003.* New York: Cambridge University Press.

Surra, C. A., Hughes, D. K., & Jacquet, S. E. (1999). *The development of commitment to marriage: A phenomenological approach.* Dordrecht, Netherlands: Kluwer Academic Publishers.

Surra, C. A., & Longstreth, M. (1990). Similarity of outcomes, interdependence, and conflict in dating relationships. *Journal of Personality and Social Psychology, 59*(3), 501–516. doi:10.1037/0022-3514.59.3.501

Swann, W. B., Griffin, J. J., Predmore, S. C., & Gaines, B. (1987). The cognitive-affective crossfire: When self-consistency confronts self-enhancement. *Journal of Personality and Social Psychology, 52*(5), 881–889. doi:10.1037/0022-3514.52.5.881

Tach, L. & Halpern-Meekin, S. (2009). How does premarital cohabitation affect trajectories of marital quality? *Journal of Marriage and Family, 71*, 298–317.

Tafoya, M. A., & Spitzberg, B, H. (2007). The dark side of infidelity: Its nature, prevalence, and communicative functions. In B. H. Spitzberg & W. R. Cupach

(Eds.), *The dark side of interpersonal communication* (2nd ed., pp. 201–242). Mahwah, NJ: Lawrence Erlbaum Associates.

Taft, C. T., Schumm, J., Orazem, R. J., Meis, L., & Pinto, L. A. (2010). Examining the link between posttraumatic stress disorder symptoms and dating aggression perpetration. *Violence and Victims*, 25, 456–469. doi:10.1891/0886-6708.25. 4.456

Takaki, R. T. (1993). *A different mirror: A history of multicultural America*. Boston, MA: Little, Brown and Co.

Teachman, J. (2003). Premarital sex, premarital cohabitation and the risk of subsequent marital dissolution among women. *Journal of Marriage and Family*, 65(2), 444–455. doi:10.1111/j.1741-3737.2003.00444.x

Temple, J. R., Weston, R., Rodriguez, B. F., & Marshall, L. L. (2007). Differing effects of partner and nonpartner sexual assault on women's mental health. *Violence Against Women*, 13(3), 285–297. doi:10.1177/1077801206297437

Terman, L. M. (1938). *Psychological factors in marital happiness*. New York: McGraw-Hill.

Testa, M. (2004). The role of substance use in male-to-female physical and sexual violence: A brief review and recommendations for future research. *Journal of Interpersonal Violence Special Issue: Toward a National Research Agenda on Violence Against Women—Part 2*, 19(12), 1494–1505. doi:10.1177/0886260504269701

Testa, M., Hoffman, J. H., & Leonard, K. E. (2011). Female intimate partner violence perpetration: Stability and predictors of mutual and nonmutual aggression across the first year of college. *Aggressive Behavior*, 37, 362–373.

Tewksbury, R. (2007). Effects of sexual assaults on men: Physical, mental and sexual consequences. *International Journal of Men's Health*, 6, 22–35. doi:10.3149/jmh.0601.22

Tharp, R. G. (1963). Psychological patterning in marriage. *Psychological Bulletin*, 60(2), 97–117. doi:10.1037/h0046726

Theiss, J. A., Knobloch, L. K., Checton, M. G., & Magsamen-Conrad, K. (2009). Relationship characteristics associated with the experience of hurt in romantic relationships: A test of the relational turbulence model. *Human Communication Research*, 35(4), 588–615. doi:10.1111/j.1468-2958.2009.01364.x

Theiss, J. A., & Solomon, D. H. (2006a). Coupling longitudinal data and multilevel modeling to examine the antecedents and consequences of jealousy experiences in romantic relationships: A test of the relational turbulence model. *Human Communication Research*, 32(4), 469–503. doi:10.1111/j.1468-2958.2006.00284.x

Theiss, J. A., & Solomon, D. H. (2006b). A relational turbulence model of communication about irritations in romantic relationships. *Communication Research*, 33(5), 391–418. doi:10.1177/0093650206291482

Thibaut, J. W., & Kelley, H. H. (1959). *The social psychology of groups*. Oxford, UK: John Wiley.

Thiessen, D. (1994). Environmental tracking by females: Sexual lability. *Human Nature*, 5, 167–202. doi:10.1007/BF02692160

Thoits, P. (2006). Personal agency in the stress process. *Journal of Health and Social Behavior*, 47, 309–323.

Thornton, A., Axinn, W., & Xie, Y. (2007). *Marriage and cohabitation*. Chicago, IL: University of Chicago Press.

Thornton, A. (1991). Influence of the marital history of parents on the marital and cohabitational experiences of children. *American Journal of Sociology, 96*(4), 868–894. doi:10.1086/229611

Tibbits, C. (1965). The older family member in American society. In H. Jacobs (Ed.), *The older person in the family: Challenges and conflicts* (pp. 1–11). Iowa City: Institute of Gerontology.

Tjaden, P., & Thoennes, N. (1998). *Stalking in America: Findings from the national violence against women survey.* National Institute of Justice and the Centers for Disease Control and Prevention.

Tjaden, P., & Thoennes, N. (2000a). *Full report of the prevalence, incidence, and consequences of violence against women: Findings from the national violence against women survey.* National Institute of Justice and the Centers for Disease Control and Prevention.

Tjaden, P., & Thoennes, N. (2000b). Prevalence and consequences of male-to-female and female-to-male intimate partner violence as measured by the national violence against women survey. *Violence Against Women, 6*(2), 142–161. doi:10.1177/10778010022181769

Tjaden, P., & Thoennes, N. (2006). *Extent, nature, and consequences of rape victimization: Findings from the national violence against women survey.* National Institute of Justice and the Centers for Disease Control and Prevention.

Tjaden, P., Thoennes, N., & Allison, C. J. (1999). Comparing violence over the life span in samples of same-sex and opposite-sex cohabitants. *Violence & Victims, 14,* 413–425.

Tjaden, P., Thoennes, N., & Allison, C.J. (2002). Comparing stalking victimization from legal and victim perspectives. In K. E. Davis, I. H. Frieze, & R. D. Maiuro (Eds.), *Stalking: Perspectives on victims and perpetrators* (pp. 9–30). New York: Springer Publishing Co.

Trask, B. & Koivunen, J. (2007). Trends in marriage and cohabitation. In B. Trask & R. Hamon (Eds.), *Cultural Diversity and Families,* (pp. 80–99). Thousand Oaks, CA: Sage.

Trivers, R. L. (1972). Parental investment and sexual selection. In B. Campbell (Ed.), *Sexual selection and the descent of man, 1871–1971* (pp. 136–179). Chicago, IL: Aldine.

Troy, A. B., Lewis-Smith, J., & Laurenceau, J. (2006). Interracial and intraracial romantic relationships: The search for differences in satisfaction, conflict, and attachment style. *Journal of Social and Personal Relationships, 23*(1), 65–80.

Tsai, M. (2006). Sociable resources and close relationships: Intimate relatives and friends in Taiwan. *Journal of Social and Personal Relationships, 23*(1), 151–169. doi:10.1177/0265407506060184

Tsapelas, I., Fisher, H., & Aron, A. (2010). Infidelity: When, where, why? In W. R. Cupach & B. H. Spitzberg (Eds.), *The dark side of close relationships II* (pp. 175–195). New York: Routledge/Taylor & Francis.

U.S. Bureau of the Census. (2010). Retrieved from http://factfinder.census.gov/servlet/DTTable?_bm=y&-geo_id=01000US&-ds_name=ACS_2009_5YR_G00_&-_lang=en&mt_name=ACS_2009_5YR_G2000_B09016&-mt_name=ACS_2009_5YR_G2000_B11009&-format=&-CONTEXT=dt.

U.S. Centers for Disease Control and Prevention. (2012). *National Health Statistics No. 49.* Retrieved from www.cdc.gov/nchs/data/nhsr/nhsr049.pdf.

Van Eeden-Moorefield, B., Martell, C. R., Williams, M., & Preston, M. (2011). Same-sex relationships and dissolution: The connection between heteronormativity and homonormativity. *Family Relations, 60,* 562–571.

Van Eeden-Moorefield, B., Pasley, K., Crosbie-Burnett, M., & King, E. (2012). Explaining couple cohesion in different types of gay families. *Journal of Family Issues, 33,* 182–201.

Van Horn, K. R., Arnone, A., Nesbitt, K., Desilets, L., Sears, T., Giffin, M., & Brudi, R. (1997). Physical distance and interpersonal characteristics in college students' romantic relationships. *Personal Relationships, 4*(1), 25–34. doi:10.1111/j.1475-6811.1997.tb00128.x

Van Lange, P. A. M., Rusbult, C. E., Drigotas, S. M., Arriaga, X. B., Witcher, B. S., & Cox, C. L. (1997). Willingness to sacrifice in close relationships. *Journal of Personality and Social Psychology, 72*(6), 1373–1395. doi:10.1037/0022-3514.72.6.1373

Vangelisti, A. L. (2006a). *Hurtful interactions and the dissolution of intimacy.* Mahwah, NJ: Lawrence Erlbaum Associates.

Vangelisti, A. L. (2006b). Relationship dissolution: antecedents, processes, and consequences. In P. Noller & J. A Feeney (Eds.), *Close relationships: Functions, forms and processes* (pp. 353–374). Hove, UK: Psychology Press.

Vangelisti, A. L. (2007). Communicating hurt. In B. H. Spitzberg & W. R. Cupach (Eds.), *The dark side of interpersonal communication* (2nd ed., pp. 121–142). Mahwah, NJ: Lawrence Erlbaum Associates.

Vega, V., & Malamuth, N. M. (2007). Predicting sexual aggression: The role of pornography in the context of general and specific risk factors. *Aggressive Behavior, 33,* 104–117.

Vézina, J., & Hébert, M. (2007). Risk factors for victimization in romantic relationships of young women: A review of empirical studies and implications for prevention. *Trauma, Violence, & Abuse, 8*(1), 33–66. doi:10.1177/1524838006297029

Vicinus, M. (2004). *Intimate friends: Women who loved women, 1778–1928.* Chicago, IL: University of Chicago Press.

Volz, A. R., & Kerig, P. K. (2010). Relational dynamics associated with adolescent dating violence: The roles of rejection sensitivity and relational insecurity. *Journal of Aggression, Maltreatment & Trauma, 19*(6), 587–602. doi:10.1080/10926771.2010.502088

Vonk, R. (2002). Self-serving interpretations of flattery: Why ingratiation works. *Journal of Personality and Social Psychology, 82,* 515–526.

Vorauer, J. D., Cameron, J. J., Holmes, J. G., & Pearce, D. G. (2003). Invisible overtures: Fears of rejection and the signal amplification bias. *Journal of Personality and Social Psychology, 84*(4), 793–812. doi:10.1037/0022-3514.84.4.793

Waller, W. (1937). The rating and dating complex. *American Sociological Review, 2,* 727–734.

Waller, W. (1951). *The family: A dynamic interpretation.* New York: Dryden.

Walters, M. L. (2011). Straighten up and act like a lady: A qualitative study of lesbian survivors of intimate partner violence. *Journal of Gay & Lesbian Social Services: The Quarterly Journal of Community & Clinical Practice, 23*(2), 250–270. doi:10.1080/10538720.2011.559148

Wat, E. C. (2002). *The making of a gay Asian community: An oral history of pre-AIDS Los Angeles*. Lanham, MD: Rowman & Littlefield.

Weaver, J. R., Vandello, J. A., Bosson, J. K., & Burnaford, R. M. (2010). The proof is in the punch: Gender differences in perceptions of action and aggression as components of manhood. *Sex Roles, 62*(3–4), 241–251. doi:10.1007/s11199-009-9713-6

Weigel, D., & Ballard-Reisch, D. (1999). The influence of marital duration and the use of relationship maintenance behaviors. *Communication Reports, 12*, 59–70.

Weinstock, J. S. (2004). Lesbian FLEX-ibility: Friend and/or family connections among lesbian ex-lovers. In J. S. Weinstock & E. E. Rothblue (Eds.), *Lesbian ex-lovers: The really long-term relationships* (pp. 193–238). Binghamton, NY: Harrington Park Press.

West, C., & Zimmerman, D. (1987). Doing gender. *Gender and Society, 1*, 125–151.

Weston, K. (1991). *Families we choose: Lesbians, gays, kinships*. New York: Columbia University Press.

Weston, R. (2008). Insecure attachment mediates effects of partners' emotional abuse and violence on women's relationship quality. *Journal of Family Violence, 23*(6), 483–493. doi:10.1007/s10896-008-9176-5

Whisman, M. A. (1999). Marital dissatisfaction and psychiatric disorders: Results from the national comorbidity survey. *Journal of Abnormal Psychology, 108*(4), 701–706.

Whisman, M. A., Uebelacker, L. A., Tolejko, N., Chatav, Y., & McKelvie, M. (2006). Marital discord and well-being in older adults: Is the association confounded by personality? *Psychology and Aging, 21*(3), 626–631. doi:10.1037/0882-7974.21.3.626

White, J., & Klein, D. (2002). *Family theories*. Thousand Oaks, CA: Sage.

White, J., Kowalski, R. M., Lyndon, A., & Valentine, S. (2002). An integrative contextual developmental model of male stalking. In K. E. Davis & I. H. Frieze (Eds.), *Stalking: Perspectives on victims and perpetrators* (pp. 163–185). New York: Springer Publishing Co.

White, J. W., McMullin, D., Swartout, K., Sechrist, S., & Gollehon, A. (2008). Violence in intimate relationships: A conceptual and empirical examination of sexual and physical aggression. *Children and Youth Services Review, 30*(3), 338–351. doi:10.1016/j.childyouth.2007.10.003

Widom, C. S., Czaja, S. J., & Dutton, M. A. (2008). Childhood victimization and lifetime revictimization. *Child Abuse & Neglect, 32*, 785–796.

Williams, L. M. (2003). Understanding child abuse and violence against women: A life course perspective. *Journal of Interpersonal Violence Special Issue: Children and Domestic Violence, 18*(4), 441–451. doi:10.1177/0886260502250842

Williams, S. L., & Frieze, I. H. (2005). Patterns of violent relationships, psychological distress, and marital satisfaction in a national sample of men and women. *Sex Roles, 52*(11–12), 771–784. doi:10.1007/s11199-005-4198-4

Winch, R. F. (1955a). The theory of complementary needs in mate selection: A test of one kind of complementariness. *American Sociological Review, 20*, 52–56. doi:10.2307/2088200

Winch, R. F. (1955b). The theory of complementary needs in mate-selection: Final results on the test of the general hypothesis. *American Sociological Review, 20*, 552–555. doi:10.2307/2092563

Winch, R. F., Ktsanes, T., & Ktsanes, V. (1954). The theory of complementary needs in mate selection: An analytic and descriptive study. *American Sociological Review, 19*, 241–249. doi:10.2307/2087753

Winstok, Z., & Perkis, E. (2009). Women's perspective on men's control and aggression in intimate relationships. *American Journal of Orthopsychiatry, 79*, 169–180.

Wolf, K. A., & Foshee, V. A. (2003). Family violence, anger expression styles, and adolescent dating violence. *Journal of Family Violence, 18*(6), 309–316. doi:10.1023/A:1026237914406

Wolfe, L. (1981). *The Cosmo report.* New York: Ann Arbor House.

Wood, J. T. (1995). Feminist scholarship and the study of relationships. *Journal of Social and Personal Relationships, 12*, 103–120.

Woods, L., & Porter, L. (2008). Examining the relationship between sexual offenders and their victims: Interpersonal differences between stranger and non-stranger sexual offences. *Journal of Sexual Aggression, 14*(1), 61–75. doi:10.1080/13552600802056640

World Bank. (n.d.). Retrieved June 15, 2012, from http://data.worldbank.org/indicator/IT.NET.USER.P2.

Wrubel, J., Stumbo, S., & Johnson, M. O. (2010). Male same-sex couple dynamics and received social support for HIV medication adherence. *Journal of Social and Personal Relationships, 27*(4), 553–572. doi:10.1177/0265407510364870

Yabiku, S., & Gager, C. T. (2009). Sexual frequency and the stability of cohabiting unions. *Journal of Marriage and Family, 71*, 983–1000.

Yeh, H., Lorenz, F. O., Wickrama, K. A. S., Conger, R., & Elder, G. (2006). Relationships among sexual satisfaction, marital quality, and marital instability at midlife. *Journal of Family Psychology, 20*, 329–343.

INDEX